EXPERIENCING AND COUNSELING

MULTICULTURAL AND DIVERSE

POPULATIONS

THIRD EDITION

Nicholas Vacc, Ed.D.
Professor and Chairperson
Department of Counseling and
Educational Development
University of North Carolina at Greensboro
Greensboro, North Carolina

Susan DeVaney, Ed.D.
Assistant Professor
Department of Educational Leadership
Western Kentucky University
Bowling Green, Kentucky

Joe Wittmer, Ph.D.
Professor Emeritus
Department of Counselor Education
University of Florida
Gainsville, Florida

ACCELERATED DEVELOPMENT
A member of the Taylor & Francis Group

EXPERIENCING AND COUNSELING MULTICULTURAL AND DIVERSE POPULATIONS
Third Edition

3 4 5 6 7 8 9 0   BRBR   9 8

Technical Development: Cynthia Long
                          Marguerite Mader
                          Sheila Sheward

A CIP catalog record for this book is available from the British Library.

∞ The paper in this publication meets the requirements of the ANSI Standard Z39.48-1984 (Permanence of Paper)

Library of Congress Cataloging-in-Publication Data

Experiencing and counseling multicultural and diverse populations /
    [edited by] Nicholas Vacc, Susan DeVaney, Joe Wittmer. -- 3rd ed.
        p.   cm.
    Includes bibliographical references and index.
    ISBN 1-56032-381-7 (alk. paper)
    1. Social work with minorities--United States. 2. Minorities-
    -Counseling of--United States. I. Vacc, Nicholas A. II. DeVaney,
    Susan B., 1947-   . III. Wittmer, Joe.
    HV3176.E96   1995
    362.84'00973--dc20   94-25102
                                                CIP

LCN: 94-25102
ISBN: 1-56032-381-7

For additional information and ordering, please write or call:

ACCELERATED DEVELOPMENT
A member of the Taylor & Francis Group
1900 Frost Road, Suite 101
Bristol, PA 19007-1598
1-800-821-8312

DEDICATION

To
Our
Colleagues

TABLE OF CONTENTS

Chapter 1

INTRODUCTION

Nicholas A. Vacc, Ed.D.
Susan B. DeVaney, Ed.D.
Joe Wittmer, Ph.D.

This book presents an overview of thirteen special populations. Published originally as *Let Me Be Me: Special Populations and the Helping Professional*, this edition has an increased number of populations represented, been revised and updated in content, and been stylistically improved. Although this edition is by no means all inclusive, those needs, experiences, and characteristics of the groups presented are representative of divergent, unique, or ethnic subgroups in American society; thus the term "diverse populations."

PURPOSE OF THE BOOK

The purpose of this book is to expose practitioners such as counselors, teachers, college professors, mental-health workers, and social workers to the unique and genuine characteristics of several of America's subgroups and to effectively assist these same professionals as they work with clients and/or students from these populations. We believe that knowledge and awareness of those factors which influence the behavior of individuals from these subgroups will assist helpers to be more effective in their work. The fundamental assumption is that helpers can improve their effectiveness if appropriate attitudes, information, and self-understanding exist.

This book also was written to partially fill the existing gap in the lack of relevant educational materials and satisfy a growing consciousness that action is needed in order to make school, work, and personal experiences more meaningful for those individuals whose racial, social, religious, and/or cultural backgrounds; sex; physical abilities; or language differ from those of mainstream society.

THE EDITORS' PHILOSOPHY FOR WRITING THE BOOK

Our belief is that the helping professional may hold the key to the process of reducing, if not eliminating, the social and emotional barriers which prevent many of the members of America's subgroups from becoming secure American citizens. To do this, helping professionals must make a concerted effort to approach the different subgroup members among their clientele, with a cognitive understanding over and above the affectual. Love and empathy are not enough! We cannot and do not refute the abundance of research findings which indicate that to be effective as a helper one must communicate warmly, empathetically, and genuinely with clients. However, if helping professionals are inexperienced in the values and conduct of special populations, these professionals will be less effective than they would be when operating with an accurate, cognitive understanding of the total milieu of these individuals.

Acute disparities are compounded when a helper with a lack of cognitive knowledge about a special subgroup interacts with a confused and bewildered group member. Functioning in a congenial familiar cultural situation, the helper may be prone to impose idealized values on the client. A lack of cognitive understanding makes one more prone to impose one's own values. In contrast, knowledgeable helping professionals can be catalysts in the process of helping others develop an appreciation of the different subgroups found in America as well as facilitating improved individual functioning within the groups themselves.

Why is a lack of true understanding of the many different subgroups still found in America today? Our feeling is that much of the misunderstanding stems from American standards determined by college graduates who often believe that everyone is like them or should be like them. This phenomenon of assumed similarity causes a lack of desire to understand accurately those who are different socially and culturally. For example, can the Amish truly not want television? As you read Wittmer's chapter concerning this subgroup, you will find that they really do not want TV in their homes. Helpers with a sound cognitive knowledge of their clients' cultural background will more easily understand the source and reasons for the behaviors which may appear odd or peculiar at times.

As you read the subsequent chapters, you will learn that the participants of most of the special groups included in the book do not want to be mainstreamed, to develop middle-class values, or be robbed of their individuality and dignity. They want their difficulties and differences to be understood rather than interpreted and evaluated. They desire to be appreciated for what they are—members of a particular subgroup who have a right to exist in America as long as they are productive, unoffending, and tax-paying citizens. Many of the special population groups addressed in this book are still sadly misunderstood; their experiences in today's schools and in society in general are a long way from being positive and productive.

Most experiences and perceptions are relevant to the group in which one was reared. Likewise, what is considered peculiar behavior in one cultural setting, may be viewed as proper and necessary in another culture. Helpers should realize that clients or students who are members of a special population may never be completely at ease with helpers. However, these clients or students will communicate if accepted on an affective level as fellow human beings and on a cognitive level as possessing a unique cultural background. Thus, we urge readers to work hard to preserve their own self-respect and the self-respect of all persons with whom they come in contact. In conclusion, the helping professional is not to stamp out mistakes nor to institutionalize, but rather to help each client or student become a productive and worthwhile individual within society, regardless of race, social beliefs, sex, age, religion, or cultural background.

HISTORICAL INFLUENCES

Special population groups frequently have been politicized and influenced by the social mood of the times. The dominant thought until the 1960s was that America was a melting pot of cultures. Its social institutions, schools, and industries reflected the democratic ideal of providing opportunity to all and upward mobility to the deserving. An assumption basic to this thought was that cultural homogeneity (assimilation) was success and cultural heterogeneity was failure. Assimilation connoted the unacceptability of minority populations' culture, language, and folkways in America. Today, a new interpretation relative to special populations is being viewed with increasing favor: that the democratic ideal, imposed by the majority on individuals through education, serves to stamp out much that is good in society simply because it is different. Ravitch (1976) stated:

> For a variety of reasons, the despair which followed the political assassinations of the Kennedy brothers and Martin Luther King, the anger which flowed from urban riots and the Vietnam War, and the cynicism which followed the Watergate disclosures—the failure theory of the radical revisionists—is strongly in the ascendancy. (p.214)

The discernable interest of American minorities for recognition and preservation of their uniqueness, for whatever reasons, has added impetus for greater understanding of America's special populations.

America, unfortunately, has a long history of oppression of minority groups. A case in point is the native American. The process of assimilation was actually funded by Congress in the early 1800s to "promote civilization among the aborigines" (Ravitch, 1976). Not until the 1930s did the government's Bureau of Indian Affairs relax its efforts for "Americanization," and then it was only for a brief period of time.

Assimilation was basic to the American system, particularly during and after World War I. Many an immigrant's children were made to feel ashamed of their family's speech, customs, and cultural values (Ravitch, 1976). During World War II, heightened patriotism and fear of subversion caused the relocation of thousands of Japanese Americans. Many Germans changed their names for fear of reprisal. Many Americans once again took note of the negative value of being different.

Not until the late 1940s, after World War II, did some significant events occur that moved society toward accepting differences. In 1947, President Truman created the president's Committee on Employment of the Handicapped to promote, on a voluntary basis, more jobs for handicapped people. In 1954, the landmark Supreme Court decision in the case of Oliver Brown brought an end to existing patterns of segregated schools. Starting with the Kennedy years in the 1960s, and more decisively during President Johnson's term of office, public policies and political forces gave impetus to the movement for individual rights. The Economic Opportunity Act and the Civil Rights Act of 1964, as well as the Elementary and Secondary Education Act of 1965, helped foster the rights of minority persons. No one act of legislation granted all "rights," but each contributed to a ripple effect for minority populations. Legislation affecting Blacks or Native Americans, for example, also affected the handicapped and refugees. Pathways were established for all special groups. Coalitions among members of special populations grew; quiet organizations became active lobbyists at all levels of government and demonstrators took to the streets.

Historical influences relative to special populations can be easily oversimplified and explained by simplistic slogans or by topographical historical counts. But, to do so is to mock what is explicitly being sought by these groups—individuality and recognition of uniqueness.

This brief attempt to synthesize some of the influences affecting special populations has been included to generate in the reader a sense of the complexity of the situational and political factors which bring us to this point in history. As stated by Ravitch (1976):

> Until late in the nineteenth century, this nation was considered by its majority to be a white protestant country; at some time near the turn of the century, it became a white christian country; after World War II, it was a white man's country. During the past several years it has become a multi-ethnic, multi-racial country intensely aware of differences of every kind...(p. 228)

The emerging sense of worth of members of special populations, then, can no longer be neglected. Learning about their different values, attitudes, desires, aspirations, and beliefs affects every citizen's life.

USERS OF THE BOOK

We urge teachers, professional counselors, and others, as they work with members of special populations, to seek out naturally existing characteristics that will aid the "different" students or clients as they learn. In other words, rather than bending the student to match the curriculum, we suggest cultivating the talents and unique cultural characteristics that already exist within that individual.

Authors of chapters in this book are writing from a particular perspective. In most cases, they either have been members of the respective subgroup or are members of that group today. We caution you not to stereotype each individual within a population strictly by the characteristics outlined within the respective chapter. For example, after reading the chapter concerning the Southeast Asian refugee, one might conclude that all such persons are reserved and shy when receiving assistance. This is not necessarily the case. You also could encounter, for example a Vietnamese client or student who is highly extroverted and wishes to shed any vestiges of the Asian culture. Thus, we urge you to avoid stereotypic generalizations of particular groups as you work with respective members.

Basic to working with individuals in a given population group are a number of assumptions which are woven into the succeeding chapters:

1. Individuals themselves rather than mass methods of working with individuals are important.

2. The individual, not the subgroup, is the unit of consideration. The individual is a person primarily and a Black, Mexican-American, or single parent, for example, secondarily.

3. The social aspects of an individual's life, including relationships at home, work, and school, are as important as that person's body and mind.

4. Accurate information is necessary as a foundation for providing services for the individual.

5. Staffing of services by adequately trained professionals via preservice and inservice programs of preparation and skill development is essential.

The process of assisting the helper to gain an understanding and awareness of the variations among individuals is a basic goal of a helping professional's instruction or training. In our opinion counselor educators, sociology professors, psychology professors, and teacher educators will find this book useful as a text for courses that are now being developed at the college level to train individuals to work with America's subgroups. The book also can be useful in inservice consultation activities with professional counselors, teachers, para-professionals, and social workers. Although the book is aimed at helping professionals, we are convinced that it also is a worthwhile reference and text for high school teachers preparing units on America's subgroups. The informative nature and authenticity of the book, we think, will greatly enhance the interest level of high school students. Helping children and adults to understand the diversity of America's population is basic to fostering a healthy American society and developing a greater understanding of and appreciation for the different societies of the world.

We recommend responding to the awareness index as you read each chapter, then thoroughly reading Loesch's epilogue. In that final chapter, Loesch provides a variety of helpful suggestions and exercises to enhance counselor preparation programs (helping professionals) with regard to special populations.

REFERENCE

Ravitch, D. (1976). On the history of minority group education in the United States. *Teacher College Record, 78,* 213-228.

Chapter 2

GETTING IN TOUCH WITH YOUR HERITAGE

James O. Fuller, Ph.D.

James O. Fuller is a Visiting Assistant Professor of Counselor Education at the University of North Carolina at Greensboro. He is the coordinator of the School Counseling Program at UNCG. His interests are in the areas of school counseling, family counseling, and multicultural issues in counseling. Before coming to UNCG as a student, he was a school counselor in Seoul, Korea, at the Seoul Foreign School, an international school for expatriate children. He earned his B.A. in Psychology at Asbury College, his M.Div. with an emphasis in counseling at Asbury Theological Seminary, and his Ph.D. at the University of North Carolina at Greensboro.

GETTING IN TOUCH WITH YOUR HERITAGE

"Without willing it, I had gone from being ignorant of being ignorant to being aware of being aware." Maya Angelou, *I Know Why the Caged Bird Sings*, p. 230.

When Socrates said "know thyself", he was probably talking about a search to discover the world of one's inner self. This was, of course, the major thrust of the "find myself" decade of the sixties in the United States. Little did Socrates know in his time, and little did we know in the sixties that "know thyself" would take a different slant for us in the nineties—the slant of learning who we are in order to more adequately deal with the differences associated with living and operating in a diverse society.

Counseling has traditionally been an activity associated with a White, homogeneous, Western society (Sue, 1992). This has been described as monoculturalism or ethnocentrism. In the United States this implies that a White, homogeneous, Western culture is "right" and superior to other cultures in the world. According to Sue, ethnocentrism was the foundation upon which our traditional theories of counseling and psychotherapy were based. In addition, ethnocentrism defined what was normal and what was not normal in counseling and psychotherapy and was responsible for the belief that differences were not to be tolerated. Following this perspective has been comfortable, successful, and secure for many people—in particular, those people whose culture was responsible for creating "the rules."

Much of the misunderstanding between Americans and people from other cultures can be attributed to Americans who believe that everyone is like them or at least should be like them. For many Americans, an assumption is "everyone shares our view of the world." Those people who tend to assume similarity also tend to lack any desire to understand persons socially or culturally different from themselves. The problem with such an attitude is that people who are guilty of assuming similarity do not usually want to change. When change does occur, it does not frequently happen haphazardly, but as a result of long-term immersion in cultures or groups different from one's own, or long-term contact with a person or persons different from one's self.

COUNSELOR AWARENESS

The need for counselors to be aware of their own cultures and population groups in order to more effectively serve people of diverse groups and cultures is a growing concern in the United States. Several demographically-related reasons for this concern exist: increasing mobility, the growth of racial and ethnic minority groups, the recognition that society is comprised of diverse groups, the aging White American population, and the declining birth rate among White Americans.

The first of these reasons is the ever-increasing mobility of the people of the world. The world has been described as much smaller than it used to be. Ever since the advent of telephones, television, airplanes, radios, and other even newer technologies, countries and peoples have not operated in solitude. More and more we are interconnected and interdependent.

The second reason counselors need to be aware of their own cultures and population groups is related to the growth rates of minority groups and the recognition of diverse groups in the United States. The 1990 Census indicates that within 20 years White Americans will constitute 48% of the population of the United States while racial and ethnic minorities will make up the remaining 52%. This fact combined with the aging White American population and the decline of the White American fertility and birth rates are striking indicators that traditional majority-based forms of counseling and therapy may not be acceptable or effective for a growing segment of the population. We, as counselors, have a responsibility to become more aware of the population groups that comprise the United States and to become aware of our values, biases, stereotypes and assumptions about human behavior. We must examine the world views we bring to the counseling encounter. Without this awareness and understanding as counselors, we may inadvertently fall into the trap of assumed similarity. Being unaware of, unwilling to change, or unable to challenge our own assumptions promotes an ethnocentric point of view.

Other counseling issues are tied to counselors' awareness of their own cultures: (1) Counselors who are not aware of their own cultural and ethnic heritage run the risk of imposing values on clients through group-learned assumptions or nonverbal behaviors; (2) counselors who are unaware of their own cultural and ethnic heritage will be limited in their treatment plans when working with diverse groups or different cultures because of a lack of understanding of the clients' perspectives and a lack of open-mindedness (whether conscious or unconscious) to differences; (3) in cross-cultural, multicultural, or diverse settings, counselors need an understanding of clients' lack of understanding in order to implement effective treatment plans; (4) with respect to effective counseling of culturally different or diverse populations, counselors need to know when to refer; and (5) counselors who are unaware of their own heritage and cultural differences run the risk of offending clients with their behavior, or of being offended by clients' behavior.

A logical assumption is that people are not intentionally unaware. The question we must ask ourselves is how we assimilate cultural characteristics while not being aware that we possess them. A follow-up question concerns how to become aware, first of our own culture or group, and then of other cultures or groups.

LEARNING A CULTURE

Cultural Encapsulation

People learn their culture through a process of "enculturation" by which an individual acquires the skills necessary to function in a particular socio-cultural system (Spradley & Phillips, 1972). Saying one is enculturated gives the impression that he/she "...has incorporated the norms of a given culture with such thoroughness that the person exemplifies that culture" (Ward, 1984, p. 54). Becoming enculturated without personal cultural awareness can lead to cultural encapsulation.

Cultural encapsulation does not come about from a malicious desire to be ingrown and unaware. It usually develops as an unconscious attempt to simplify the confusion and contradiction presented by the overwhelming variety of experience found in the world. With regard to counselors, cultural encapsulation can result from four sources: (1) lack of exposure to diverse groups, whether by choice or by happenstance; (2) attaching little importance to noted cultural differences between themselves and their clients; (3) allowing themselves to be convinced that certain methods of counseling and therapy are universally applicable; and (4) lack of willingness to explore and question their beliefs (particularly with regard to stereotypes, biases, and assumptions). All four of these sources result from a lack of awareness of one's own culture and ethnicity, understanding of other cultures and groups, and the fact that important differences exist among cultures.

The process of cultural encapsulation may be hidden from the encapsulated individual. Munroe and Munroe (1975), in their book on cross-cultural development, described humans as being as unaware of their developing culture as a fish is unaware of the water in which it is swimming. In some ways, counselor training programs contribute to encapsulation by emphasizing the tried and true methods of counseling and therapy and by minimizing the importance of training counselors to recognize and respond to differences among groups. By unintentionally or intentionally avoiding these important topics and allowing ethnocentric thinking to persist, training programs implicitly teach cultural bias.

For counselors remaining in a state of encapsulation, a certain sign of impending failure in the therapeutic relationship is for a counselor to be aware of differences but disregard them. It is possibly even more dangerous for a counselor to be unaware that differences exist. In either case, in a world where counseling across cultures or diverse groups is an ever-increasing necessity, to **not** challenge one's assumptions will inevitably lead to an inability to communicate effectively across cultures.

Culture Learning Model

When asking "How does one learn a culture?" it appears that three ways are available for people to learn cultures. One is by infusion, that is, the unintentional gathering of cultural components and their assimilation into a working pattern of thinking and behavior. In this form, our culture is second nature in that we are not even conscious of it. Next we learn our cultures intentionally. During this process our "second nature" culture is brought into consciousness. This cultural learning usually happens in schools, at seminars and workshops, and by means of reading material or audio-visuals. In other words, this form of culture learning involves more formal aspects of education but is based on the unintentional learning of the first phase. The third means involves learning about cultures other than one's own. This process involves parts of both of the first two means of culture learning. The formal aspects of education can be a jumping off point for learning the technical aspects of other cultures including customs, mores, traditions, and language. The unintentional aspect of learning comes into play when one becomes more comfortable with the new culture, reaching the point where new information is infused rather than consciously added.

Infusion

With the exception of physiological differences such as disabilities or neonatal drug dependency, most people enter the world on fairly equal footing. That is, most newborn babies are culturally similar: they share styles of behavior with other human babies. Gradually, through experience, they learn the culture into which they were born. They cry, smile, eat, crawl, walk, and talk in concert with cultural admonitions.

Within a very few years babies are proficient enough to attend to their culturally-appointed, necessary, age-appropriate tasks. Through this process of learning, communicating, and incorporating (assimilating) children become a part of the culture in which they live and the culture becomes a part of them. This is the process which my culture-learning model labels as infusion, or being unintentional, and is representative of how all people learn their first culture. In this mode, culture learning is subtle and quiet. It is similar to learning to breathe—natural and easy, and not usually highlighted as a focal point of life and development. It is within this time of development a person begins to notice within-culture differences. Logically, one would need to understand those in one's own culture who are different, but not significantly different, before attempting to cope with a second culture which might present much more notable and significant differences. Therefore, within-culture understanding begins at the infusion stage.

The intentional method or mode of learning culture involves schools and other means of formal education. In this mode people move from the cloudy state of being and existing in a culture to understanding and being more knowledgeable about a culture. This is the opportunity to think about and make explicit parts of one's culture that formerly have been blended and unconscious, be able to know and understand one's cultural milieu.

The major contributor to the intentional mode is school, where formal history, including underlying cultural assumptions, is studied, examined, and discussed. These assumptions represent beliefs about government, interpersonal relations, geography, arts and literature, and politics. Although school may be a primary avenue for implementing the intentional mode, the teaching of culture is not the primary focus of school. Culture learning can be accurately described as an unseen aspect of the curriculum. Values, assumptions, and biases, to a great degree, are taught. For the most part, this is not a result of conscious intention, but happens when people interact. Coming together in an institution or organization or in ordinary, every day interpersonal situations adds to the experience of culture learning. The unintentional mode, therefore, puts one's life into place, including activities, habits, and values, and the intentional mode allows the aspects of one's life to be identified, discussed, and evaluated.

Learning another culture is dependent to a great extent upon how well an individual can understand his/her cultural roots, including biases, stereotypes, values, and communication patterns. The deeper the understanding of one's own culture, the better the individual will be able to interact with and, ultimately, learn another culture. Contrary to what many people might think, learning another culture is different from learning one's own culture: there must be intentionality. Once a person is sufficiently enculturated in a first culture, second culture learning comes about as a result of education. If an individual has not sufficiently learned his/her own culture, the differences encountered in another culture can easily become frustrations rather than understandable differences to which he/she can adjust. Conversely, if one has learned intentionally and sufficiently his or her own culture, that learning can be a foundation for dealing with aspects of another culture.

One additional aspect of culture learning that might occur is enculturation to the second culture, learning a second culture to the same extent that the first culture is learned. Many people believe that this is not possible, rarely possible, or not preferred even if possible. Enculturation into a second culture is a two-way operation—an individual must desire to become fully enculturated, and that individual also must be allowed by the culture to become fully enculturated. In most cases, one or the other of these requirements is not met. In addition to the above, this enculturation necessitates abandoning one's original culture.

For the counselor, the first three levels of this paradigm are most important: (1) to understand that one is a cultural individual with values, biases, stereotypes, and communication patterns that are molded by culture awareness; (2) to know what these values, biases, stereotypes, and communication patterns are in order to understand the process of molding or identification that has taken place; (3) and to understand the differences between his/her culture and other cultures in order to learn and understand the idiosyncratic nature of other cultures. In this way the counselor will be able to situationally join with persons of other cultures for the purpose of counseling.

ACHIEVING SELF-AWARENESS

To the extent that the counselor and client bring to counseling their own personal cultures, any counseling relationship can be considered a cultural episode. Counselors should not only be interested in the facts about clients' cultures but should be interested in what the clients' perceptions are of their cultures. A major focus of cross-cultural counseling is the cultural episode occurring when aspects of the counselor's culture, aspects of the client's culture, and the counseling situation are combined. From within this combination emerges the newly created, unique, and shared culture of the counseling experience.

That the client's culture should be examined in order to enhance the quality of the counseling process is a wide-spread notion. Incorporated into this point of view is the attitude among some professionals that the counselor's background influences the counseling process in a direct way through the counselor's perceptions, expectations, understanding of the symptoms expressed, understanding of potential stressors, and awareness of available resources. Therefore, in order to be effective with clients, counselors should take their own cultural backgrounds into consideration, but they also should learn as much as possible about the client's cultural background. Counselors should go beyond their own self-reference criteria and consider issues and problems in counseling from the client's cultural perspective. Sue, Arrendondo, and McDavis (1992) defined a counselor who is culturally skilled as one who is in the process of becoming personally aware of cultural assumptions, biases, stereotypes, and limitations.

ATTITUDES, ASSUMPTIONS, AND BIASES

As mentioned earlier, White Americans often have difficulty considering themselves as members of a culture group. Many are surprised by the depth of their identification with "whiteness" or White Anglo-Saxon Protestant (WASP) traditions and values. "Identification with the WASP culture is usually accepted by WASPs themselves as a matter of fact and without real awareness of the subtle influences on them or of how the culture might be viewed by non-WASPs" (Axelson, 1985, pp. 368-369). In informal classroom experiments conducted by Axelson, college students were asked "Who are you?" WASP students answered, "American", "person", "adult", "man/ woman", "[job title]", or some other general answer. Nonwhite students or White minority students answered with more ethnically-related answers such as "Black," "Asian," or "Italian-American." On the other hand, when the White students were asked what they were not, they tended to answer with ethnically-related answers.

VALUES

In a general sense, Americans hold different values from much of the rest of the world. Thomas and Althen (1989) reported some differences between American values and non-American values as shown in Table 2.1.

TABLE 2.1
Illustrative Values of Americans and Non-Americans as Reported by Thomas and Althen (1989).

American Values	Some Non-American Values
Personal growth and change are valuable/desirable.	Conformity to time-tested ways of behaving.
Individuals have control over life circumstances.	Life circumstances are directed by external forces.
Personal problems are soluble.	Problems fated to occur.
Professional people can help other people solve problems.	One's problems are beyond the control of other people.
People (counselors) can be genuinely interested in welfare of strangers.	Only one's close friends and relatives can be trusted.
Open discussion of problems can be beneficial.	It is dangerous to reveal oneself to others.
Emotional disturbances have their roots in the past.	Emotional disturbances have their root in external forces or situations.
People are (more or less) equal.	There is hierarchical ranking of people in society.
Males and females are (more or less) equal.	Males are superior.

When considering values, counselors must be aware that they cannot enter the counseling process value free or value-neutral. If counselors enter with either of these two assumptions, they will run the risk of coercing clients to make decisions or behave in ways that are consistent with their own (the counselors') values rather than the clients'. They will also run the risk of making value judgments about clients and viewing clients as right or wrong, moral or immoral, instead of different.

Counseling goals also are affected by the counselor's values. Counselors who say they have no goals will inadvertently impose their (unknown) goals on clients. Since counselors do assume some degree of authority in the counselor/client relationship, since counseling is not value free, and since the values that are being transmitted are those counselors learned in their background and training, clients may want to assume counselors' values or at least attribute more credence to them than they would in a non-counseling setting. Another reaction that clients may have is to reject help altogether because the counselor's value system and theirs are so far apart. In many cases, neither counselors nor clients will take responsibility for setting the goals for counseling. Accordingly, the results of counseling are tenuous. A well-stated axiom applies here: "If you don't know where you're going, you'll end up somewhere else." Counselors are responsible for knowing what their values are, for knowing what their goals for the counseling process are, and for not imposing their values or goals on clients.

"It is a demanding task to transcend the values, biases and convictions that form our cultural contexts; it is far more difficult to recognize, own, and modify the cultural roots, depths, and patterns that shape our unconscious and automatic behavior" (Augsburger, 1986, p. 24).

STEREOTYPES

Stereotypes are defined as the application of personal theories of personality to others. These personal theories of personality consist of collected beliefs and perceptions about classes of individuals, groups, or objects. They are not to be equated with prejudice, which is defined as "...preconceived judgment or opinion without just grounds or sufficient knowledge" (Axelson, 1985, p. 120). Stereotypes may be considered similar to prejudice, however, when based on inaccurate or false information. Stereotypes, like prejudice, can be positive or negative. They can impede the counseling process by providing obstacles to viewing clients as individuals with individual characteristics. Stereotypes also can hinder the creativity of the counselor by providing a foundation for counseling that may or may not be accurate. On the other hand, stereotypes can provide hypotheses to be used in understanding individual clients. A goal for counselors is to be aware of the stereotypes they hold and then to make those stereotypes work for them. This involves discovering the necessary information to make stereotypes more accurate. Culturally-aware counselors will test their stereotypes by being aware of them, open to new experiences, receptive to new ideas, capable of looking at old facts in new ways, and willing to change old stereotypes if the hypothesis does not hold (Axelson, 1985).

COMMUNICATION DIFFERENCES

Often the statement is made that the occasion of learning another language is a prime opportunity to learn about one's own language. It has also been said that learning a second language can be severely hindered by the lack of knowledge and understanding of one's own language. These same statements can be made with regard to knowing one's own culture and being able to then learn and understand another culture.

Communication, including language, is certainly a major part of the counseling process. Counseling in a cross-cultural or multicultural situation is complicated and is sometimes hindered by communication barriers. Language barriers alone would be enough to impede the counseling process, but communication is much more than just language. Much communication can be designated "communication from the environment," based on selective perception of input. The major framework for making input selection is provided by our culture. The process of selection involves a sort of "mental map" which serves as a filter through which input passes. Information which is unintelligible or foreign to us is filtered out while other input is allowed to pass through and become part of the communication (and the counseling process). Hoopes (1981) labeled this foreign input as "noise" in a cross-cultural communication situation. Noise represents obstacles to effective communication. For example, many Asians do not desire intense eye contact. A counselor who is practicing his/her best counseling style, as learned in most counselor education programs in the United States, will want and attempt to maintain eye contact at all times. To the Asian client, this attempt may cause noise in the process. Personal distance also can be culturally determined. Some cultures consider close proximity to be appropriate only in intimate relationships. In others, standing or sitting close is the norm. Counselors who sit close and lean toward the client may be inadvertently invading the client's personal space. In some instances clients' respect for the counselor's position or job title influenced them to act or respond in certain, culturally-prescribed ways not necessarily helpful to the counseling process. For example, if the position of counselor is revered in a culture, clients may be inclined to respond as they believe the counselors want them to respond. None of these examples represent the certain death of the counseling relationship, but any one or any combination could prove to be a hindrance. When counselors are unaware of differences that are present in cross-cultural situation, the hindrances can accumulate and counseling can be less effective.

When we are operating in a culture different from our own, we have few clues for decoding environmental communication messages. Language/communication difficulties make up a major part of cultural adjustment for a client, and those difficulties can be recreated in the counseling arena. Counselors should be aware of their own "environmental communication" in order to be able to better assist clients in handling their counseling issues, and possibly in handling communication issues in general from the dominant culture. If a client cannot resolve communication difficulties, reactions may range from mild discomfort to radical emotional dislocation that would render the client unable to function in that environment (Hoopes, 1981).

Much of the resolution of communication difficulties lies in developing an understanding of the cultural code of the dominant culture. Cultural code refers to the concept that everything within the range of human interaction has meaning. A culture's code includes interpretations of silence, smiles, touch, dress, taste in music, and much more. For the client, unfamiliarity with the dominant culture's code can result in disorientation and culture shock (Hoopes, 1981). It is vital that counselors understand their own cultural code in order to be able to work with clients without imposing their values, offending the client, being offended by the client, or misinterpreting clients' nonverbal behavior. In some cases the counselor may be able to ask the client what physical arrangements would be most comfortable. Being aware of cultural differences presents the counselor with an opportunity to empower the client to (1) educate the counselor about his/her (the client's) culture, and (2) to work on his/her counseling issues in an environment that is more natural to the client.

SUMMARY

This chapter has dealt primarily with the need for counselors to examine and be aware of their own cultures, including attitudes, biases, stereotypes, values, and communication patterns.

The following material presents activities that can be used for purposes of examination, discussion, and understanding of one's cultural and philosophical roots.

EXPERIENTIAL ACTIVITIES

Individual Activities

Cultural Self-analysis

Examine your cultural heritage in terms of the following questions.

1. What is your national background, racial group, or membership in a diverse population or group?
2. What was your religious affiliation during your childhood?
3. What is your religious affiliation now?
4. What is your gender?
5. What is your age?
6. Based on your income and job, what is your current socioeconomic status?
7. In what geographic region were you reared?
8. In what geographic region do you currently reside?

Examination of Your Personal Culture

1. What is one thing you are proud of regarding your culture?
2. What is one thing that embarrasses you about your culture?
3. What is a trait, practice, or tradition that you admire about a culture other than your own?
4. Describe a time when you were hurt by someone's prejudice in words or action? Describe feelings involved.
5. Describe a time you hurt someone because of your prejudice in words or action? Describe feelings involved.

6. What is a stereotype, prejudice, or act of discrimination you learned in your youth?

7. What is a stereotype, prejudice, or act of discrimination you changed as you grew older? Why did you change?

8. Describe an incident regarding race relations in your work or school setting and how you responded to it.

9. Thinking back on the events of question 8, what would you do differently (if anything) if it was to occur now? Why?

10. Describe a time you saw an act of prejudice and did something about it?

11. Describe a time you saw an act of prejudice and did nothing about it?

12. In thinking back on the events of questions 9 and 10, would you handle things differently now? Why?

Group Activities

Identifying Cultural Differences

Recall a specific incident when you felt very uncomfortable around a group of people who were different from you.

1. Describe three feelings experienced at that time.

2. Describe any gestures or activities that could have been used to help you feel more at ease. That is, what could have been done to make you feel more comfortable? How would you have responded?

A Special Event

Special events are approached differently in different cultures and population groups. Describe a special event from your childhood. Begin with the preparations that were made before the event. Then describe what you remember about your involvement before the event, during the event, and after the event.

If you cannot remember a special event from your childhood, describe the experience of someone else—a child, a sibling, a niece or nephew, neighbor, or friend.

What Is Your Worldview?

Walsh and Middleton (1984) described worldview as being a perceptual framework through which a person sees the world. Worldviews are divided into eight different general categories: family, the arts, environmental concerns, legal institutions, health care, education, politics, and religious institutions. Briefly describe how you view each of these eight categories from the standpoint of your present cultural/population group context. For example, some people describe a family as a man and a woman, living together in a monogamous relationship, with children who are either biologically or legally (in the case of adoption) their own. Other people might add or subtract from these components when describing a family.

From your standpoint, describe and explain the general purpose(s) for:

1. The family.
2. The arts.
3. Environmental concerns.
4. Legal institutions.
5. Health Care.
6. Education.
7. Politics.
8. Religious institutions.

Outside Class Activities

Identifying Your Own Ethnic/Cultural Origins

This exercise begins with the assumption that understanding one's own background, including how one's group membership affects one's biases, perceptions, behavioral habits, and assumptions, will enhance the counselor's understanding of the client population and will enable the counselor to work more effectively and empathetically with persons of differing cultures, races, ethnicities, life-styles, and religions. Use the following questions to begin to understand how your group membership has contributed to your psychological and cultural make-up.

1. Describe your affiliation with any particular subpopulation (i.e., a group that differs based on a feature or features that distinguish it from other groups).

2. Who was significant in teaching or transmitting to you your subgroup identity? What impact does your identification with that group have on your present life? In other words, what does it mean to you to be a member of this group?

3. Are there other groups that are like your group? Name them. In what way(s) is/are they similar and different?

4. What is the most satisfying thing about being a member of your subgroup? What is least satisfying?

5. What is the attitude of your subgroup concerning ways to approach personal or emotional problems? How would members of your group attempt to solve such problems?

6. How do you think members of your family would react if you were to seek the help of a professional counselor or therapist? How would they react if you were to ask them to participate in family counseling?

Another Culture's Worldviews

After completing this exercise for your own culture or population group, repeat it with reference to the other population groups described in this book. By doing so, you may be able to discover some of the hidden (or maybe not-so-hidden) differences between yourself and others, differences which are based on divergent worldviews and not on a "right" or "wrong" approach to the world.

REFERENCES

Augsburger, D. W. (1986). *Pastoral counseling across cultures.* Philadelphia: The Westminster Press.

Axelson, J. A. (1985). *Counseling and development in a multicultural society.* Monterey, CA: Brooks/Cole Publishing.

Hoopes, D. S. (1981). Intercultural communication concepts and the psychology of intercultural experience. In M. D. Pusch (Ed.), *Multicultural education.* LaGrange Park, IL: Intercultural Press.

Munroe, R. L., & Munroe, R. M. (1975). *Cross-cultural human development.* Monterey, CA: Brooks/Cole.

Spradley, J. P., & Phillips, M. (1972). Culture and stress: A quantitative analysis. *American Anthropologist, 74,* 518-529.

Sue, D. W. (1992). The challenge of multiculturalism: The road less traveled. *American Counselor, 1,* 6-14.

Sue, D. W., Arrendondo, P., & McDavis, R. S. (1992, April). Multicultural counseling competencies and standards: A call to the profession. *Journal of Multicultural Counseling and Development, 20*(2), 64-68.

Thomas, K., & Althen, G. (1989). Counseling foreign students. In P.B. Pederson, J.G. Draguns, W.J. Lonner, & J.E. Trimble (Eds.), *Counseling across cultures,* (pp. 205-241). Honolulu: University of Hawaii Press.

Walsh, B.J. & Middleton, J.R., (1984). *The transforming vision.* Downers Grove, IL: InterVarsity Press.

Ward, T. (1984). *Living overseas.* New York: The Free Press.

Chapter 3

OLDER ORDER AMISH: CULTURALLY DIFFERENT BY RELIGION

Joe Wittmer, Ph.D.

Joe Wittmer, reared in the Old Order horse-and-buggy Amish faith in Indiana until age 16, holds a Ph.D. from Indiana State University in Psychological Services. Prior to earning the Ph.D. in 1968, he was a teacher-counselor and guidance director in Fort Wayne, Indiana schools. Dr. Wittmer also worked in the National Teacher Corps Program in the slums of Gary, Indiana, for two years. He is currently Professor Emeritus in the Department of Counselor Education at the University of Florida.

Dr. Wittmer's professional interests include writing and consultation in interpersonal communication. He has co-authored nine books and has published more than eighty-five articles in refereed journals. His two most recent books are The Gentle People: Personal Reflections of Amish Life (1991) and Valuing Diversity and Similarities: Bridging the Gap through Interpersonal Skills (1992).

Dr. Wittmer has been vice-chairperson of the National Committee for Amish Religious Freedom since 1970 and has been actively involved in litigation activities concerning their religious freedom.

AWARENESS INDEX

Directions: Please test your knowledge by responding to the following questions before proceeding to the text in this chapter.

Compute your score from the scoring guide at the end of this Awareness Index.

Select the best response for each item.

1. Approximately how many Old Order horse-and-buggy Amish are in America today?

    a. 40,000

    b. 60,000

    c. 80,000

    d. 100,000

2. When Amish parents have a marriage-age daughter they do which of the following

    a. paint the barnyard gate blue.

    b. move the hex signs off the barn onto the house.

    c. put an ad in the Amish newspaper.

    d. behave similarly to most American parents.

3. Today, the Amish are located

    a. basically in Pennsylvania.

    b. throughout 20 states, Canada, and several South American countries.

    c. a. and b. above, plus Europe.

    d. none of the above

4. Another common name for the Amish is

    a. the Amana.

    b. the Mennonites.

    c. the Plain People.

    d. all of the above

5. The Amish left Europe for America

    a. to escape religious persecution.

    b. at the invitation of William Penn.

    c. in search of religious freedom.

    d. all of the above.

6. Amish parents forbid their children to

    a. salute the flag.

    b. pledge allegiance to the flag.

    c. attend educational movies at school.

    d. all of the above.

For each item mark true or false.

T F 7. The Old Order Amish are rapidly growing in numbers.

T F 8. The Amish family organization is strictly patriarchal.

T F 9. Divorce is non-existent among the Amish.

T F 10. The first language of all Amish is German.

T F 11. The Amish are offshoots of the Mennonites.

T F 12. The problems with high school education caused several thousand Amish to migrate to South America during the late sixties and early seventies.

T F 13. Hex signs on barns are popular among the Amish.

T F 14. Amish farmers are exempt from social security payments.

T F 15. Tourism offers little monetary benefits to the Amish by their own choice.

T F 16. A 1972 Supreme Court decision exempted the Amish from compulsory high school education.

T F 17. The Amish produce and market a popular brand-name refrigerator.

T F 18. In the absence of any type of indoor plumbing, it is common for the Amish to have BO.

T F 19. Upon marriage, Amish men grow a full-beard.

Scoring Guide for Awareness Index

1. d, 2. d, 3. b, 4. c, 5. d, 6. d, 7. T, 8. T, 9. T, 10. T, 11. T, 12. T, 13. F, 14. T, 15. T, 16. T, 17. F, 18. F, 19. F

INTRODUCTION

I think they are beautiful people. They are so sober. The way they think, the way they feel, the way they dress—it is all one unit. They mind their own business and live their own life and I think this is beautiful.

These words are from Mauricio Lasansky, the artist of the famous intaglio portrait, "Amish Boy," in his description of the more than 100,000 Old Order Amish people scattered throughout 20 states. Many people confuse the Old Order Amish with the Mennonites, Amana, Hutterites, Beachy's and other religious off-shoots of the early Anabaptists. This chapter is about the Old Order, no electricity, horse-and-buggy-driving Amish.

To pinpoint the exact number of Old Order people in America today is difficult. However, we do know that more than 22,000 children were enrolled in Amish schools (grades one through eight) during 1990-1991 (*Blackboard Bulletin*, 1993). Thus, I estimate somewhere around 100,000 living in the U.S.A. with another 10 or 15 thousand more living in Canada and South America. The Old Order Amish Americans are expected to double in number during the next 15 years (Wittmer, 1991).

ABOUT THE WRITER AND GROWING UP AMISH

I am often asked what being Amish is like. Most Americans know them only by newspaper reports as a simple, virtuous people who live on farms, use no electricity, automobiles, trucks, tractors, radios, television or other such "necessities" of modern life. Their broad-brimmed black hats, black buggies, and past tussles with educational authorities have further stereotyped the Amish as anachronisms in the space age.

Religion on our Indiana farm was a seven-day-a-week affair. The way we dressed, the way we farmed, the German we spoke—our whole life-style was a daily reminder of our religion, as it is for all Amish.

The fourth of six children, I learned the Amish way by a gradual process of kindly indoctrination. At five I was given a corner of the garden to plant and care for as my own and a small pig and calf to raise. Amishmen are either farmers or in related occupations such as blacksmithing and buggy-making. My father had no doubt that I would someday be a God-fearing farmer like himself, and my mother often added in her German dialect, "and a nice black beard like your father's, you will have yet."

Because Amish parochial schools were not yet in existence, I entered the strange world of public schools at age eight. My parents deliberately planned this late entry into school so that I would be sixteen, minimum age for quitting, in the eighth grade. High school to the Amish is a "contaminating" influence that challenges the Biblical admonition to be a "peculiar people." Old Order Amish children are not permitted more than eight years of formal education. The Amish also resist education below the eighth grade if it originates in modern consolidated schools. America was at war with Germany when I entered the first grade.

Without radios and newspapers or relatives fighting (all Amish are conscientious objectors), I had little opportunity at home to keep up with its progress. School was another matter.

Boys played war games and talked constantly about the war and the branch of service they someday would join. Often I was asked where I would serve. I knew that as a conscientious objector I would never go to war. I often wished that I could help the non-Amish children gather sacks of milkweed pods, used to make parachutes for American flyers. However, I was taught to engage in activities that would further the war effort was sinful. Because I did not participate, I was often the object of derision.

The ordeal of Amish students reached its cruel peak during the daily pledge to the flag, which for religious reasons, our parents taught us not to salute or to pledge allegiance. The jabs of the students and the disappointed looks of the teacher as we remained seated cut me deeply. How could I explain that the Amish believe in praying for all governments, which, they hold, are ordained by God? How could I explain that hate is not in the Amish vocabulary? Explain it, moreover, in a German accent, for German was the first language of all Amish youth, the church requiring it to be spoken at home.

In retrospect, I can understand all too well the feelings of the non-Amish students. I can understand also why the Amish have established their own schools. What was at stake was not the feelings of Amish youth, but a way of life.

The average person often has difficulty understanding the pressures on a nonconformist in the public school system. Many activities are strictly off limits to the Amish youth, not only dancing and other "worldly entertainments", but also class pictures and educational movies. When such activities were scheduled, we Amish children were herded into another room usually to the chiding and laughter of our classmates.

My most vivid memories of boyhood days concern hostility and harassment endured by my parents and others in the Amish community because of our non-resistance stance to the war. Often "outsiders" attacked us when we rode in our buggies. They threw firecrackers, eggs, tomatoes, even rocks. Soldiers home on leave burned our fodder shocks, overturned our outdoor toilets, broke windows, and stole buggies. A favorite tactic was to sit in a car trunk and hold onto a buggy while the car sped down the road. The buggy was turned loose to smash into bits against a road bank. After witnessing many such acts of vandalism I became terrified of non-Amishmen. Because the Bible admonished them to be "defenseless Christians," my father and the other elders of the community refused to summon law officials to their defense. By Scripture they lived and by Scripture they would die if necessary. They turned the other cheek.

Although turmoil and conflict occurred outside the Amish community, peace was the watchword within its borders. We worked hard and we played hard, though without the competition of the outside world. We worked as a unit for ourselves and for the Amish community. We played together. We ate together—no meal was started until all members were present, and dinner was never interrupted by Walter Cronkite. Thrashing days, barn raisings, and public auctions were a more than adequate substitute for radios, comic books, and organized sports. Security and love abound within the Amish way of life.

Why, then, did I, at sixteen, make the decision to continue in school—the first step away from Amish origins? The answer is not simple. It includes (1) a passion for knowledge and (2) a growing resentment toward my Amish heritage, sparked by the years of derision and scorn in public schools. Somewhere on my way to a Ph.D. I fulfilled the one and outgrew the other, leaving still some unanswered questions with which psychiatrists wrestle.

Perhaps my Amish kinsmen community claimed me. And, indeed, the campus on which I teach is a far cry from my father's farm. And "a nice black beard like your father's" I do not have. But there is no animosity, no shame, among the Amish that I have left. And though I live within mainstream society, I am also vice-chairman of the National Committee for Amish Religious Freedom, the organization which defended the Amish right not to attend high school all the way to the Supreme Court and won a unanimous decision.

ABOUT THE AMISH

The Amish want no part of the values and ways that exist in the modern world about them; they wish to be left alone to live life away from the mainstream of the secular society.

The Old Order Amish strive continually to remain different from "English" as non-Amish are called. They shun the use of modern technological luxuries and travel via horse-drawn carriages. Their homes are extremely plain and lack running water, electricity, refrigerators, and most other conveniences that are found in the modern American home. Their within-group conversation is in a German dialect, and they wear home-sewn garb reminiscent of the 18th century.

> *...I know why we don't have TV like the outsiders do. We are different like God wants. The outsiders can have their TV because it's not good for you. Mom and me were in Sears one day and I saw TV a bit. Mom said they use bad words and dance on TV. We didn't watch any more. I don't want TV ever in our house...Amos, 4th grade.*

This excerpt as well as others which follow, was taken from essays written by Amish elementary school children in response to an assignment: What It's Like to Be Amish. Appreciation is extended to the Amish school teacher for sending me the essays. She wishes to remain anonymous.

Values of peace, total nonviolence, and humility are in evidence in any Amish community. They do not teach the skills of violence and technology. An Amishman realizes early in life that he is totally non-resistant and that he will never go to war. These values, lived by the Amish adults, gain the allegiance of the Amish youth, as less than five percent leave the sect. Further, no indigence, divorce, or unemployment exists. There is very little delinquency and no record of an Old Order Amishman ever being arrested for a felony and none has appeared on a welfare roll. The Amish also value calmness and tranquility—it is difficult to be in a hurry while driving a horse and buggy!

...Our horse is almost red. He is a nice horse and he takes us where we want to go. Some horses kick, but ole Jamie doesn't. I sit in the back of the buggy and I get scared when the cars come. They get close and make dust. Once Uncle John's got hit and the driver died. I was sad. Uncle John was hurt ...Rebecca, 3rd grade.

Mainstream society's emphasis on high-powered cars, computers, and contraceptive devices is conspicuously absent from the horse-and-buggy Amish world. The Amish constantly live by the scriptural admonitions to "Come out from among them, and be ye separate," and "Be ye a peculiar people." They live in isolated communities attempting to stay apart from the secular influences of the "outsider's" world. However, the Amish feel the pressing-in of America's emphasis on technology, violence, and twentieth century progress.

All Amishmen are oriented toward one goal—that of eternal life, and they equate their personal pursuance of this ultimate goal with present methods of attaining it. Industry, careful stewardship, the sweat of the brow, and beards on married men are all means to an end—eternal life.

Uniforms of any type are taboo among the Amish, but dress is uniform. Youngsters are attired as miniature adults. No change in style is to be considered, and status is not attributed to type of clothing worn. This alleviates coveting and self-pride while building group cohesion. Thus, a deviate is highly conspicuous and the similarity serves as a boundary-maintaining device.

...We wear plain clothes because the Bible says we should. Sometimes the outsiders stare at you but they never have said anything to me about my clothes. We can be a witness for others by being plain...But, just wearing plain clothes doesn't make you a Christian. I think sometimes we forget that...Elizabeth, 7th grade

An Amish man begins growing a chin beard the week before his marriage, but the upper lip and neck are kept clean shaven.

This custom is in keeping with their non-conformity to "worldly" values and ways; an "outsider" with a moustache is often in evidence. A straight line is shaved across the back of his neck and his hair is bobbed in a "crockline" appearance. An Amishman doesn't part his hair, and it is never "tapered" on the sides. The men wear large broad-brimmed black hats, suspenders, homesewn shirts without buttons or pockets, homesewn pants without hip pockets or zippers, and homesewn underwear without stripes. All shirts are sewn in such a manner so as to necessitate being put on and removed by slipping over the head.

...My dad said when he was little one time he was with my grandpa and some outsider boys called them "bushhogs." Then the boys said baa-baa like a goat. I think that is funny. Dad has whiskers but nobody went baa-baa yet...Noah, 4th grade.

Amish women do not wear make-up of any sort nor shave any part of their bodies. They wear dresses that are full-blown and not adorned with buttons, hooks and eyes, press buttons, or zippers. The only means of keeping their dresses intact is straight pins. They do not wear lacy under clothing and bras are prohibited. The female's hair is never cut and is always parted in the middle.

To an Amishman the "world" begins at the last Amish farmhouse. He has not acquired the "worldly" need for a tractor with which to farm. He may rely on a tractor for belt power, but it will be mounted on a steel-wheeled wagon and pulled from job to job by horses. He also uses horses to plow his fields and to pull his black buggy. Work is a moral directive. Labor saving devices are mere temptations and "something new." Something new or different is of the Devil while tradition is sacred. Although these customs may seem stern from the outside looking in, the Amish are healthy and happy. They have not acquired the methods of the "world" to attain their happiness or to fulfill their needs.

As a former Amishman, it is difficult to explain the feeling of being truly different from the dominant, surrounding society. Amish youngsters are reared very carefully and various methods are employed to protect them from the contaminating influences of the "outsider." The fact that one is different and peculiar is a continuous indoctrinating process for the young. They develop a strong conscience. Once indoctrinated, a person indeed finds difficulty in altering oneself to accept the values and ways of others without experiencing extreme psychic pain.

> ...Being Amish means not doing what the world does. It means living a plain life for God on earth. It means being happy without the things outsiders have...Elam, 5th grade

ABOUT THE FAMILY

The family system is the primary unit which organizes the dominant patterns of value orientation in the Old Order Amish culture. Older members of the family funnel the cultural heritage to the younger offspring. Within the Amish family setting the child learns to respond to authority, to play roles in the cooperative structure, and to obey the norms of the sect. Sibling rank is based according to age and the older siblings' roles include disciplining the younger children. The Amish family organization is strictly patriarchal. The father rears his son in the same manner he was reared by his father. The father-son relationship is excellent and the generation gap seldom exists.

Women of the family take a back seat to the men in most endeavors and the Amish male rarely does the tasks of a female, although women are expected to help with most all male tasks. Only on special occasions such as butchering, cooking apple butter, and weddings, does the husband participate in household tasks. However, women and adolescent girls frequently help with the harvest of crops, especially during cornhusking.

Marriage is supported by kinship and religious sanction. Although varying degrees of cooperation are present between the husband and wife in the fulfillment of their roles, the Amish generally adhere to the biblical tradition in which the husband is in direct charge over both his wife and children. Male and female roles clearly are differentiated and the woman's place is perhaps best typified by the biblical admonition: "The head of the woman is the man." Amish married couples do not reveal overt affection for one another in public. An Amish husband refers to his wife as "her" and she makes reference to "him." However, there is mutual respect and seldom does arguing occur in presence of children. Divorce is non-existent and no written or unwritten provisions exist for securing either divorce or separation. And, although procreation may be upper-most in their minds, it is the opinion of the writer that Amish couples permit themselves to enjoy sex.

Most Amish couples have several children and realize that as they grow older the children will care for them. The older one becomes, the wiser one becomes. The Amish never use nursing homes; it's nice to grow old. The youngest son brings his bride to his parents' farm upon his marriage. At this time, a second residence —grossdawdy haus—is built for the parents, often adjacent. The old folks get the new homes in the Amish community! The management of the farm is then turned over to the son, and the parents retire. Relationships between the two families are cordial, and even the mother-in-law/daughter-in-law relationship, which is so troublesome for other cultures with patriarchal family customs, appears amicable.

ABOUT CHILDREN AND GROWING UP

Amish couples do not practice birth control of any type and pray for children. It is indeed a happy occasion when a child is born to Amish parents. A new baby is showered with love and neighbors come from miles around for sees koffee—"sweet coffee". Sweet coffee is the custom of visiting and eating at the home of the proud Amish parents. Neighbors provide the food. There is no Godfather ceremony or gifts. A baby means another corn husker, another cow milker, but, most of all, another God-fearing Amishman. The birth is always seen as a blessing of the Lord. Thus, Amish parents feel that their children really don't belong to them; they belong to God.

Few Amish couples are without offspring. Families usually range from eight to ten children; two Amish families in my former community had sixteen children. My Old Order sister has fifteen. Couples without children almost always adopt, often from outsiders.

A baby is an integral part of the family from the moment of birth. People marvel at the attention, the love, and the affection given to the newborn Amish infant. Even when asleep the baby will be in someone's arms. For the first several months of life he or she will be held constantly by some member of the family. The baby goes where the parents go, even to the fields to work, and also will attend the long and tiresome church services when just a few weeks old. The Amish baby is considered too precious to be left in a nursery or with a baby sitter.

They may spoil babies, but Amish parents seldom refer to an infant as being spoiled. Infants can do no wrong; they remain blameless. If they have adjustment problems, the parents and community erred. An Amish baby is always diapered on someone's lap, usually the mother's or an older sister's. Amish parents do not read books on child rearing and do not stick to strict time schedules; if babies cry, something is wrong and if hungry, they are fed regardless of the hour.

Every Amish baby, if physically possible, is breast fed. No turmoil ever occurs concerning whether to breast feed or not. It is simply the only thing to do. Breasts are not viewed as sex symbols and nursing may occur whenever Amish are gathered socially, including church. Breast feeding is done without any apparent shame, but never in the presence of an outsider. To outsiders the Amish mother may appear to be hiding her infant from the eyes of the world; when in public the baby is entirely covered with a blanket. An Amish woman always wears a black shawl over her shoulders, and a mother carefully tucks the baby away under her shawl, often making the child unnoticeable. The Amish child is to be protected, even at an early age, from the "world."

Food from the table is shared with the baby at a very early age. It is not unusual to see a four month old baby being fed mashed potatoes directly from the table while sitting in the mother's lap. Eating time is an important time and activity for an Amish family. They believe that everyone, including the new baby, eats better in a group. The new baby also sleeps with the parents for the first few months of life. Along with the security this practice affords, it also is convenient for breast feeding and provides warmth in the poorly heated homes. Psychologically, this practice may contribute more to the Amish youths' apparent security than any other factor. It is difficult to pinpoint the age at which weaning occurs, but usually around age two.

Toilet training usually begins around age two with no apparent harshness or anxiety attached to the endeavor. Amish babies are held constantly, and of course, in the absence of rubber pants (which are considered worldly) they often leave their mark on the holder's lap. Although this may draw a snicker from an outside observer, the wet spot warrants no attention or concern from the Amish people present. In the absence of modern, closed-in bathrooms, waste containers for human elimination are evident in all Amish bedrooms. To the Amish, human elimination is simply a natural activity and thus toilet training is facilitated by the process of imitation and observation. This activity should not be construed to mean that there is no privacy; however, much less concern over privacy is associated with toilet activity than in the outsider culture and bedroom doors are not fitted with locks.

ABOUT AMISH ORIGIN

The Amish sect was born out of the religious turmoil of the Anabaptist movement in 16th Century Europe. To say the least, the sect's emergence was turbulent. The Anabaptists refused to baptize their offspring before the age of reason and also refused to bear arms. They were a unique group during that time in history. They were not directly involved in the fierce fighting (in the name of religion) that surrounded them and were in total disagreement and disfavor with the Catholics, Martin Luther, and the entire Reform movement. The Anabaptists yearned to return to a primitive, earlier brand of Christianity. To bring back this primitive Christianity, the Anabaptists literally accepted the Bible as their dictate. They made it clear to both church and State that they would stop taking oaths, would not baptize their offspring before the age of reason, would not drink, and would never again pick up a sword. Further, this return to primitive religion brought the wrath of the Reformers, the Catholics, and several Protestant groups upon the Anabaptists. The Anabaptists were denounced as heretics and subjected to the death penalty when caught.

Despite much suffering and death, the Anabaptists prevailed. They migrated throughout Europe in their attempts to avoid persecution. Mennonites were found in Holland and North Germany, the Hutterian Brethren in Moravia, and the Swiss Brethren in Switzerland. In the early 1600s a division occurred within the Anabaptists in Holland. The name *Mennonite* was later applied to them. The rift came about regarding the practice of shunning or *Meidung*—total avoidance, both physically and spiritually, of the excommunicated member. In 1632 ministers from several different areas in Europe met in Holland in an attempt to heal the breach within their church. Menno Simon, a former Catholic priest, was the leader of the Anabaptists in Holland. His followers became known as Mennists. The ruling bishop of the Mennonite group did not enforce shunning. A deep split developed within the Church. The leader of the emerging group which enforced the Meidung, an aggressive young Swiss bishop named Jacob Amman, took it upon himself to excommunicate all those Mennonite bishops and ministers not enforcing the Meidung. Amman's followers became known as Amish.

History records that thousands of Amish and members of other Anabaptist sects were martyred for their religious convictions during the 15th and 16th centuries throughout Europe. Anabaptists were especially persecuted for their rejection of infant baptism and their refusal to bear arms, which was considered treason. One historical event alone saved the Amish from extinction—William Penn's tour of Europe offering Pennsylvania as a haven from religious persecution. The Amish accepted the invitation to take part in Penn's religious experiment and came to America in the early 1720s to settle in Pennsylvania. No Amish are left in Europe today. The *Martyrs Mirror* (Bracht, 1938), a 1,582-page book found in most Amish homes today, contains a careful account of hundreds of Amish martyrs with details of how they met their deaths. Accounts are recorded of the severing of hands, tongues, ears, and feet along with many eyewitness accounts of drownings, crucifixions, live burials, stake-burnings, and suffocations. These accounts are related over and over again to Amish children by their parents and elders. This past persecution is still an important element in Amish historical memories helping to keep alive their present sense of distinctiveness and contributing to their group cohesion.

ABOUT THE AMISH AND PROGRESS

...Sometimes I wonder what the world is coming to. Everybody in the outsider community seems to be in a hurry when you meet them. I read in the Budget that this is why they have so many heart attacks. They are no longer satisfied with cars and airplanes as they are building rockets to ride in. Will they ever be satisfied? For me the buggy is quick enough...Esther, 7th grade

How long can the Amish survive? Urbanization is threatening the Amish way of life, particularly as farming becomes more mechanized. The economic problems of a people committed to a primitive technology while embedded in a highly technological society are immeasurable. For example, one of the Amish farmers' largest economic supplements is the selling of fluid milk to the local dairies. The demands of milk inspectors, however, have made it almost impossible for an Amishman to continue to sell milk to these dairies. When Indiana passed a law drastically lowering the required temperature of milk, it would have eliminated the 3000 non-mechanized Amish milk producers had an interested group not intervened on their behalf. The law was later changed to the Amish milkers' benefit. My opinion is that the Amish will survive and maintain their distinctiveness as long as they can keep the figurative wall between themselves and secular society. Although the Amish are growing in numbers, failure to maintain this wall brought about their disappearance in Europe, a circumstance that also could occur in America.

Many Old Order Amish members have gone along with the new milk parlors and gasoline engine operated cooling systems, but the notion of milking machines is not compatible with the Amishman's belief in non-conformity. The milk buyers, however, no longer wish to buy milk that has been produced by hand. Further, the Amish continually have refused to allow their milk to be picked up on Sunday while dairies require the Amishmen milk seven days a week or not at all.

In the past the Amish farmer has enjoyed lower overhead than his non-Amish neighbor simply because he used horses and had more "hands" around to help. The horse drawn equipment used to cost much less than the mechanical type. However, due to scarcity, this type of equipment is increasing in price every day. Also, an Amish farmer never accepts a subsidy of any type from the government. Observing his outsider neighbor accepting government subsidy for not growing a particular crop, for example, is personally stressful and difficult to understand.

The Amish settlements most threatened by urbanization are those located near metropolitan areas. In central Ohio (Madison County) an Amish community is faced with the spread of urban life from the state capital of Columbus. Many Amish farms are selling for as much as $6,000 per acre. And, if they are close to large metropolitan areas, they often bring up to $10,000 per acre. Amish farmers have always supported one another financially and used to outbid their non-Amish neighbors for land within the settlement. Now, however, the going prices are more than they can afford to pay. Also, more and more farm auctions are being held on Sunday to eliminate the sabbath-keeping Amish bidder. Thus, many Amish people have found themselves dividing their acreage into much smaller plots and taking jobs in industry on the side. Others are moving to Central and South America in search of new lands. As a matter of fact, several Central and South American countries are successfully recruiting the Amish today, offering them inexpensive land, no military inscription, and total religious freedom.

Almost half of the Amish people in Starke County, Ohio, one of the larger Amish settlements in America, have given up farming during the past twenty years. Some have maintained a small farm for cattle and pasture to graze their driving horses while turning to the traditionally approved occupations of masonry and carpentry. However, many are now pursuing work in church-approved factories, a practice which in the past was strictly taboo, while many other families are moving to other locations.

I'm confident that factory work, in time, will erode many of the values the Amish have so long treasured. Industrial work is a departure from tradition made necessary by the changing economy. Factory hours are shorter and pay checks are higher, but factory work is especially detrimental to the Amish farm family organization. Also, joining the Union is strictly forbidden by the Amish church. During 1980 a group of Amishmen lost their factory jobs in Ohio because of the closed-shop situation in that state. Some Amish churches that recently permitted factory work have now reversed that decision. And, many outsider factory owners are perplexed when, because of a new rule made on Sunday work hours, not one of their hard-working Amishmen shows up for work the following Monday morning.

Not only has urbanization and progress brought about a change for many Amishmen, but also it is changing the life-styles of many Amish females. It has never been unusual for a few young man to leave the Amish church for the more liberal Mennonite way of life or even to join an outsider church, but now some young women are following suit. In the past, a woman leaving the Amish church was unheard of. Why this sudden shift? Most Amish elders blame it on "working out" in modern outsiders' homes. When young women work as maids for another Amish family they earn between $25 to $35 per week. However, they learn quickly that they can earn the same amount in one day by doing housework in town for outsiders. Also, some young Amish women, much to the disdain of the elders, are taking jobs in factories. My own mother, at age 80, gave up her job as maid among the outsiders.

America's emphasis on education also threatens the Old Order Amish sect's way of life. The Amish teach their young that formal education is worthwhile up to a point, but that too much is un-Christian and only for the foolish. If a fear exists among

Amish parents, it is that of losing their children through too much formal education. The parents yearn for complete jurisdiction over their children's activity and have it everywhere except in the public school classroom.

Against formal education beyond the eighth grade (and sometimes below that level if it requires attending a modern consolidated school), the Amish are especially opposed to the "godless" science, the competitive atmosphere, and the alien teachers found in the modern school. They prefer the old-fashioned one-room school with its limited facilities, since this type is more in keeping with their simple domestic life. The Amish want to train their youth at home in the care and operation of farms and, to them, this requires no more than eight years of reading, writing, and arithmetic. Because most states require that a child attend school until 16 years of age, the Amish initiated a vocational plan of their own for all students beyond the eighth grade but not of legal quitting age. The vocational plan came under repeated legal attack by state and local school authorities across the country.

These school battles were fought in communities in Michigan, Ohio, Iowa, Pennsylvania, Kansas, and several other states. In Iowa, in 1966, deputy sheriffs chased Amish children through cornfields in an attempt to bus them to a public school after school officials had demanded that the Amish comply with the state's attendance laws. The jailing of many Amish parents with fines totaling nearly $10,000 failed to alter their beliefs.

One of the most publicized legal encounters took place in Kansas in a 1967 test case. An Amish farmer, convicted of sending his fifteen year old daughter to the sect's vocational school instead of the local high school, disregarded a centuries-old stricture against litigation and permitted the then recently formed National Committee of Amish Religious Freedom to take his case to the State Supreme Court. By a four to three vote, the court refused to hear the case. This ruling created a precedent; many subsequent cases were lost as lower courts continually ruled against the Amish. The troublesome predicament ended on May 15, 1972 when the Committee won a unanimous U.S. Supreme Court decision exempting the Amish from state laws compelling their children to continue schooling beyond the eighth grade. In essence, the Court indicated that compulsory, formal education beyond the eighth grade would greatly endanger, if not destroy, free exercise of the Amish religious beliefs. The ruling affirmed a 1971 judgment by the Wisconsin Supreme Court. Legal scholars indicate that this case was the first time in the history of America that compulsory education laws had been challenged successfully.

Although the school controversy was the basic reason for the emigration of several thousand Amish to Central and South America in the late 60s and early 70s, there are currently more eminent ones. Impingement, persecution, and harassment come from several different sources. Local, state, and national legislators often pass new laws without the consent, knowledge, or consideration of different minority groups. A case in point was a law passed in Indiana requiring a triangular reflectorized emblem to be affixed to the back of all slow moving vehicles. The Amish viewed this three-cornered emblem as a hex symbol, or "the mark of the beast" as described in the Bible, and refused to affix it to their buggies (Contrary to popular belief the Amish do not affix HEX signs to their barns!). They further felt that the gaudy emblem would glorify man rather than God. In an attempt at compromise the Amish offered to use neutral color reflector tape. Several Indiana Amish farmers were placed in local jails for following their religious scruples. They never raised their voices and served their jail sentences without any apparent feelings of animosity. Finally a compromise was reached.

The Social Security system also caused immeasurable problems for the Amish, who view it as a form of insurance, a practice that is religiously taboo. Even though they would never collect one cent. Many Amish farmers had good cattle and horses confiscated by the Internal Revenue men during the middle sixties for failure to pay social security. When the IRS men came to an Amish farm to confiscate livestock, the nonaggressive Amish unselfishly assisted them in choosing the livestock they felt would best make up for their lack of paying social security. They were extremely kind to the IRS men and local newspapers carried stories about them being taken to the house, given coffee, and fed. In one case they loaded the livestock and went fishing with the Amishman in the farm pond. Other news accounts revealed how the government men left (with the confiscated livestock) with tears in their eyes. However, unlike many other controversies involving the Amish, this one had a happy ending—President Johnson attached a rider to the Medicare Bill exempting all Amish farmers from paying social security. But the problem keeps coming up. In a 1987 case, the courts ruled against an Amish farmer for not withholding social security payments from Amish employees on his farm. Thus, in a strange interpretation of the Medicare Bill rider, an Amish farmer does not himself have to pay social security, but must pay it on behalf of his Amish employees!

One of the Amish counties most threatened by urbanization and progress during the 1990s is Lancaster County, Pennsylvania— the Amish heartland. This is the county first offered as a sanctuary to the Amish by William Penn when he toured Europe. The Amish in this beautiful area of Pennsylvania are the target of several thousand tourists per year. Tourists travel through the county's back roads in tour buses or rented buggies and are often a nuisance to the Amish. The Amish write about their tourist problems to the *Budget* (the Amish weekly newspaper) telling about the rudeness of tourists. Recently, an Amish scribe wrote to the *Budget* describing how a busload of tourists trampled his garden in pursuit of a picture of his family as they worked in the garden. In all fairness, most tourists are respectful of the Amish. It is those ignorant of the Amish values and ways who cause problems.

Traveling through Lancaster County one finds an endless string of "Amish" motels, "Amish" food, "Amish" restaurants, "Amish" gift shops, "Amish" museums, "Amish" amusement parks, and so forth. Tourism in this one Amish community is now a multi-million dollar a year business! In the winter time, one can travel through Lancaster County going through such tiny Amish villages as Paradise, Intercourse, and Blue Ball, which have been left undisturbed for over 100 years. There one sees the horse and buggy driving Amish, water wheels, windmills, and other sights reminiscent of 200 years ago. But in the summertime the mood changes to a carnival atmosphere as bumper to bumper traffic and billboards proclaim, "It's real—it's genuine, you're here. Visit the house and farm occupied by the

German-speaking Amish. Stop and talk to these genuine Amish people." A tourist's inquisitiveness can quickly become a nuisance to the Amish who strive to avoid publicity and photographs at all costs (Wittmer, 1991).

> *...the tourists often bother us. They have cameras and we don't want pictures. The other night dad was milking and the man kept trying to take dad's picture. He kept hiding his face...Ester, 5th grade.*

I urge anyone who plans to tour an Amish community to please take care to learn about the uniqueness of some of the Amish values and ways prior to your visit. In addition, leave your camera in your car! The Amish will appreciate it.

> *...I don't know what the tourists want at school. They just want to look at us maybe. I wish they would leave us alone...Esther, 5th grade.*

The movie *Witness*, an intriguing suspense/love story set in Lancaster County, may have heightened many viewers' understanding of the centrality of religion in the Amish life-style. However, the filming marked a new high in symbolic and real life intrusion and harassment for the Amish. Filming the movie set off a furor among Amish and non-Amish alike. The Amish were strongly opposed, but most kept their views to themselves. One can only imagine the turmoil created among the Amish in Lancaster County when the sound trucks and taboo movie cameras arrived. The National Committee for Amish Religious Freedom tried to stop the filming but to no avail. However, as one Amish bishop explained to the writer, "Fortunately, no Amish person will ever see the movie!" Unfortunately, tourism increased dramatically because of the movie.

Tourism offers almost no monetary benefits to the Amish by their own choice. They are not in the selling business, nor the hotel and motel business. One of the most damaging aspects of tourism is that Lancaster County has now been "discovered" and recently married Amish farmers cannot find land to purchase. People who are benefiting the most from the Amish leaving the farms are the local industry owners. Amish men have been groomed to awaken at 4:00 AM and work is a moral directive whether on the farm or in a factory. They make excellent factory workers, but usually unhappy ones.

It should be acknowledged that, although they live a difficult life and are sometimes oppressed, the Old Order Amish continue to do well in America. Locke (1992) best described this dichotomy when he stated:

> Unlike most oppressed groups in the United States today, the Amish are not deprived of their ability to secure enough to eat and live in suitable quarters. However, to some outsiders, the Amish choice of a way of life may seem much like poverty. The Amish can live very cheaply by dressing plainly; by building or making most of their clothes, houses, and barns; by not using electricity; and by not owning any modern conveniences or machines. If anyone in the community is in need, everyone comes to that person's assistance. Their simple way of life, coupled with a tradition of community aid, has enabled the Amish to be both healthy and prosperous. (Locke, p. 31, 1992)

It is difficult to measure the total effect that America's progress has on a people such as the Amish who are committed to a primitive technology in the midst of a modern world bent on secularization. Nevertheless, the Amish are a tenacious people and are intent on maintaining their way of life. Family and closeness to one another is everything to the peaceful Amish. With those ties they have survived in America for well over 200 years. Now, the land offered to them by William Penn is cluttered, costly, and offers little accommodation for their way of life; however, they will move wherever is necessary to preserve the faith and sustain the family. As their King James Bible indicates, "If they stop up your wells, move to new lands." It is sobering to realize that some peace-loving Amish people are finding it necessary to emigrate from America in search of religious freedom during the 1990s! Yet, it is a fact of life— it is difficult not to be a modern man in America today (Wittmer, 1991).

ABOUT COUNSELING
THE OLD ORDER AMISH CHILD

Parts of this section are from "Counseling the Old Order Amish Child" by J. Wittmer and A. Moser (1974). *Elementary School Guidance and Counseling, 8,* 263-271. Reprinted by permission.

What role does public education play in the threat to the Amish way of life? In the past, most Amish communities were content to send their children to the local public elementary schools. Approximately 5,000 still attend today. However, the emphasis on science and evolution, the apparent increase of violence and drug usage, and educational TV have contributed to a sudden increase in the number of Amish parochial elementary schools.

Public school personnel who come into daily contact with Amish children can lessen the Amish people's perceived threat. This lessening of threat is especially so with elementary school counselors, since many varied methods or approaches can be used effectively when working with these "peculiar" children. Some common counselor functions, however, might be ineffective with Amish children.

Rebecca is a young child who attends a public elementary school. In her broken English, she says, "It makes me wonder why outsider kids make fun when a movie is on by the teacher and we make quick to leave the room"

Amos, a young boy attending the same school and who, like Rebecca, speaks German as a first language, also wonders about his relationships at school. "The Englisher boys are mad with me for not pledging the flag. Dad says a graven image it is. Why do they git me, already?"

And Elam, another child in the same school, says, "The coach he says that shorts I must wear next PE class. What should I tell him, yet?"

How would you respond to these children? Would you tell little Rebecca that she might enjoy the movie if she stayed in the room? Would you suggest that Amos should be patriotic and join in the pledge of allegiance? And Elam? Would you tell him that he should put on the PE shorts because physical education is good for his health?

Are Amish children different from non-Amish children? Because the Amish are suspicious of outsider investigations, very few studies have been completed concerning their personalities, but of the few available studies, all but one study have been about Amish children. The research, summarized in Hostetler and Huntington (1992) indicates that Amish youth are significantly more introverted and submissive than non-Amish youth. These studies also describe the Amish personality as being quiet, responsible, and conscientious. The first and only research concerning the personality of Amish adults (Wittmer, 1970) suggested that the adult Amish personality parallels that of Amish elementary school children. An uniqueness exists about the Amish personality whose elements are common to all members of the sect. This model personality or psychic unity among the Amish people is largely due to common childhood experiences and child-rearing practices.

Hostetler and Huntington (1992), who studied Amish children for more than 20 years, found further evidence of homogeneity when more than 60% of the total Amish population they studied fell within two personality types on the Meyers Briggs Type Inventory: (ISFJ) Introversion, sensing, feeling, judgment, and (ESFJ) extraversion, sensing, feeling, judgment. One of the most interesting findings in the Hostetler-Huntington studies dealt with the *happy time drawings* of Amish children. The Amish drawings always included work-related activities, whereas non-Amish drawings frequently showed competitive activity and hostility. Further, the drawings revealed that regulation and conformity, rather than spontaneity, were dominant Amish characteristics. One important finding for teachers and counselors was the de-emphasis of the self and the importance of the group. The family, the church, and the community are seen as having more significance than the individual.

About the Effective Counselor

The counselor who is effective with Amish children will be genuine and empathic, but also will follow the guidelines presented.

De-emphasize the concept of self. The Amish child is taught to be cooperative rather than competitive, innovative, or aggressive. To the Amish, a child is not a unique individual. He or she is simply one member of a God-fearing group and should be treated as such. Individual resolution is undesirable. Humility is a virtue, and pride, especially self-pride, is a cardinal sin. Amish children do not show pride in dress or appearance (No mirrors are in the home) or self-accomplishments (They never recite memorized prayers aloud as this would show pride in one's ability to memorize). Yet Amish children, like other children, have basic psychological and developmental needs. They desire to be wanted, to be needed, and to gain acceptance from peers and authority figures. If Rebecca seems unmoved by your praise for a task well done, don't confuse her reactions with indifference. Her reactions most likely coincide with her culture's sanctioned behavior.

Amish youth seek academic achievement and most teachers report that Amish children are good students. This fact may appear contrary to denial of self-accomplishment. However, work is a moral directive within the culture. The Amish child works hard in school and achieves but does not talk about these accomplishments and does not expect praise for doing those things that are expected. For example, when an Amish boy does an excellent job of cleaning the barn, his father simply states, "The barn is now clean." However, any attempt on the part of educators to introduce competitive activities in order to achieve educational goals could only mean, in Amish terms, the loss of humility, simple living, and God's love!

Recognize the limitations of tests. Can you imagine the frustration of taking a test that requires you to identify a gas tank correctly being removed from a car, a well-known cartoon character, or a particular control dial on an electrical appliance when you've never seen them before? Amos, for example, sees school as a bewildering environment, and most of his experiences there are new. The Amish child will most likely never have heard of the Michael Jackson, Sesame Street, or the Miami Dolphins. When using the school's rest room for the first time, the child will not understand how a commode functions. For Amos, it is likely to be a perplexing experience.

Speed is rarely stressed in the Amish culture and children are admonished by their elders to do careful, accurate work. Amish children are told to work steadily and to do well what one does, rather than do a great deal and make careless mistakes. Children are taught never to skip anything that they do not understand. They are to ponder it, to work at it, until they have mastered it. Thus, a teacher or counselor who administers a speed test to an Amish child could increase unnecessary psychological stress and fail to gain a true picture of the child's skill.

Amish children are at a disadvantage when taking any standardized test, especially if they are being compared to non-Amish children. The Amish see no purpose in formal schooling beyond the elementary grades. Performing well on a standardized test in order to gain a better job or enter high school or college has no special meaning and is useless as a motivational scheme. In addition, testing is often taboo within an Amish community, and educators should seek the consent of Amish parents before administering any test. Educators also will find that Amish parents are not interested in knowing their children's achievement test scores or a comparison of their child's scores with those of other children in the United States, or for that matter, in the classroom.

Understand culturally different groups' varied worlds of work. The world of work of Amish children is rather limited. Both children and parents are uninterested in career exploration. The vocational preferences of Amish children, for example, tend toward service occupations and manual work. These children emulate the work roles of Amish adults and want to be farmers or farmers' wives. Studies reveal (Hostetler & Huntington, 1992) that Amish boys prefer farming or farm related work, whereas girls prefer housekeeping, gardening, cooking, cleaning, and caring for children. These vocational aspirations and dreams are realistic and attainable within the limits of Amish culture. One should note that the feminist movement has not brought about any changes in the Amish life-style. The Amish still interpret the King James Bible literally, especially those sections concerning the submissive role of women.

Respect the need for social distance that Amish children have with non-Amish children. A very real concern among Amish parents today is the possibility that their children will form close, personal friendships with non-Amish children and become too comfortable with the ways of the outside world before they totally understand their own Amishness. Any attempt on the counselor's part to have Amish children form friendships (such as mixed group counseling) with non-Amish children will be contrary to the wishes of Amish parents.

Avoid probing into home or Amish community problems. Because institutions such as the home and the church are held in high esteem, Amish children enjoy participation within these institutions. The possibility of bringing shame on their family will inhibit talking about family or cultural problems. For example, even though an Amish child may be overwrought concerning an excommunicated family member, it would be even more shameful to discuss it with a non-Amish person.

Realize that a caring relationship is not enough. Affective understanding alone is not sufficient when counseling Amish children. The effective counselor also will be knowledgeable of the customs, traditions, and the values existing in the Amish child's unique environment. The acute disparities in culture will most certainly be compounded if a counselor lacks knowledge and then interacts with a confused and bewildered Amish student.

Accept the fact that an Amish child's parents may have asked him or her to avoid counselors. Amish parents are responsible for training their children and consider themselves accountable to God for doing it correctly. Thus, your counseling or talking with them concerning values or morals may appear disrespectful to an Amish parent. If the home is responsible and obligated for moral and religious training, then you may appear to be a meddler.

Amish adults do not seek counseling from professional counselors. At times, however, an Amish adult will seek the advice of others within the commune, especially ministers. Thus, school counselors and teachers should realize that Amish parents are extremely leery of any outsider with advice for them or their children. They will quietly listen to these suggestions, but will definitely not incorporate them until after they have sought council with at least three Amish adults. Using three adults to solve problems and/or make decisions is a common Amish practice. For example, if a dispute develops between two Amish farmers, three men are selected to arbitrate and find the solution. Their decision is final.

The Amish are only one distinct religious minority group found in public schools. They are easily recognized, but other such groups are not. Mennonites, Hutterites, Christian Scientists, and many other groups may in appearance blend into a school's population. But their values, beliefs, and attitudes, like those of the Amish, play a significant part in attitudes toward school and the way in which they learn. In summary, to be an effective counselor with an Amish child in a public school setting you will need to learn about the values and ways of the Amish culture. It often will be necessary to keep your own cultural biases in check. Be genuine and empathic. Don't bend the child to match the curriculum. Let the curriculum meet the Amish child's needs.

EXPERIENTIAL ACTIVITIES

Individual Activity

1. Some individuals known by the Amish as "seekers" attempt to become "Amish." Although always accepted few have remained Amish. What do you think are the reasons for the almost 100% attrition rate of such individuals?

2. How might certain cultural values held by the Amish be exploited by the majority culture? Select three such values and explain how exploitation might occur.

3. Which Amish characteristics given in this chapter contrast the most with your own? Would these differences affect communication between you and an Amish person? How? How would those differences affect your ability to effectively counsel with an Amish person?

4. Assume the role of an Amish person and write a short essay titled, "Living in Modern Day America."

Group Practice Activity

Instructor's Note

Read the following fantasy aloud to the class participants. Then place them into groups of 5 or 6 and request that they take turns sharing their respective fantasies. Suggest that they use appropriate counseling responses during their discussion. Specifically request that they not interpret another's fantasy. However, self interpretation may be appropriate during the small group discussion.

A Structured Fantasy

You're feeling relaxed now; you're very calm. It's in the middle of the week, just prior to bed time. You find yourself sitting in your comfortable chair very relaxed. Your eyes are closing... You are tired, very tired, and decide to go to bed. You enter a very restful sleep, a very restful sleep; it's just one of those nights when you feel very good, very sleepy, very restful (pause 15 seconds). Now, visualize yourself awakening the next morning. You see yourself entering your bathroom. Now, take a careful look in the mirror. You see there's been a rather startling transformation during the night... You woke up as a member of the Old Order Amish culture!

You went to bed as a member of one culture and you woke up Amish. (pause) How does it feel? (pause) Now, you find yourself walking outside and meeting your best friend. How does your friend react? (pause) Now, visualize yourself walking across the campus. How do people react to you? You meet your favorite instructor. What happens? How do you feel? What is the overall reaction towards you? (pause) OK. Open your eyes now." (Adapted from Wittmer, 1992).

Outside Class Activities

1. Read the following poem, recently written by a sixteen-year-old Amish female, and then respond to the two questions that follow. Place your responses in writing and be prepared to discuss them during a future class session.

A Buggy Ride

Who'd want to drive a motor car
    When he could have a horse?
There may be many others who
    Would take a car, of course.
They do not know the joy of it,
    A horse and buggy ride.
The feel of wind upon your face,
    No stuffy seat inside.
Along the road we hear birds sing.
    And watch a squirrel dash,
And just enjoy the scenery
    Instead of rushing past.
The sound of horses's trotting feet
    Is music to the ear.
No car is ever half as nice
    At any time of year.
True, winter's snows are very cold
    And rain makes me quite wet.
The wind can be uncomfortable—
    Our fingers freeze, and yet
I still would choose a buggy ride,
    In spite of cold or heat.

> I shall insist that it is true,
> A buggy can't be beat.
>> -R. Wenger (reprinted with permission)

  a. What insights did you gain regarding the Amish from reading the above?

  b. What struck you most about the poem?

2. Think about your concepts and experiences from this chapter on Old Order Amish. As you do respond to the following questions:

   a. What did you learn that has the strongest implications for the Amish person?

   b. With someone different by religion?

   c. For multicultural counseling in general?

REFERENCES

Blackboard Bulletin, Editor. (1993, January). Amish schools. Aylmer, Ontario: Pathway Publishers.

Bracht, J.V. (1938). *Martyr's mirror.* Scottdale, PA: Mennonite Publishing House.

Hostetler, J., & Huntington, G.E. (1992). *Amish children: Education in the family, school, and community.* Ft. Worth: Harcourt Brace Jovanovich.

Locke, D.C. (1992). *Increasing multicultural understanding.* Newbury Park, CA: Sage Publications.

Wittmer, J. (1970). Homogeneity of personality characteristics: A comparison between Old Order Amish and non-Amish. *American Anthropologist, 72,* 1063-1068.

Wittmer, J. (1991). *The gentle people: Personal reflections of Amish life*. Minneapolis: Educational Media Corporation.

Wittmer, J. (1992). *Valuing diversity and similarity: Bridging the gap through interpersonal skills*. Minneapolis: Educational Media Corporation.

Wittmer, J., & Moser, A. (1974). Counseling the Old Order Amish child. *Elementary School Guidance & Counseling, 8*, 263-271.

Chapter 4

ASIAN AMERICANS

David Sue, Ph.D. and Diane M. Sue, Ph.D.

David Sue, Ph.D., is currently Director of the Mental Health Counseling Program at Western Washington University. He received his undergraduate degree at the University of Oregon and completed his doctorate at Washington State University in 1973. Dr. Sue has research and clinical interests in Asian Americans and counseling process variables. Dr. Sue frequently collaborates with his brothers, Derald and Stan, on articles concerning Asian Americans.

Diane Sue, Ph.D. who is an Intervention Specialist for Burlington-Edison School District in the state of Washington, received her doctorate in Educational Psychology from the University of Michigan, Ann Arbor. Dr. Sue's special interest include classroom management strategies, consultation, and minority populations.

AWARENESS INDEX

Directions: Mark each answer true or false. Compare your answers with the scoring guide at the end of the test.

T F 1. Most Japanese voiced strong objections to the United States government concerning their forced evacuation to detention camps during World War ll.

T F 2. The incidence of poverty among elderly Chinese is much higher than it is for elderly African Americans and Spanish-speaking populations.

T F 3. College enrollment rates for Chinese and Japanese between the ages of 18-24 is quite high, but the percentage of these individuals who actually complete college is surprisingly small.

T F 4. Most studies indicate the Chinese and Japanese groups have highly similar values and family structure.

T F 5. Asian Americans appear to have as varied a choice of careers as their Caucasian counterparts.

T F 6. Most Asian American clients feel more comfortable in a structured counseling environment than one that is unstructured.

T F 7. Most second and third generation Chinese and Japanese children in the United States use English as the primary language in their homes.

T F 8. Asian American clients often seek counseling or therapy.

Scoring Guide for Awareness Index

1. T   2. T   3. F   4. T   5. F   6. T   7. F   8. F

PERCEPTIONS, SENSITIVITY, FEELINGS

The following poems were written by fifth and sixth grade children from Franklin School in Berkeley, California as part of a class project. They illustrate the perceptions, sensitivity, and feelings of a minority group in America. (D.W. Sue, 1973, pp. 397-399.)

I'm an Asian and I'm proud of it. I'm a person although some people don't look upon me as one. They call me names and think it's funny! Sure I get called names. Do you think I like it? After all, how would you feel if someone called you a "Ching chong Chinaman" or a "Nip"? They can't even tell us apart.

They say things about our culture like, "They write so funny." Even our language they make fun of by going Ching, cho, chu.

I'm an Asian. I've got dignity, but the thing I don't have is friendship.

Robert Chung

Asians are silent people
Never speaking of distress
Bearing much in their heart
The burden of the silent one.

Standing up to their rights
Trying to prove loyal by working hard.
America, a place of hopes...
For White people only!

Leah Appel

I am an Asian. Asians are proud people and I am proud to be Asian. Many people call me Caucasian, especially Blacks. I have been called names, as many people have. Asians have been placed in concentration camps, discriminated against and bombed. Yet at this moment, they are fighting and dying for their country in Vietnam.

People who don't know the Asian history say things like "All Chinese are laundry men" and "All Japanese are gardeners." Of course, I know it was the only menial labor available when the immigrants first came to America.

I hate that song with, "Japanese eyes slant down and Chinese eyes slant up." Last year I was the only Asian in my class. As an insult they called me "Chinese spies." It is enough to make you sick.

But, I am proud to be Asian and I want all to know.

Naomi Nishimura

*Yellow is the sun coming
up in the morning And the sun coming down
in the evening
Yellow is a house being painted
Yellow is the color of some pencils
Yellow is the sunset,
Yellow is the sunrise.
Yellow is the color of some paper.
It's the peeling of a
grapefruit or lemon,
Yellow is the shine
of a light.
Yellow is a banana.
Yellow is a color that
is very bright to
everyone
Yellow is me!*

Jon Mishima

POPULATION

As of 1990, approximately 7.3 million Asian Americans were living in the United States, accounting for approximately 2.9% of the total population (U.S. Census Bureau, 1993). Asian Americans continue to be one of the fastest growing minority groups. Their population is predicted to reach 20 million by the year 2030 (Ong, 1993). Difficulties arise in an attempt to characterize Asian Americans because this population is comprised of so many different groups. At least 30 distinct subgroups exist with the Asian American population, each within unique values, customs, religion, and language. Compounding the problem are the differences that exist within specific Asian American groups in terms of acculturation, primary language, and generational status in the United States.

The Asian American population consists of both recent immigrants (approximately 2,400,000 arrived between 1981 - 1988) (*U.S. Dept of Justice*, 1989), many of whom are of refugee status, and individuals who have been in the United States for many decades. Tremendous diversity exists among the Asian American population with respect to cultural assimilation, knowledge of the English language, socioeconomic status, and educational background. The unique needs of Southeast Asian refugees are addressed elsewhere in this book.

THE CHANGING FACE OF ASIAN AMERICANS

The makeup of the Asian American groups have changed dramatically in the last 10 years. In 1980, the largest Asian populations were the Chinese (812,178), Filipino (718,894), and Japanese (716,331). In 1990, the most populous ethnic groups were the Chinese (23%), Filipino (19%), Japanese (12%), Asian Indian (11%), Korean (11%), and Vietnamese (8%). Because of the large influx of immigrants, the majority of Asian and Pacific Islanders are foreign born with the exception of Japanese Americans. The diversity of Asian Americans groups, each with different cultural norms and values, prevents adequate representation of each of the groups in this chapter. The focus of the present chapter, therefore, will be primarily on the Chinese and Japanese groups, which currently comprise two of the largest Asian-American populations in the United States and which have the earliest history of entry into this country. According to the *U.S. Census Bureau* (1988) the Chinese are the largest Asian American subgroup and are located in the greatest concentration in San Francisco/Oakland, California, New York City, and Los Angeles/Long Beach California. Japanese and Filipino Americans live primarily in Hawaii or California. Large populations of Korean Americans live in California and New York. The Vietnamese are concentrated in California and Texas.

BRIEF HISTORY OF ASIAN IMMIGRATION IN AMERICA

Asian American groups immigrated to the United States for much the same reasons as other immigrant groups—the pursuit of financial security and an improved standard of living. The first Asian group to migrate heavily to the United States was the Chinese in the 1840s. The immigration was triggered by the discovery of gold in California coupled with a disastrous crop failure in China. In contrast to other immigrant groups, the Chinese were sojourners—individuals who did not seek to settle permanently but who desired an opportunity to earn some money and return to China. The Chinese immigrants, who were primarily males, worked as laborers in gold mines and on railroads or were employed at other less desirable jobs such as laundry work. They were subjected to massive discrimination and prejudice soon after arriving. These attitudes resulted in the Exclusion Act of 1882 which prevented the legal immigration of Chinese from 1882 until 1944, when the act was repealed. This ban resulted in the separation of husbands from their wives for decades and a highly unequal sex ratio. In 1890, over 100,000 Chinese males and only 3,868 Chinese women were in the United States (Wong, 1973). Not until the 1960s was a closer balance attained. Today the elderly males still form a higher percentage than their female counterparts (Office of Special Concerns, 1974; U.S. Census Bureau, 1980).

Immigration of the Japanese in large numbers began in the 1890s from Hawaii and Japan. They also were lured by the promise of better conditions and wealth in the United States and filled the demand for an inexpensive source of labor to replace the Chinese. Many Japanese males came to the United States to live and later sent away for picture brides from Japan. As laborers, they worked on railroads and in canneries. Because the great majority were from the farming class, many worked on unwanted lands or found work as a agricultural laborers.

Although the Japanese were considered more desirable than the Chinese because they brought their families, prejudice and discrimination quickly followed. In 1906, the San Francisco Board of Education issued an order segregating Japanese from White school children (Masuda, 1973). The Gentlemen's Agreement limited immigration and the Alien Land Act of 1920 (which was directed primarily against the Japanese) prevented them from purchasing land. An editorial in the *San Francisco Chronicle* in 1920 reflected the attitude of White Americans at the time (Ogawa, 1973):

> The Japanese boys are taught by their elders to look upon...American girls with a view to future sex relations...What answers will the fathers and mothers of America make...? The proposed assimilation of the two races is unthinkable. It is morally undefensible and biologically impossible. American womanhood is far too sacred to be subjected to such degeneracy. An American who would not die fighting rather than yield to that infamy does not deserve the name...(p. 7)

Feelings against the Japanese culminated in the location of over 110,000 persons of Japanese ancestry into detention camps during World War II. Effects of these camps resulted in financial ruin for many Japanese families, disrupted the family structure, and served to break up Japantowns.

The 1917 Immigration Act excluded all Asian immigration with the exception of those from the Philippines, which was an American territory. Filipinos were considered a source of cheap labor and were brought over to work on Hawaiian plantations. After the Korean war, refugees from Korea were admitted. With the Immigration Act of 1965, nearly one third of the immigrants were from the Philippines, Korea, China, and India. The conflict in Vietnam brought a large number of refugees and immigrants from Vietnam, Laos, and Cambodia. These new Asian Americans also encountered prejudice and discrimination (Leung, 1990).

SPECIAL PROBLEMS

As a group, Asian Americans have not received widespread attention from educators, counselors, or state and federal officials. The prevailing view that Asian Americans are model minorities and problem free has resulted in limited financial and moral support. Although special concern sessions were held for Blacks, Spanish-speaking, and Native Americans at the White House Conference on Aging in 1971, Asian Americans were not included until a request was made by Asian American groups (Asian American Elderly, 1972). This exclusion occurred in spite of statistics from the Office of Special Concerns (1974) that the incidence of poverty among elderly Chinese was much higher than that for elderly Black and Spanish-speaking populations. Similarly, Asian-Americans were originally not included in the National Institute for Mental Health Center for Minority Group Programs since problems among this population were unknown (Brown & Ochberg, 1973). Asian Americans are frequently not categorized as minorities and are often not eligible for affirmative action programs. One Asian American applying for admission to graduate school was told that in order to qualify as a minority group member he would have to furnish information indicating that he came from a disadvantaged background. However, among Asian adults aged 25 or older, there are four times as many with no education or kindergarten only as other adults in the United States (U.S. Census Bureau, 1985). In addition, Asian Americans achieve less in nonacademic settings than would be predicted by their educational level (Sue & Okazaki, 1990). Although Asian Americans make up 4.3% of professionals, they only account for 1.4% of managers (Schwartz, Raine, & Robins, 1987).

Counselors and educators tend to feel that Asian Americans experience few adjustment difficulties, a view which has been supported by the popular press. In a *Psychology Today* article, "The Oriental Express," McLeod (1986) pointed out the "success" of the 700,000 Indochinese refugees who have settled in the United States since 1975; the majority were either employed or attending school. Approximately 27% of children of boat people attending school in the U.S. have an A average. The article also pointed out, however, that 40% of those who had held white collar or professional jobs in Asia were underemployed in America. Not all Asian and Pacific Island groups are doing well. Sixty percent of Samoans and 44% of other Pacific Islanders in Seattle high schools have grade point averages below 2.0 as compared to 24% of White high school students (Stephens, 1986). In fact, gang activities involving Cambodian, Filipino, Laotian, Samoan/Tongan, and Vietnamese are a serious matter in some urban communities. In Seattle, for example, the number of cases of Asian gang related activities has increased dramatically in the 1990s (Goldsmith, 1993).

Although the model minority image has persisted for almost two decades, more recent press coverage has begun to highlight Asian American concerns, including subtle forms of discrimination in education and employment settings (Hassan, 1986-87). In a 1980 U.S. Commission on Civil Rights report it was concluded that, although some Asian Americans are highly successful, Asian Americans earn far less than White Americans with equivalent educational levels and discriminatory employment practices continue.

Housing

Problems among Asian Americans are not highly visible because many of them occur in Chinatowns. Twenty percent of all Chinese housing is overcrowded. This percentage is 33% in New York City. San Francisco's Chinatown spans 42 square blocks and contains 885 persons an acre, which is ten times the national average (Yee, 1970; Loo & Ong, 1984). Exacerbating the problem is the continuing influx of Asian immigrants to already overcrowded communities.

In the literature about the Chinese, a frequent misconception involves the mistaken belief that the Chinese (both in the United States and abroad) prefer crowded living conditions and live under these conditions with no ill effects. Loo (1991/1992) found that Chinatown residents were less hopeful, rated their quality of life as low, were less happy, and less satisfied with their education, jobs, health, family life, leisure time, and marriage than were other Americans. An interview study undertaken in San Francisco's Chinatown indicated the negative impact of the living condition. The vast majority (99%) of respondents reported negative attitudes toward overcrowding in the home and in the neighborhood. Not only were these attitudes consistently expressed, respondents also were able to articulate stressors associated with crowded living conditions including psychological stresses ("makes me feel short-tempered"; "I get in a bad mood"; "Crowding kills your personality"; "It makes me yell at my kids"; "distrust of others"; "I become unreasonable"), and environmental or health risks ("no fresh air," "unsanitary," "too much noise") (Loo & Ong, 1984, p. 72).

Those working with individuals who live under extremely crowded conditions need to realize that frequently few, if any, housing alternatives exist. We need to remember that such living conditions are often the result of social, economic, and linguistic disadvantages experienced by the client, and that a client's sense of helplessness may be quite real.

Testing and Education

For many Asian Americans, entering school with strange and confusing surroundings can be a frightening experience. A lack of facility with English provides an additional disadvantage. Up to three-fourths of various Southeast Asian groups indicate that they do not speak English *well* or *at all* (Government Accounting Office, 1990). Information from the Office of Special Concerns (1974) indicated that among Japanese families having lived in the United States for at least three generations, 62% of the children spoke Japanese at home. Among Chinese children under the age of fourteen, 96% of those foreign-born speak Chinese and 70% of the second generation children speak Chinese in their homes. Facility with English will continue to be a problem for future generations of Asian Americans. Because of this difficulty, Asian-Americans may be at a disadvantage with respect to tests such as the *Graduate Record Examination* and the *Miller Analogies Test* which depend heavily on familiarity with English.

Another educational concern has emerged recently related to alleged discrimination in college admission procedures (Hassan, 1986-87). Asian American groups have recently challenged admission practices at competitive schools, contending that Asian American applicants have the lowest acceptance rate of any group, despite the fact that their grades and overall academic standing are higher than the majority of applicant subgroups (Ho & Chin, 1983).

Personal Stress and Conflict

Constant exposure to the values and norms of the host culture, as well as the lack of information about the culture of Asian Americans among other Americans, may produce stress and conflict. This may result in the demeaning of one's group and the acceptance of the values of the larger society. Asian American children feel less positive about their own physical characteristics than do their White peers (Pang, Mizokawa, Morishima, & Olstad, 1985). Foreign born Asian college students are more other-directed than their white counterparts and report greater levels of interpersonal distress and psychological maladjustment, even though they have lived in the U. S. for an average of 10 years (Abe & Zane, 1990). Chinese-American college students also display a higher fear of negative evaluation and social avoidance than Caucasian college students (Sue, Ino, & Sue, 1983; Sue, Sue, & Ino, 1990).

PERSONAL AND COUNSELING NEEDS
OF ASIAN AMERICANS

Traditional cultural values have a significant impact on the psychological characteristics of Asian Americans, particularly those individuals who are the least acculturated. Value conflicts, loneliness, passivity, conformity, deference, and reserve are found with greater frequency in Asian students than in Caucasian student groups (Ayabe, 1971; Sue, Ino, & Sue, 1983; Sue, Sue, & Ino, 1990; Sue & Zane, 1985). Although traits such as passivity, deference, and reserve might be interpreted negatively from a Western cultural perspective, these traits are strongly supported by Asian values. Although indicators show increasing assimilation and changes in social roles within Asian populations (Fong, 1973; Levine & Montero, 1973), Asian Americans will continue to show unique personality and interest patterns for generations to come. A critical issue for mental health professionals is to understand these cultural values since they relate to rapport building, symptom expression, and comfort with various therapeutic techniques. Additionally, appropriate conceptualization of the presenting problem frequently necessitates a solid grasp of cultural values and interpersonal dynamics within a specific cultural group.

Values

Chinese and Japanese groups share many similar values. In both cultures, the families are patriarchal. Parent to child communications are formal and flow downward. Relationships among family members are well defined and members' positions are highly interdependent. Good behaviors such as filial piety (respect and obligation to one's parents), achievement, and obedience are defined with precision because an individual's behavior reflects upon the entire family. Control of the children is maintained by fostering feelings of shame and guilt. These values account for the importance of structure and deference in Asian American families.

In working with an Asian American client, often the counselor will discover that the client has conflicts between traditional and Western values. Traditional values support obedience to parental desires (as they relate to occupational goals, choice of friendships, leisure time activities, etc.), whereas Western values support individual freedom of choice in these pursuits. Asian American clients may be in a situation where familial expectations involve the financial support of aging parents, including the expectation that an aging parent be taken into one's home. Conflicts may arise when the client does not have the financial means for such support or when the more acculturated client has conflicts between Western goals of personal fulfillment and traditional values of family responsibility. The obligation often is felt most strongly by the eldest son. Sue and Morishima (1982) presented the case of Mae C., who immigrated from Hong Kong several years earlier:

> At the advice of a close friend, Mae C. decided to seek services at a mental health center. She was extremely distraught and tearful as she related her dilemma. Since arriving in the United States, Mae met and married her husband, who was also a recent immigrant from Hong Kong. Their marriage was apparently going well until her husband succeeded in bringing over his parents from Hong Kong. While not enthusiastic about having her parents-in-law live with her,

Mae realized her husband wanted to help them and that both she and her husband were obligated to help their parents.

After the parents arrived, Mae found that she was expected to serve them. For example, the mother-in-law would expect Mae to cook and serve dinner, to wash all the clothes, and to do other chores. At the same time she would constantly complain that Mae did not cook dinner the right way, that the house was always messy, and that Mae should wash certain clothes separately. Mae would occasionally complain to her husband about his parents. The husband would excuse his parents demands by indicating "They are my parents and they're getting old." In general, he avoided any potential conflict; if he took sides, he supported his parents. (pp. 76-77)

This case illustrates the impact that cultural values may have on counseling needs and the necessity of understanding the significance of these values for all involved.

Independence and Self-reliance

Chinese and Japanese children feel a much greater sense of obligation towards the family and parents than do Caucasians. As Hsu (1953, p. 72) observed, "The most important thing to Americans is what parents should do for the children; to Chinese, what children should do for their parents." In Chinese stories, personal sacrifices for the sake of filial piety are rewarded. While in American stories such as Cinderella and Hansel and Gretel, the children defeat evil adults. Family expectations of unquestioning obedience often produce problems when Asian children are exposed to American values of independence and self-reliance. These conflicts may be revealed during counseling sessions:

John's parents had always had high expectations of him and constantly pressured him to do well in school. They seemed to equate his personal worth with his ability to maintain good grades. This pressure caused him to spend endless hours studying, and generally he remained isolated from social activities. John's more formalized training was in sharp contrast to the informality and spontaneity demanded in Caucasian interpersonal relationships. His circle of friends was small, and he was never really able to enjoy himself with others. John experienced much conflict because he was beginning to resent the demands and the pressure his parents put on him. His deep seated feelings of anger toward his parents resulted in passive aggressive responses such as failure in school and physical symptomatology.

As Sue and Sue (1990) pointed out, the case of John illustrates possible conflicts faced by Asian students between their loyalty to the family and desires for personal independence. Learned patterns of emotional restraint and formality interfere with social interactions, and feelings of guilt and depression result when one fails to live up to parental expectations.

Educational Expectations

The pressure to succeed academically among Asians is very strong. From early childhood, outstanding achievement is emphasized because it is a source of pride for the entire family. Chinese mothers are more likely than White mothers (41% versus 11%) to rate school achievement as very important (Sollenberger, 1968). This finding was surprising since 47% of the mothers and 52% of the fathers in the study sample had received no more than elementary school education and were from the lower socioeconomic class. Reflecting the emphasis on education is the finding that college enrollment rates for Asian Americans between the ages of 18 and 24 and the percentage completing college is higher than any other group in the United States (Government Accounting Office, 1990). Parental expectations for achievement can be an additional stress factor in recent immigrant students, who were found to compensate for their lack of English proficiency by taking reduced courseloads and studying more hours. As a result, they indicated feelings of isolation, unhappiness, and stress (Sue & Zane, 1985).

Emotional Restraint

In most Asian cultures restraint of emotions is emphasized because emotions are viewed as potentially disruptive forces on the family structure. Moreover, emotional expression is considered a sign of immaturity which should be suppressed. Most Americans, however, feel that expressing emotions is indicative of individuals who are mature and accepting of themselves. The conflict produced by these differences in values is illustrated in this example of an Asian placed in a group counseling situation.

> The Japanese group member is deterred from directly confronting other group members because he has been taught that it is impolite to put people on the spot...The admission and display of personal inadequacy, even in a counseling group, is a sign of familial defect...In most situations the Japanese person tends to be non-expressive. He has been raised (sic) since childhood not to show his emotions. Thus, although he may be moved by what is occurring in the group, he is almost instinctively restrained from revealing his concern, and his facial expression remains passive...One Caucasian characterized this behavior as a sign of noncaring, and it brought forth this exclamation from him, "Doesn't this have any effect on you? Don't you care at all?" (Kaneshige, 1973, pp. 408-410)

Kaneshige suggested that in group situations involving Asians extra effort should be made to produce a non-threatening climate. Confidentiality must be stressed and responses from Asians should be actively elicited while minimizing interruptions by other group members.

Career Choices

Sue and Frank (1973) found that in regard to choice of career fields, Chinese and Japanese students were more likely than the general student body to show interest patterns and career majors in nonsocial science fields such as engineering, chemistry, biology, and physics. Similar findings were obtained from a sample of Chinese-American students attending a large midwestern university (Sue, Ino, & Sue, 1983; Sue, Sue, & Ino, 1990; Sue & Zane, 1985). The under-representation of Asians in the social science areas may be due partly to culture since forceful self-expression is not encouraged. However, an element of discrimination and prejudice may exist against Asians in the social science fields. Many well meaning counselors may unintentionally restrict the career choices of Asians in the social sciences because of the stereotypic notions that Asians are good in the physical sciences and poor in people relationship areas. An explanation offered for the higher representation of technical majors among Asian Americans is that less discrimination and more objective evaluation of skills and abilities occurs in technical areas, where verbal skills or assimilation of Western values are less likely to be assessed. As with any group that has faced restricted career choices, careful exploration of all possible fields must be presented to Asian American students.

Variations in Acculturation

Mental health professionals must remember that a client may be acculturated in some areas but not in all areas. Acculturation can be assessed on the basis of the number of years an individual has lived in the United States; age at the time of immigration; the political, economic, and educational background of the country of origin; and the individual's professional background (Lee, 1982). In general, the earlier the age at the time of immigration and the longer the length of time in the United States, the higher the level of professional attainment. Likewise, the more similarity between the United States and the country of origin, the more acculturation we can expect. On the other hand, Sue and Zane (1985) highlighted the critical importance of awareness of individual differences in the backgrounds of ethnic minority clients and warned that overgeneralization or overreliance on cultural explanations may hinder a therapeutic relationship as much as failure to acknowledge cultural factors.

Typical Presenting Problems

On the whole, Asian Americans are less likely to seek mental health counseling than are other groups (Sue, 1992). From an Asian cultural perspective, emotional difficulties experienced by a family member are seen to reflect negatively upon the entire family unit. For this reason, until the problem becomes quite severe the emotionally-stressed individual or family member may be reluctant to acknowledge the need for mental health counseling. Those who do seek treatment understandably tend to be more disturbed, on the average, than non-Asians seeking treatment (Sue & Sue, 1987). Depression is more common among Asian American groups, particularly Koreans, than among the general population (Kuo, 1984). Among recent

Southeast Asian refugees posttraumatic stress disorder is prevalent (Sue & Sue, 1990).

Some recent investigations suggest that Asian Americans' conceptualization of mental illness may differ from traditional Western views and that this may have an impact on typical presenting problems. Asian Americans are more likely to believe that mental illness is associated with organic variables and that mental health involves willpower and the avoidance of morbid thoughts (Lum, 1982; Sue, Wagner, Ja, Margullis, & Lew, 1976). Rather than describing specific emotions, Asian Americans (including refugees) are likely to talk about somatic complaints such as headaches, insomnia, fatigue, heart palpitations, dizziness, or general aches and pains during therapy sessions (Brown, Stein, Huang, & Harris, 1973; Sue & Sue, 1987; Bokan & Campbell, 1984).

IMPLICATIONS OF CULTURAL VALUES FOR TRADITIONAL COUNSELING

Many counselors do not understand why Asian American clients do not actively participate in the counseling process and often label them "repressed" or "resistant" (Sue & Sue, 1990). Such reactions illustrate the problems that exist when the helping professional and the client differ in racial or ethnic backgrounds or when the professional lacks understanding of the client's cultural background or degree of acculturation.

Differences in value orientations and expectations may be responsible for premature termination of therapy among minority group members. Sue and McKinney (1975) found in their study of 17 mental health centers that more than 50% of the Asian American clients dropped out of therapy after only one session compared to 29% of Caucasian clients. Sue and Zane (1985) argued that an essential component is for therapists to gain credibility with clients within the first few sessions of treatment. If this does not happen, premature termination may occur. Conceptualization of the problem, means of problem resolution, and goals for treatment are all critical issues and can all be affected by cultural factors. Credibility may be reduced by failure to acknowledge cultural factors or by overgeneralization of cultural knowledge. The importance of meaningful gain early in the therapeutic process also has been emphasized as a method of increasing credibility and avoiding premature termination (Sue & Zane, 1985).

To obtain an adequate understanding of the effects of cultural values on counseling, one may examine some of the characteristics of traditional forms of counseling and contrast them with the values of Asian Americans. Sue and Sue (1990) identified three types of goals or expectations in counseling that may be sources of conflict with minority group members.

First, most counselors expect their clients to exhibit openness and psychological mindedness. To do so, however, the client must be fluent in English and aware of Western cultural concepts of the counseling process. Because many Asian Americans come from a bilingual backgrounds, they may be disadvantaged in this form of verbal expression. Asian clients also have learned to restrain emotional expression and feel that this repression is a sign of maturity. Additionally, Asian clients may have an expectation of what should happen in a counseling session, looking at counseling as an advice-giving process rather than an insight-oriented process. These factors can hinder verbal communication, and a counselor who is inexperienced with clients from Asian groups may conclude erroneously that the individual is resistant or repressed.

Second, the process of counseling involves the revelation of intimate details on the part of the client. The cultural upbringing of Chinese and Japanese clients may be in opposition to this goal. Discussion of personal problems is thought to reflect poorly on the whole family as well as the individual, and the pressure not to reveal personal matters to strangers is strong. In addition, the Asian client comes to the counseling situation expecting advice or practical solutions rather than insight into the nature of his or her problem. Many Asian Americans believe that mental health is contingent on the avoidance of morbid thoughts and that mental illness has an organic basis (Tsai, Teng, & Sue, 1981). Problems may be presented in the form of somatic complaints or educational and occupational difficulties. A focus on personality dynamics at the beginning of counseling may be misunderstood and serve to drive the client away. History-taking, without adequate explanation, also may be offensive to the client (Tsui & Schultz, 1985).

Third, the counseling environment is often an ambiguous one for the client. Often the therapist listens while the client talks about the problem. In many cases, little direction is given. The unstructured nature of the counseling environment adds stress for Asian American clients who prefer concrete, tangible, and structured approaches to problems. The pattern of communication also may be unsettling. Asian Americans may have been reared in an environment in which communication flows downward from an authority figure. The counselor may be expected to initiate and direct the conversation. In a situation where the Asian American client is asked to initiate conversations, the counselor will likely receive only short phrases or sentences. A counselor may respond negatively to Asian American clients, not knowing that, for them, silence and deference may be a sign of respect.

These factors indicate the importance of flexibility on the part of the counselor working with Asian Americans. Because an Asian American client will already feel ambivalence in seeking therapy, a subtle approach is required. Confrontation will increase already present feelings of guilt and shame. Instead of immediately focusing on personal matters, the counselor may follow the lead of the client and discuss the presenting problem even if it is considered to be superficial. Sue and Sue (1972) presented a case in which meaningful material was obtained after the individual completed the Edwards Personal Preference Schedule. The presenting problem revolved around vocational counseling. The counselor's impression was that the client was in conflict over parental expectations of him as the oldest son. Direct approaches to discuss this problem were not successful; however, a discussion of test results in a non-threatening manner provided the opening.

COUNSELOR: Let's explore the meaning of your scores in greater detail as they relate to future vocations. All right?

CLIENT: Okay.

COUNSELOR: Your high score on achievement indicates that whatever you undertake you would like to excel and do well in. For example, if you enter pharmacology, you'd do well in that field (client nods head). However, your high change score indicated that you like variety and change...You may tend to get restless at times...Maybe feel trapped in activities that bore you.

CLIENT: Yeah.

COUNSELOR: Do you see this score (Abasement score)?

CLIENT: Yeah, I blew the scale on that one...What is it?

COUNSELOR: Well, it indicates you tend to be hard on yourself...For example, if you were to do poorly in pharmacy school...you would blame yourself for the failure...

CLIENT: Yeah, yeah...I'm always doing that...I feel that...it's probably exaggerated.

COUNSELOR: Exaggerated?

CLIENT: I mean..being the oldest son.

COUNSELOR: What's it like to be the oldest son?

CLIENT: Well...there's a lot of pressure and you feel immobilized. Maybe this score (points to change scale) is why I feel so restless. (Sue & Sue, 1972, pp. 642-643.)

This approach led to a discussion of the student's resentment toward his parents for the pressure to succeed and eventually to a successful resolution of the problem. The provision of structure as well as a careful explanation of the counseling process can do much to facilitate mutual understanding. As rapport and trust build, a counselor will have greater freedom to explore potential areas of conflict.

If group therapy is used with Asian American clients, expectations of client behavior should again take into account cultural values (Ho, 1984). A group leader might be viewed as an authority figure who will give direct guidance, and the members will have the greatest comfort with structured, goal-directed work with clear objectives. Again, confrontation techniques are likely to be highly counterproductive. Exposure of family conflicts or an open exchange of ideas and opinions also might be difficult for Asian clients. Ho also recommended that groups be as homogeneous as possible with respect to language, ethnicity, generational status, and cultural variables within the native country. Cross-sex groupings may be difficult, particularly for clients with minimal acculturation. Adequately preparing each client to participate in a group session (discussing confidentiality, problem-solving, honest interpersonal exploration, and common feelings of first time group members) is also important. Additionally, periodic scheduling of individual conferences with each group member can be beneficial in monitoring comfort level with group processes.

Finally, some words of caution should be presented. Most Asian Americans are able to successfully manage cultural conflicts. Great variability exists among Asian Americans in the degree to which they are influenced by cultural expectations. Many Asian Americans, for example, are as assertive as Caucasians. Mental health professions must be careful not to rely on generalizations about Asian Americans as a group but must instead seek to understand the specific background of each client. The understanding of Asian values and culture may sensitize individuals to potential conflicts and conflict areas, but counselors will still have to rely on their clinical judgement and knowledge of individual differences.

EXPERIENTIAL ACTIVITIES

Individual Activity

What stereotypes do people still hold regarding Asian-Americans? From your perspective create a list of ten such stereotypes and briefly indicate the reason or roots of each. Which of the stereotypes have changed in recent years? Are stereotypes of Asian Americans still portrayed by the mass media? How might these stereotypes affect expectations and communications?

Group Activity

Divide the participants into small groups of 5 or 6.

Ask each group to select a discussion leader.

Give the group about 10 minutes during which time each person describes leadership qualities.

Give the group about 10 minutes, during which time each person describes Asian American communication styles. How do the two differ?

Are there instances where an Asian communication pattern might be more effective?

How might these differences affect your communication and assessment of one another?

How might Asian American groups consider the communication pattern described by majority group members?

Outside Class Activity

Attend a cultural event with another person whose ethnic or cultural background differs from yours. Attend an Asian International Meeting or one with Asian Pacific Islanders.

REFERENCES

Abe, J. S., & Zane, N. W. S. (1990). Psychological maladjustment among Asian and White college students: Controlling for confounds. *Journal of Counseling Psychology, 37,* 437-444.

Asian-American Elderly. (1972). *The White House Conference on Aging* (1971). Washington, DC: U.S. Government Printing Office.

Ayabe, H.L. (1971). Deference and ethnic differences in voice levels. *Journal of Social Psychology,* 85, 181-185.

Bokan, J.A., & Campbell, W. (1984). Indigenous psychotherapy in the treatment of a Loatian refugee. *Hospital and Community Psychiatry, 35,* 281-282.

Brown, B.S., & Ochberg, F.M. (1973). Key issues in developing a national minority mental health program at NIMH. In C. Willie, B. Kramer, & B.S. Brown (Eds.), *Racism and mental health: Essays.* Pittsburgh: University of Pittsburgh Press.

Brown, T.R., Stein, K.M., Huang, K., & Harris, D.E. (1973). Mental illness and the role of mental health facilities in Chinatown. In S. Sue & W. Wagner (Eds.), *Asian-Americans: Psychological perspectives* (pp. 212-234). Palo Alto, CA: Science and Behavior Books.

Fong, S.L.M. (1973). Assimilation and changing social roles of Chinese-Americans. *Journal of Social Issues, 29,* 115-128.

Goldsmith, S. (1993, January 28). Asian gangs: A community fights back. *Seattle Post-Intelligencer,* pp. A5-A6.

Government Accounting Office. (1990). *Asian Americans.* Washington, DC: Human Resources Division.

Hassan, T. (1986-87). Asian-American admissions: Debating discrimination. *The College Board Review* (No. 142), 18-21; 42-46.

Ho, D., & Chin, M. (1983). *Admissions: Impossible bridge, 51,* 7-8

Ho, M.K. (1984). Social group work with Asian/Pacific Americans. *Social Work with Groups, 7* (3), 49-61.

Hsu, F.L.K. (1953). *American and Chinese: Two ways of life.* New York: Abeland-Schuman.

Kaneshige, E. (1973). Cultural factors in group counseling with interaction. *Personnel and Guidance Journal, 51,* 407-412.

Kuo, W. (1984). Prevalence of depression among Asian-Americans. *Journal of Nervous and Mental Disease, 172,* 449-457.

Lee, F. (1982). A social systems approach to assessment and treatment for Chinese-American families. In M. McGoldrick et al. (Eds.), *Ethnicity and Family Therapy,* New York: Guilford Press.

Leung, P. (1990). Asian Americans and psychology: Unresolved issues. *Journal of Training and Practice in Professional Psychology, 4,* 3-13.

Levine, G.N., & Montero, D.M. (1973). Socioeconomic mobility among three generations of Japanese Americans. *Journal of Social Issues, 29,* 33-48.

Loo, C. M. (1991/1992). Award address. *Asian American Psychologist,* pp. 1-2.

Loo, C., & Ong, P. (1984). Crowding perceptions, attitudes and consequences among the Chinese. *Environment and Behavior, 16,* 55-87.

Lum, R.G. (1982). Mental health attitudes and opinions of Chinese. In E.E. Jones & S.J. Korchin (Eds.), *Minority Mental Health* (pp. 164-190). New York: Praeger.

Masuda, M. (1973). *The Japanese. Discrimination against Asians.* Seattle: State of Washington.

McLeod, B. (1986). The Oriental express. *Psychology Today, 20,* 48-52.

Office of Special Concerns. (1974). *A study of selected socioeconomic characteristics of ethnic minorities based on the 1970 census, Volume II: Asian-American.* Washington, DC: Department of Health, Education, and Welfare.

Ogawa, D. (1973). The Jap Image. In S. Sue & N. Wagner (Eds.), *Asian-Americans: Psychological perspectives.* Ben Lomand, CA: Science and Behavior Books.

Ong, P. (1993). *The state of Asian Pacific American.* Los Angeles: Asian Pacific American Public Policy Institute.

Pang, V. O., Mizokawa, D. T., Morishima, J. K., & Olstad, R. G. (1985). Self-concepts of Japanese-American children. *Journal of Cross-Cultural Psychology, 16,* 99-109.

Schwartz, J., Raine, G., & Robins, K. (1987, May 11). A "superminority" tops out. *Newsweek,* pp. 48-49.

Sollenberger, R.T. (1968). Chinese-American child rearing practices and juvenile delinquency. *Journal of Social Psychology, 74,* 13-23.

Stephens, A. (1986). *Disproportionality Task Force Preliminary Report.* Seattle, WA.: Seattle Public Schools.

Sue, D., Ino, S., & Sue, D.M. (1983). Non-assertiveness of Asian-Americans: An inaccurate assumption? *Journal of Counseling Psychology, 30,* 581-588.

Sue, D., & Sue, S. (1987). Cultural factors in the clinical assessment of Asian-Americans. *Journal of Clinical and Consulting Psychology, 55,* 479-487.

Sue, D., Sue, D.M., & Ino, S. (1990). Assertiveness and social anxiety in Chinese-American women. *Journal of Psychology, 124,* 155-164.

Sue, D.W. (1973). Asians are .... *Personnel and Guidance Journal*, *51*, 397-399.

Sue, D.W., & Frank, A.C. (1973). Chinese and Japanese American college males. *Journal of Social Issues, 29,* 129-148.

Sue, D.W., & Sue, S. (1972). Counseling Chinese-Americans. *Personnel and Guidance Journal, 50,* 637-644.

Sue, D.W., & Sue, D. (1990). *Counseling the culturally different* (2d Edition). New York: John Wiley & Sons.

Sue, S. (1992). Ethnicity and mental health: Research and policy issues. *Journal of Social Issues, 48,* 187-205.

Sue, S., & McKinney, H. (1975). Asian-Americans in the community health care system. *American Journal of Orthopsychiatry, 45,* 111-118.

Sue, S., & Morishima, J.K. (1982). *The mental health of Asian-Americans.* San Francisco: Jossey Bass.

Sue, S., & Okazaki, S. (1990). Asian-American educational achievements. *American Psychologist, 45,* 913-920.

Sue, S., Wagner, N., Ja, D., Margullis, C., & Lew, C. (1976). Conception of mental health illness among Asian-American and Caucasian-American Students. *Psychological Reports, 38,* 703-708.

Sue, S., & Zane, N.W.S. (1985). Academic achievement and socioemotional adjustment among Chinese university students. *Journal of Counseling Psychology, 32,* 570-579.

Tsai, M., Teng, L.N., & Sue, S. (1981). Mental health status of Chinese in the United States. In A. Kleinman & T.Y. Lin (Eds.), *Normal and abnormal behavior in Chinese culture, pp. 291-310.* Hingham, MA: Reidel Publishing.

Tsui, P., & Schultz, G. (1985). Failure of rapport: Why psychotherapeutic engagement fails in the treatment of Asian clients. *American Journal of Orthopsychiatry, 55,* 561-569.

U.S. Census Bureau, Department of Commerce. (1980). *Census of the population: Supplementary report. Race of the population by states.* Washington, DC: U.S. Government Printing Office.

U.S. Census Bureau, Department of Commerce. (1985). Survey of income and program participation (SIPP). Washington, D.C.: Government Printing Office.

U.S. Census Bureau, Department of Commerce. (1988). *We, the Asian Pacific Islander Americans.* Washington, DC: U.S. Government Printing Office.

U.S. Census Bureau, Department of Commerce. (1993). *Statistical abstract of the United States.* Washington, DC: U.S. Government Printing Office.

U.S. Department of Justice (1989). *Statistical yearbook of the Immigration and Naturalization Service.* Washington, DC: Government Printing Office.

Wong, K.C. (1973). The Chinese. *In Governor's Asian-American Advisory Council, Discrimination against Asians* (pp. 2-5). Seattle: State of Washington.

Yee, M. (1970, February 23). Chinatown in crisis. *Newsweek,* pp. 57-58.

Chapter 5

OLDER PERSONS

Harold C. Riker, Ed.D., and Jane E. Myers, Ph.D.,

Harold C. Riker is Professor of Education Emeritus, Counselor Education Department, University of Florida, Gainesville. He is a Faculty Associate of the Center for Gerontological Programs and Studies and a member of its steering committee. Dr. Riker received his B.A. and M.A. degrees in English literature and history from the University of Florida and his Ed.D. degree in Student Personnel Administration from Teachers College, Columbia University.

Active in local, regional, and national professional associations, Dr. Riker is currently a member of the State Advisory Council on Aging and the State Committee on Housing for the Elderly. He has served as a member of the Governor's Committee on Aging and as a delegate to the White House Conference on Aging.

Jane E. Myers, Ph.D., CRC, NCGC, LPCC is a professor of counselor education at the University of North Carolina at Greensboro. She received her graduate training in gerontological counseling at the University of Florida. She has worked as a rehabilitation counselor, administrator of aging programs, and rehabilitation and counselor educator. She also has directed two national curriculum development and training projects in gerontological counseling. Dr. Myers has written and lectured extensively in the field of gerontological counseling and was the Founding President of the Association for Adult Development and Aging.

AWARENESS INDEX

Directions: Mark each item as true or false. Compute your score from the scoring guide at the end of this Awareness Index.

T F 1. An older person is one who has attained 55 years of age.

T F 2. Older persons are very much alike.

T F 3. The number of older persons is increasing rapidly.

T F 4. Over 21% of all older persons have incomes below or near the poverty level.

T F 5. Physical impairment is largely limited to those who are 65 years of age and above.

T F 6. Stereotypes of older persons often become self-fulfilling prophecies.

T F 7. Counselors are likely to have some degree of prejudice against older persons.

T F 8. Self acceptance is an important counseling need of older persons.

Scoring Guide for Awareness Index

1. F   2. F   3. T   4. T   5. F   6. T   7. T   8. T

OLD OR NOT?

Age is a quality of mind. If you have left your dreams behind,
If hope is cold, If you no longer look ahead
If your ambition fires are dead,
Then you are old.

But if from life you take the best,
and if in life you keep the just,
If love you hold;
No matter how the years go by
No matter how the birthdays fly,
You are not old.

—Author Unknown

TWO CASES

Two delightful women illustrate the range of differences among older persons.

Mrs. G.

Mrs. G. is 72 years of age and lives alone in a college town where her husband was a member of the faculty before his sudden and unexpected death. She is White and from a professional, middle-class family. Mrs. G. is usually busy, primarily with other busy women about her same age. Together, they are involved in helping others through a number of community agencies. Mrs. G. enjoys a warm relationship with a son and his family who live in the same town. She has a number of friends in other communities where she and her husband have lived, and maintains an active correspondence. Mrs. G. is a vigorous person who finds happiness and support in her family, her friends, and her service for others. She finds that age has brought new opportunities. Mrs. G. has lived through her grief and has joined a small group of widows who, after a short training period, are active in assisting older, recently widowed women to work through their sense of loss and fear of the future.

Mrs. C.

Mrs. C., on the other hand, represents a very different segment of U.S. society. In her mid-nineties, she is Black, poor, and dependent for her existence on food stamps and supplemental security income provided by the Federal Government. When her children were very young her husband deserted her, and she assumed the full burden of their support. Now in their 70s, these children remain strongly attached to their mother who has helped to rear their children and their children's children. Both sons have returned to live with Mrs. C. along with a daughter who is her primary caretaker.

Mrs. C. spends much of her time in bed watching television. When she leaves the house, it is to see the doctor or attend church. Somewhat hard of hearing, she has a slight tremble in her voice and arthritis in her hands. Her physical environment is impoverished.

For over 60 years, Mrs. C. worked as a house maid; for most of those years she was with one family who regarded her as a family member. Since her retirement this family no longer contributes to her support. She has been sustained and supported by the bonds of love and loyalty that have held her family together.

WHO ARE OLDER PERSONS?

In the sense that every person is older than someone else, all persons are older. In the sense that attitudes toward life and living influence aging, those persons who habitually look backward to the past rather than forward to the future are older, regardless of their chronological age. By stating that persons sixty years of age and over are eligible for benefits under the Older Americans Act, the U.S. Congress has so defined older persons. Because retirement from jobs has traditionally been set at 65 years of age, those who are 65 and over often are described as older persons. As retirement age increases the definition of *older* may be expected to change as well.

In order to define older persons as a special population, the chronological age of 65 and above is used in this chapter, principally because much of the demographic information about older persons is based on this age group. At the same time, one should recognize that those who are 40 years of age or more are often classified as older, particularly by employment agencies. Persons in this age group experience longer periods of unemployment than those who are younger.

Several points should be made about older persons. First, they are a diverse group, with wide variations in family background, education, income, abilities, and interests. Second, each person is an individual, very much like he or she has always been, only more so. In other words, arrival at a certain age, whether forty, sixty, or sixty-five, in no way marks fundamental change in personality, interests, or abilities. And, third, the rapid rise in numbers of older persons has created a special and growing segment of the total population with particular needs, interests, and concerns which demand attention and response on the part of the U.S. society.

THE AGING OF AMERICA

U.S. citizens are living longer. As early as 1800, the median age was 16; by 1970, it was just under 28; by 2000, it will reach 35 (Graying of America, 1977). Between 1900 and 1991, the average life expectancy of men and women increased by more than 50%, from 47.3 to 75.4 years. For men, life expectancy in 1983 was 71.0; for women, 78.2. Currently, 75% of the U.S. population can expect to reach 75 years of age; in 1900, 40% could do so (U.S. Senate Special Committee on Aging, 1986.) Men who arrive at 65 years of age can anticipate living for 15.3 more years; women can expect 19.0 more years (American Association of Retired Persons, AARP, 1992).

The number of older persons is increasing dramatically. In 1900, about 3 million persons age 65 and over were counted by the U.S. Bureau of Census. This number expanded over 10 times to more than 31 million in 1991 (AARP, 1992). The 1985 total was about 28.5 million, and the estimate for 2000 is almost 35 million, a ten-year growth of nearly 22% (AARP, 1992). Of particular interest is the increase in the numbers of older persons by age groups. During the period 1900 to 1991, the 65 to 74 age group grew eight times; the 75 to 84 group grew 13 times, and the 85 plus group increased 25 times (AARP, 1992).

Demographic Characteristics

An appalling fact about the aging population is the sizeable number who live at or below the poverty level. As of 1991, approximately 3.8 million were below the poverty level, described as an income of $6,532 for an older person living alone or $8,241 for an older couple. Over 20% of the older population is described as poor or near poor (AARP, 1992). In an inflationary period, with rising costs and the declining value of fixed incomes, older persons are especially vulnerable to financial difficulties. To assume that a person can maintain a decent standard of living on $6,532 a year, or $125 per week, is, to say the least, unrealistic.

Race, Sex, and Marital Status

On the basis of race, approximately 89% of persons 65 years of age and over are White; 8% are Black; 3% are of other racial origin. Persons of Hispanic origin represent 4% of the older population. The sex ratio is weighted toward females, who represent 59% of the total. The current sex ratio among older persons is 148 women for every 100 men. In 1991, one-half of all older women were widows (48%) and one-fifth of the men were widowers. Only 41% of older women are married compared to 77% of older men, and 5% of all older persons are divorced (AARP, 1992).

Older persons have substantially less formal education than do those under 65 years of age; however, the educational level of the older population is rising steadily. Two decades ago, 63% of the older person group had some high school education or less compared to 26% of those under 65 years of age (Harris & Associates, 1975). Steady growth in the educational level of older persons is reflected in a rise in the median number of years of schooling from 8.7 to 12.2 years in the period from 1970 to 1991.Between 1970 and 1991, the percentage of older people who completed high school rose from 28% to 58%, with 12% of older persons having four or more years of college. The number of years completed varies considerably according to ethnic origin. In 1992, the percentage who completed high school was 61% for Caucasians, 28% for Blacks, and 26% for Hispanics (AARP, 1992).

Employment

The percentage of employed older persons has dropped steadily. In 1900, 63.1% of men over 65 were employed; by 1989 this percentage had fallen to 16.6%, and by 1992 to only 15.8% (AARP, 1992). Among the factors involved was encouragement by the Federal Government for workers to retire early in order to create more jobs for others. Organized labor also bargained for pension plans that would permit early retirement, opening up employment and promotion opportunities for younger workers. Inability to find or keep regular work has led some older workers to use their retirement options. However, efforts are being made to encourage older persons to continue working if they have the interest and capability to do so. Mandatory retirement has been banned legally, and employers are encouraged to hire older workers.

Trends toward earlier retirement apparently do not reflect the preferences of a substantial proportion of workers and retirees. According to a 1979 Harris study, 51% of the surveyed employees expressed a preference to keep working rather than to retire; 48% in the 50 to 64 age group preferred to keep working after age 65; and 56% of the retired group wished they had not stopped working.

Health

Most older persons, about 86% of them, reported one or more chronic diseases which limit their daily activities, yet only 32% reported their health as fair or poor (AARP, 1992). The most commonly stated conditions were arthritis (53%), high blood pressure (42%), hearing impairments (40%), heart disease (34%), cataracts (23%), orthopedic impairments (19%), visual impairments (14%), arteriosclerosis (12%), and diabetes (10%). In spite of such conditions, these persons remain generally active and independent. At least 85% live in their own communities, with about 5% in institutions such as nursing homes. At the same time, the 65+ age group is responsible for about 25% of our country's health costs and makes use of as much as 25% of all drugs. Worth noting is that 72% of those in the 45 to 64 age group also may have one or more of the chronic diseases listed previously (Butler, 1975). Physical impairment, therefore, is by no means limited to those who are 65 years of age and above. In fact, statistics concerning functionally disabled persons indicate that one-third are below age 16, one-third are aged 16 to 64, and one-third are aged 65+ (Rehab Group, 1979).

In the past, aging and disease were often regarded as part of the same process. More recently, the importance of distinguishing among changes resulting from aging, disease, and social-psychological factors has been recognized. For example, Comfort (1976) concluded that, in general, physical changes are not as significant to the aging process as are *sociogenic* factors. Sociogenic factors are those which are imposed on individuals by the negative stereotypes about aging maintained through the culture of which they are a part. If indeed aging is to some considerable extent socially imposed, changes in negative stereotypes should receive high priority.

STEREOTYPES OF OLDER PERSONS

A basic problem experienced either directly or indirectly by older Americans is discrimination because of age. Younger persons often consider older persons inferior to themselves. This kind of discrimination enables younger persons to deny the possibility of their own aging. The irony of this situation is that these younger persons eventually find themselves the victims of their own prejudice.

An insidious effect of ageism, as Butler (1975) has described prejudice against older persons, is that many older persons accept and believe in their inferiority and the weaknesses attributed to them. Older persons place their peers in a category of inferiority. What, then, are some of the common stereotypes?

Stereotype of Unproductiveness

Older persons are believed to become unproductive and, hence, useless, a point of view long supported by the concept of mandatory retirement. However, the facts are that, given the opportunity, many older persons continue to be productive and actively involved in work and/or community life. Contrary to popular belief, older workers can be as effective as younger workers, except perhaps in jobs requiring prolonged physical stamina or rapid response behaviors. Older workers are dependable, maintain excellent attendance and safety records, and require minimum supervision after job requirements are learned. In terms of creativity, some persons remain active in their 80s and 90s. Examples include Pope John XXIII, working at church reform; Christopher Wrenn, designing St. Paul's Cathedral in London; and Michelangelo, completing St. Peter's Cathedral in Rome.

Stereotype of Disengagement

One theoretical explanation of the behavior of older persons is that they gradually withdraw from customary life activities and become more concerned with self. Such withdrawal can be selective so that relationships with some persons are retained, but the emphasis is on less interaction with others and on living with memories of the past. While this theory of disengagement explains the behavior of some older persons, it by no means has application to all. The fact is that many older persons are very much involved in the life of their communities, to the extent than an activity theory has been stated to account for this type of behavior. A continuity theory suggests that individuals tend to continue in retirement behaviors they have followed throughout their life span while the liberation theory considers old age to be a privileged time economically, socially, and psychologically (Fry, 1992). Of course, the stereotype of disengagement can mislead older persons to believe that they should withdraw from others after active work experience.

Stereotype of Inflexibility

Older persons are commonly believed to be set in their ways, insistent on following specific patterns of behavior, and unwilling to consider change. At least two factors may be involved. The first could be preference for what is familiar and customary. The second could be fear resulting from awareness of a slowdown in personal reaction time coupled with an acceleration in the tempo of life in the world around them. However, healthy older persons do respond positively to change, shifting points of view and altering life styles as part of their continued personal growth. The ability to change and adapt seems to be related more to lifelong behavior patterns than to age.

Stereotype of Declining Ability to Learn

The notion that persons can no longer learn when they grow older is expressed by the popular saying, "You can't teach an old dog new tricks." A common belief is that intelligence slides downward from adult years through old age. Actually, healthy older persons can continue to increase their ability to organize their thinking and can successfully complete training and college degree programs with notable efficiency. Apparently, decreases in reaction time which universally occur in later life are unrelated to intelligence. Rather, slower reaction time contributes to slower learning rates. Older people learn as well as younger ones, if given more time to master new tasks.

Stereotype of Senility

The term *senile* is loosely and inaccurately applied to older persons who are forgetful, confused, or unable to maintain attention to one topic for any period of time. Both older and younger persons experience anxiety, grief, and depression; yet when the former give evidence of these problems they are sometimes assumed to have brain damage! Overuse of drugs, malnutrition, psychosocial stresses, and undiagnosed physical ailments may produce behavior labelled senile. Prompt diagnosis and treatment generally relieve all symptoms. A major complicating factor is the lack of willingness on the part of physicians to treat older persons. Many of their diseases are in fact *iatrogenic*, or physician induced (Butler & Lewis, 1983).

Permanent brain damage, correctly described as senility, is irreversible. However, much of what is called senility can be successfully treated, but may be ignored for the unstated reason that older persons are sometimes regarded as dispensable. Alzheimer's Disease is a progressive form of mental deterioration which lasts for an average of 10 to as many as 20 years before death occurs. Its symptoms include loss of memory, inability of the person to make changes quickly, and destruction of minds and personalities. Eventually, total care is required. Certain drugs show promise, but a cure is not yet known.

Stereotype of Declining Interest in Sexual Activity

The stereotype of loss of sexuality in later life has two elements. The first is the frequent belief that sexual relationships for persons over 65 years of age are improper. For example, a typical description of older men involved in sexual activity is "those dirty old men." Lustiness in younger men becomes lechery in older ones.

The second element is the common impression that older men and women lose with age their physiological capacities for sexual activity. On the contrary, healthy older persons who have maintained some degree of continuity of their sex lives continue to enjoy sexual relationships throughout most of the life span. Physiological changes do occur, but they tend to be gradual, and the body usually accommodates to them. At the same time, because of the emotional problems which can develop in this area of sexual relationships, accurate information and warm understanding on the part of both partners are important to the mental and physical health of those involved.

Although age does not place a time limit on sexuality or sexual capacity, a common emotional problem among older persons is fear of impotence. Sexual activity, however, provides feelings of well-being and positive self-regard and recent studies indicate that about 80% of older persons are sexually active.

Fewer than 30% find that sexual responses and feelings diminish with age (Hittner, 1987).

Stereotype of Serenity

Popularized by fiction and the news media, untroubled serenity often is pictured as the reward of those who grow old. Grandma bakes cookies in the kitchen while Grandpa rocks contentedly on the front porch. The apparent conclusion to be reached is that the storms of active life are over. Actually, older persons often face more stressful conditions than any other age group, exhibiting a remarkable ability to endure crises. Their resilience suggests that living longer has prepared them, somehow, to handle new stress.

The youth-oriented society of this country has effectively segregated its older membership, perpetuating a host of false beliefs about aging, and dooming many older persons to life with little hope and declining enjoyment. Stereotypes about aging seem to undermine important personal qualities of self-confidence and self-worth and to forecast a dismal, decaying future which hardly seems worth the effort. The social prejudice confronting older Americans implicitly denies the possibilities for continued personal growth and explicitly imposes barriers for those striving to develop their own capabilities.

COUNSELING NEEDS OF OLDER PERSONS

Counseling needs vary widely among older persons. For sizeable numbers, these needs are minimal, but for perhaps as many as 30%, needs for counseling range from moderate to great. Myers (1978) developed a classification system for the counseling needs of older persons which includes four components: personal concerns, interpersonal concerns, activity concerns, and environmental needs. She later added special categories of older persons as important areas of concern for counselors. Certain demographic categories, including age, gender, and race, seem to be related to the needs of older persons for counseling (Myers, 1984, 1991).

Personal Concerns

Personal difficulties to those over 65 include psychological concerns related to death and dying, mental health, and independence; physical concerns related to health; and psychological and/or physical concerns related to acceptance of the aging process and acceptance of oneself as one who is aging. These concerns combined with the changes and losses of aging contribute to decreased self-esteem and increased difficulty in decision making for many older persons. Other areas of personal needs, as identified by Ganikos (1977) in a study of older adult persons, include personal adjustment and adjustment to life situations.

A major area of counseling need is for assistance in resolving personal problems and/or continuing or renewing progress toward self-fulfillment. Personal problems often grow out of personal losses such as loss of a spouse, friends, job, health, and youth, and generalize to feelings of loneliness, worthlessness, and depression. The passage of time awakens the older person to the realization that youthful dreams remain unfulfilled and that death is inevitable. Two frequently asked questions are "Who am I?" and "Why am I here?"

As older persons find and are helped to find answers to these questions, additional needs arise. Such needs revolve around the development or renewal of realistic, short-term goals for living. Of particular value is training in decision making skills to enable older persons to consider alternative courses of action and resolve problems with a greater sense of purpose. An important element of purpose is focusing on the present in terms of life-style.

Interpersonal Concerns

The interpersonal dimension of counseling the older adult includes psychosocial factors such as relationships with significant others. Studies of life satisfaction among older persons have demonstrated that support networks are essential to the maintenance of self-esteem and morale. Factors that correlate with high life satisfaction include marital status (married) and frequent personal and telephone visits with friends and family. Group memberships are important to psychosocial wellness. Such memberships serve to mitigate isolation and provide identification with peers. The presence of at least one close relationship, usually with a spouse or children, has repeatedly been found to be the single dominant factor determining general satisfaction over the life span.

Family relationships are not always positive, however, and counselors can intervene when difficulties arise. Some 67% of older persons lived in family settings in 1991, including 13% who lived with children, siblings, or other relatives (AARP, 1992). Family members who become caretakers for older persons may experience numerous stresses, which are intensified when the older person has a physical or emotional impairment (Myers, 1990). These stresses can lead to abuse, an increasingly common problem. Estimates are that 10 million older persons each year are victims of abuse (Myers & Shelton, 1987). The frail elderly tend to be most at risk for physical, psychological, and financial abuse. Group activity, often can relieve family members of the stress involved in caring for aging relatives.

Activity Concerns

Within the third category of needs are concerns related to work, leisure time, and utilization of skills. Work involves the concerns arising from gainful employment and retirement.

For many Americans, retirement from a full-time job has been viewed as the beginning of the end of life. For some, this view has been correct: they have declined rapidly in associations with others, in activities, in interests, and in health. Why? High among the possible factors is loss of the sense of personal worth derived from the job. In U.S. society, employment has long been the focal point for self-definition, association with others with similar interests, social contacts, and development of a personal value system. To deny employment to those who want to keep working and have the capabilities for doing so is, in fact, to destroy a significant support for life itself.

Decline in the availability of labor is leading business and industry to encourage employees to remain on the job rather than retire. Dramatic increases in the costs of pension plans and special services for older persons are leading planners to suggest that the age for retirement be raised beyond the traditional 60 to 70 years. In addition, inflation has added so much to the costs of living that income to supplement pension payments is becoming essential. On the other hand, many companies are offering early retirement packages as a cost cutting measure. For them it is less expensive in the long run to hire younger, cheaper workers than to retain the older worker who is more expensive in terms of salary, vacation time, and health care.

Environmental Needs

Environmental concerns are those that relate to independence in meeting environmental demands and obtaining needed services. For some older persons to live independently they must obtain government or private agency assistance, transportation, shopping assistance, help with meal preparation, and/or housekeeping or chore services. To effectively work with older clients in managing environmental needs, financial and budgeting service, or legal advice, counselors must develop a wide referral network.

Needs Related to Demographic Categories

Ganikos (1977) was one of the early researchers to identify demographic variables which seemed related to needs for counseling. One such variable was age. The younger subjects in her study, with an age range of 59 to 65, reported greater educational and vocational needs than the older subjects, age 65 and above. Younger widowed persons seemed to have greater educational needs than older widowed persons.

Other variables affecting expressed counseling needs were gender, marital status, and educational level. Study participants who were not married and in the lowest education groups (0 to 11 years of schooling) indicated more counseling needs related to personal adjustment than married subjects in the highest education groups (college and graduate school). In terms of adjustment to life situations, females reported greater needs than males, with both groups being at the middle educational level (high school and college). These results were supported in an extensive literature review by Myers (1984), who also noted that low income correlated highly with needs for counseling among older persons. Older minority persons exist in a situation best described as *multiple jeopardy*. They are at risk because of their minority status, because of their age, sometimes because of their gender, and often because of their health status and income. They are a minority within the minority of older persons. Their quality of life usually is low, and their needs for counseling are correspondingly high.

Needs of Older Women

Older women have some special problems. Because they live longer than men, 48% of women 65 years and over are widowed (AARP, 1992). Because society frowns on their dating and marrying younger men and because older men tend to choose younger wives when they remarry, older women have limited access to male partners. Hence many, if not most, older widows continue to live alone. Many have never worked except as housewives; those who have worked usually have received low wages. Older women often live on limited incomes with few, if any, opportunities for social activities, particularly after the loss of the husband. Identity may develop as a central issue, and loneliness is a common problem. Relationships with sons or daughters may change, with conflicts arising from differences of opinion regarding degrees of responsibility for each other. Older women are overrepresented in the 31% of noninstitutionalized older persons who live alone—some 42% of older women compared to only 16% of older men (AARP, 1992). When disabled, they are far more likely to receive institutional care. They also have a greater tendency to live in poverty.

DEVELOPMENT OF SERVICES FOR OLDER PERSONS

The principal vehicle for federal, state, and local government assistance to older persons is the Older Americans Act passed by the Congress in 1965 and subsequently amended several times.

This Act defined a national policy for older persons and included these specific objectives:

> an adequate income; the best possible physical and mental health; suitable housing; full restorative services; opportunity for employment without age discrimination; retirement in health, honor, dignity; pursuit of meaningful activity; efficient community services when needed; immediate benefit from proven research knowledge; and freedom, independence, and the free exercise of individual initiative...(Butler, 1975, p. 329).

The Older Americans Act provided for the Administration on Aging, one of the major agencies now functioning under the auspices of the Department of Health and Human Services. For at least the first seven years of its existence this agency suffered from insufficient funds and limited authority. During fiscal year 1966, Congress appropriated $6.5 million to carry out the provisions of the Act. By the end of the first year of operation most of the States had qualified for grants based on approved state plans. In a number of years following 1966, this Act was amended and funding increased. For fiscal year 1969, appropriations amounted to $31.9 million; for 1973, $213 million; for 1978, $720.4 million; and for 1985, $1,027 billion (Ficke, 1990).

The 1978 amendments represented a strong Federal effort to encourage the comprehensive coordination of services to better serve older persons. Title III, Part B, was re-written to include social services, senior centers, and nutrition services. Congregate meals and home-delivered meals were funded and preretirement and second-career counseling for older persons was made available. Legal services, such as assistance with taxes and finances, were continued under the definition of social services. The Administration on Aging's proposed regulations implementing the 1978 amendments amplified the term counseling to include welfare and the use of facilities and services (Administration on Aging, 1979, p. 45042).

Organizations to Benefit Older Adults

Many services provided older persons by federal, state, and community agencies have two common objectives: to improve and expand quality of life and to extend personal independence, delaying or avoiding dependence on long-term institutional care. Holmes and Holmes' (1979) study of human services for older persons described in detail most of the following services: information and referral services, multi-purpose senior centers, homemaker and home health services, legal services, residential repair and renovation services, services for employment and volunteer work, daycare for older persons, nursing home services, and counseling services. The U.S. Administration on Aging, which administers the Older Americans Act; the Agency on Aging, which coordinates related activities in the federal regions; and the Area Agencies on Aging, planning and service divisions designed to coordinate social and nutrition services comprise the *Aging Network*. In addiition, hundreds of organizations working to benefit older persons compete for grants funded by public and private agencies; many exert political pressure on elected representatives to support legislation favorable to their programs and concerns. A smaller number are engaged in multiple programs and activities.

The American Association of Retired Persons, with an approximate membership of 33 million, is the largest organization of its kind in the world. Dedicated to the well-being and activities of retired persons, AARP is built on a well-developed network of local, state, regional, and national units which maximize membership participation. In each state, a joint legislative committee considers political issues affecting older persons and initiates specific recommendations for legislative action on both the state and federal level.

The Gerontological Society is another sizeable national organization which is actively involved in the development and dissemination of information regarding aging and older persons. Its three branches focus on biological sciences, clinical medicine, and behavioral sciences. Its two journals, the *Gerontologist* and the *Journal of Gerontology*, are useful resources in the field of aging. The American Society on Aging and the National Council on the Aging are two additional professional associations having similar purposes. A variety of regional and state professional associations affiliate with these groups. Within the American

Counseling Association, the Association for Adult Development and Aging is the focal point for counseling older adults.

THE HELPING PROFESSIONAL'S ROLES

For many years counseling has been associated primarily with helping younger persons. Considering older persons as possible counselees opens a new area of opportunity for helping professionals. At the same time, problems quickly emerge.

Counseling Older Adults

Counseling may be defined as "the process through which a trained counselor assists an individual or group to make satisfying and responsible decisions concerning personal, educational, social, and vocational development" (U.S. House of Representatives, 1977). This definition makes the important points that counseling is a process involving a relationship, one or more decisions on the part of the counselee, and positive action which can result in the counselee's further development. Counseling older persons, known as gerontological counseling, is perhaps best identified as helping individuals to overcome losses, to establish new goals in the process of discovering that living is limited in quantity but not quality, and to reach decisions based on the importance of the present as well as the opportunities of the future.

For many reasons, however, older persons tend to be reluctant clients for counseling. Today's older persons were reared prior to the emergence of couseling as a profession and are unlikely to have had experience with counseling in their earlier years. For many, discussing personal matters outside the family was strictly discouraged and seeking professional help considered a demonstration of inadequacy. For others mental health care is equated with significant psychiatric illness. To seek counseling, therefore, would be an admission of serious mental disturbance.

In some instances, stereotypes about the aging process have so influenced the behaviors of older persons that change is difficult if not impossible. For example, one stereotype is that older persons are inflexible, unpleasant, difficult, and hard to get along with. At a time when an older person is losing family members and friends who move away or die, that person may believe that the circle of family and friends is shrinking because of his or her behaviors. This conviction, reinforced by the stereotype, can become a self-fulfilling prophecy. Counselors must recognize and appraise the degree to which older persons have been influenced by these stereotypes.

In addition, prejudice against older persons is likely to be held, often unknowingly, by counselors and other helpers. For example, when older persons are confused, forgetful, or depressed, the helper may consider these behaviors typical or expected. These conditions however may be of medical or situational origin and can often be corrected. Likewise, the helper's reaction to the older person who is ill and unlikely to recover may be "Nothing I can do will make any difference." This attitude ignores the importance of the older person's emotional state in the immediate present. Approaches to the problem of ageism include expanding the helper's knowledge base, increasing frequency of association, stimulating sensitivity to older persons as unique human beings, and maintaining personal awareness of the subtle existence of ageism. Despite the best intentions of counselors and other helpers, however, some degree of prejudice against older persons is inevitable because of the common fear of death and entrenched societal attitudes.

Often the mental health system itself prevents older persons from receiving the services they require. Therapists tend to hold negative views of older persons and their growth potential and are reluctant to use time and resources in counseling them. Current estimates are that more than 25% of older persons could benefit from mental health care for significant problems. Yet, only about 6% of persons seen in community mental health clinics are over age 65 (Burns & Taube, 1990). If this condition continues, more than 80% of older persons needing mental health care will never receive it (Butler & Lewis, 1983).

Despite these difficulties gerontological counselors assume a variety of roles: information and referral counselors, counselors for independent living, counselors for personal growth in aging, preretirement counselors, employment counselors, financial counselors, leisure activities counselors, marital and family counselors, counselors for nursing home patients, counselors for the terminally ill, bereavement counselors, trainers for peer counselors, consultants, and advocates. As a result, the competencies required to become certified as a gerontological counselor by the National Board for Certified Counselors (NBCC) are extensive and diverse (Myers & Sweeney, 1990; NBCC, 1992). To consider the numerous roles of gerontological counselors separately is to risk overlooking the fact that these roles are closely interrelated. More important, the needs of older persons are meshed, with the significant consequence that older persons must be understood and helped as whole, functioning, and unique human beings.

Regrettably, this point of view seldom prevails today. Current federal legislation places heavy emphasis on the physical needs of older persons, with considerably less attention paid to mental and emotional needs. Thus, the efforts of the Aging Network have been largely directed toward meeting physical needs. Possibly a more balanced approach to meeting the needs of older persons might have more effective results in the long run. From the viewpoint of gerontological counselors, an assessment of total needs is indispensable to corrective action in the life of the older individual. For example, helping professionals who work with older persons must be knowledgeable about available support systems and the client's access to them. Success in helping older persons may well rest on the recognition that emotional needs and physical needs are inevitably interrelated. When older persons are the clients, the helping professional's scope of information and interventions must indeed be broad.

Support Systems

The *educational support system* functions to explain the aging process to young people in order to combat the fear of growing old and the discrimination caused by the negative stereotypes of older persons. A second function is to develop lifelong educational programs which will enable older persons to keep abreast of social, economic, and political changes in the world. Through these endeavors older Americans can develop and maintain a competence level that will make it possible for them to participate meaningfully in community life.

The importance of a strong *social support system* is universally recognized. Because this system tends to grow smaller as people grow older, efforts must be made to replenish and revitalize it as necessary. One possibility is to encourage older persons to remain active in part-time employment, leisure activities, civic affairs, and educational programs. Another is to suggest that older persons move into housing projects or form small living groups which have membership responsibilities.

Health insurance and hospital care are basic elements of the *health support* system. Lifetime health care training and lifetime programs for physical exercise historically have been neglected and need further development. In addition, medical training should include greater attention to geriatric medicine and close working relationships with professional counselors so that physical and mental health care can be coordinated effectively.

The *services support system* includes access services such as transportation; information and referral; in-home services such as home health aide, visiting, and telephone reassurance; legal services; nutrition services; multipurpose senior centers; and housing. Additional efforts are needed to coordinate these services in order to maximize their results for older persons. Congregate housing and community care programs represent positive steps in this direction.

TRAINING GERONTOLOGICAL COUNSELORS: SPECIAL OR SPECIFIC CHARACTERISTICS?

Counselors of older persons are, first and foremost, counselors. Thus, the generic skills required of all counselors are necessary for their repertoire. All counselors must have basic counseling and communication skills, knowledge of theories and techniques of counseling, familiarity with vocational development theories, methods of assessment, and group counseling strategies. Counselors of older persons must have all of these general skills, as well as others involving special training geared to the specific needs of older persons.

Knowledge of the needs, concerns, and life situations of older persons can be gained through integration of concepts about aging and the needs of older persons into each of the core counselor preparation areas. For example, theories of aging can become part of the curriculum in the core course on counseling theories. Assessment methods for older persons can be addressed in psychological testing courses (Myers & Blake, 1986). A good resource describing the many generic and specialty skills required of gerontological counselors is *Infusing Gerontological Counseling into Counselor Preparation* (Myers, 1989).

In the absence of integration of information about older persons into core courses, or perhaps in addition to such integration, specialty courses in preparation of gerontological counseling are needed. The authors believe that a sequence of courses will best meet the training needs of gerontological counselors, and the senior author has developed such a sequence at the University of Florida. The five courses in this program for training counselors to meet the needs of adults across the life span are Counseling Needs of Older Persons, Theories and Techniques of Counseling Older Persons, Mid-Life Counseling, Pre-retirement and Retirement Counseling, and Practicum in Counseling Older Persons. The practicum is a supervised work experience in a setting where older persons are the primary clientele. Continuing education coursework is recommended for gerontological counselors to help them keep abreast of new developments in the field and apply these to their work. Counselor education programs may seek specialty accreditation in gerontological counseling through the Council for Accreditation of Counseling and Related Educational Programs (CACREP).

As today's counselors-in-training plan for work with older clients, they may find few opportunities available to meet their needs. Creativity, coursework in departments other than counseling, and attendance at professional conferences help to overcome gaps in training. Counselor educators, even in the absence of available coursework, can assist trainees through individual coursework and practicum experiences to examine their attitudes toward older persons and motivation for wanting to work with this population.

A helpful procedure is for both students and educators to remember that, just as gerontological counselors are first of all counselors, older persons are first of all persons. They have the same needs and emotions as persons of all ages, although the circumstances of aging may present differences in degree and experience. Counselors of older clients must be aware of their attitudes toward the needs and potential of older clients. If those attitudes are negative, they will be communicated to the older person and inhibit rapport. If one firmly believes that persons possess the potential for growth and change regardless of age, then he or she can be a successful counselor to older individuals.

EXPERIENTIAL ACTIVITIES

Individual Activity

What are some common words used to describe older persons? Older women? Older men? How do these words reflect stereotypical beliefs? What is the impact of these stereotypes on older persons?

Group Activity

Divide into groups of 5 to 6 persons. Ask one person to be the leader and one person to be the recorder. List all the losses that individuals may experience in later life. Then choose one loss and discuss how counselors can intervene to help older persons adjust and develop a satisfying life-style in spite of that loss. Have each group report their list and suggestions to the full group.

Outside Class Activity

Visit a senior center, congregate nutrition program, or senior housing project. Visit an older person there and inquire about life as an older person. How is life different now than in younger years?

REFERENCES

Administration on Aging. (1979, July 31). Grants for state and community programs on aging. *Referral register, Part II.* Washington, DC: U.S. Government Printing Office.

American Association of Retired Persons. (1992). *A profile of older Americans, 1992.* Washington, DC.

Burns, B.J., & Taube, C.A. (1990). Mental health services in general medical care and in nursing homes. In B.S. Fogel, A. Furino, & G. Gottlieb (Eds.) *Protecting minds at risk.* Washington, DC: American Psychiatric Association.

Butler, R. (1975). *Why survive? Being old in America.* New York: Harper & Row.

Butler, R., & Lewis, M.I. (1983). *Aging and mental health: Positive psychosocial approaches.* St. Louis: Mosby.

Comfort, A. (1976, Spring). *Age prejudices in America.* State Government no pagination.

Ficke, S.C. (Ed.). (1990, July). *An orientation in the Older Americans Act* (rev. ed.). Washington, DC: National Association of State Units on Aging.

Fry, P.S. (1992). Major social theories for aging and their implications for counseling concepts and practices: A critical review. *The Counseling Psychologist, 20,* 246-329.

Ganikos, M. (1977). *The expressed counseling needs and perceptions of counseling of older adult students in selected Florida community colleges.* Unpublished doctoral dissertation, University of Florida, Gainesville.

Graying of America. (1977, February 28). *Newsweek,* pp. 50-52.

Harris, L., & Associates. (1975). *The myth and reality of aging in America.* Washington, DC: The National Council on the Aging.

Hittner, C.B. (1987). The truth about senior sexuality. *Golden years. 9(2).*

Holmes, M., & Holmes, D. (1979). *Handbook of human services for older persons.* New York: Human Sciences Press.

Myers, J. (1978). *The development of a scale to assess counseling needs of older persons.* Unpublished doctoral dissertation, University of Florida, Gainesville.

Myers, J.E. (1984). *Counseling older persons: An information analysis paper based on a computer search of the ERIC data base November 1966 through May 1984.* Ann Arbor: University of Michigan.

Myers, J.E. (1989). *Infusing gerontological counseling into counselor preparation: Curricular modules and resources.* Alexandria, VA: American Counseling.

Myers, J.E. (1990). *Adult children and aging parents.* Alexandria, VA: American Counseling Association.

Myers, J.E. (1991). *Empowerment for later life.* Ann Arbor, MI: ERIC/CAPS.

Myers, J.E., & Blake, R. (1986). Professional preparation of gerontological counselors: Issues and guidelines. *Association for Counselor Education and Supervision, 26,* 137-145.

Myers, J.E., & Shelton, B. (1987). Abuse and older persons: Issues and implications for counselors. *Journal of Counseling and Development. 65,* 376-380.

Myers, J.E., & Sweeney, T.J. (1990). *Gerontological competencies for counselor and human development specialists.* Alexandria, VA: American Counseling Association.

National Board of Certified Counselors. (1992). *National certified gerontological counselor: Application and information.* Greensboro, NC: Author.

Rehab Group. (1979). *A digest of data on persons with disabilities.* Washington, DC: Author.

U.S. House of Representatives. (1977). HR Bill 1118, Counseling Assistance Act of 1977. Washington, DC: U.S. Government Printing Office.

U.S. Senate Special Committee on Aging (1986). *Aging America, 1985-86 Edition.* Washington, DC: U.S. Department of Health and Human Services.

Chapter 6

MEXICAN-AMERICANS

Donald L. Avila, Ed.D., Antonio L. Avila, Ph.D.

*At the time this chapter was written, **Donald Avila**, the senior author, was a professor of Educational Psychology in the Foundations of Education Department at the University of Florida where he taught personality theory. His area of specialization was self-concept theory. We were all deeply saddened by Don's death. He is missed as are his many contributions to the profession.*

***Antonio Avila**, the junior author, is a practicing school psychologist in Gainesville, Florida, where he is employed by the Alachua County School System.*

AWARENESS INDEX

Directions: Mark each item true or false. Compute your score from the scoring guide at the end of this Awareness Index.

T   F   1. Mexican-Americans have a lower educational level and literacy rate than Blacks.

T   F   2. Mexican nationals and Mexican-Americans feel that they have many problems in common.

T F 3. Many Mexican-Americans long to return to the old country.

T F 4. There was a good deal of intimate fraternization between the Spanish and the natives of the lands they conquered in North America.

T F 5. The speaking of Spanish is often banned in our public schools.

T F 6. When counseling Mexican-Americans, it is best to spend a fairly large amount of time exploring each individual's personal history.

T F 7. Group counseling is effective with Mexican-Americans.

T F 8. One of the most important aspects of counseling Mexican-Americans is helping them learn new values.

T F 9. Standardized tests are useful when counseling Mexican-American for individual guidance, but not for comparisons with members of other ethnic groups.

T F 10. Mestizo is the Spanish word for alien.

T F 11. Mexicans often try to pass for some other nationality.

Scoring Guide for Awareness Index

1. T 2. F 3. F 4. T 5. T 6. F 7. T 8. F 9. T 10. F
11. T

A LITTLE HISTORY

The best place to start anything is at the beginning, and the Mexican-American begins with one of the most incredible stories in the history of the world—the conquest of Mexico.

On February 19, 1519, Hernando Cortes, eight hundred troops, fourteen cannons and sixteen horses landed on the Yucatan Peninsula of Mexico (Prescott, 1934). In less than three years this handful of men conquered an entire empire numbering millions of people and established not only a new nation, but also a new breed of human beings.

How was this feat possible? How could a relatively few individuals have such a tremendous impact on history? Several factors contributed, but three were major ones. The first, understandable; the other two, uncanny.

The first circumstance that allowed this small band to accomplish what seems like an impossible task is not unusual—a state of affairs that has caused many empires to fall. At the time of Cortes' arrival, Mexico consisted of many separate tribes under the loose control of the Aztec Empire. Although considered a unified people, great disharmony existed among the separate tribes. Many of them had been conquered by the Aztecs, and like many of the peoples conquered by Rome, still resented their conquerors. Consequently, when Cortes came to the Mexican shores, he was able to recruit fairly large numbers of natives to his cause.

A second key to the success of the conquistador involved the experience of the natives. Although the Aztecs were civilized in many ways, in others they were barbaric and crude. The native armies consisted of foot soldiers armed with clubs, knives, and swords. They had never heard gun powder ignite nor seen horses. Rumors of these new weapons made them reluctant to fight. When they did engage in battle with the Spanish, the explosions of rifle and cannon and the awesome sight of huge animals and their riders terrified many natives, causing them to flee in fear.

Judging the impact of the third and perhaps strongest factor in Cortes' success is difficult, but the impact was considerable. The Aztec religion held that a white, bearded god once ruled Mexico and would one day return. Clearly, many of the natives thought Cortes was that god, and they either failed to resist the Spaniard or joined his cause because of this belief. The Aztec Emperor himself, his judgment clouded by the uncertainty of Cortes' divinity, made many blunders that contributed to the empire's downfall. He neither wanted to give his nation to plunderers nor offend a god. Consequently, a nation was conquered by little more than a group of bandits.

The establishment of a new nation and a new breed of people was much more straightforward and natural. Having subdued the natives, Cortes' men began to fraternize with them, and that fraternization created a new being—the Mestizos. Mexico City became the first Mestizo city in history. The current ancestral heritage of Mexico is reported to be 55% Mestizo, 29% Indian, and 15% European.

Now the Mexican-American story begins. Three major causes contributed to the migration of the Mexican to what is now the southwestern and far western portions of the United States. First, the Spanish search for booty, conversion, and expansion did not end in Mexico. While acquiring Mexico and most of Central America, the Spaniards sent bands of priests, soldiers, and unidentifiable scoundrels north for farther conquest. The people living in these lands were mostly small tribes of rather primitive and unaggressive Indians and offered little resistance. As usual, these adventurers began settling the land by converting, plundering, and again breeding with the locals (Longstreet, 1977).

Later, in what might be called the second phase of Mexicanization, these Mestizos decided that independence from Spain was in order. But freedom was not easy. Years of war, oppression, and poverty followed the decision to free themselves from Spain and establish an independent nation. Thus, because of the warfare and poverty, thousands left their native land and headed north in search of greener pastures.

What then is the modern Mexican-American ancestry? That's not an easy question. Today to trace one's ancestry in any true linear fashion is nearly impossible and a pure strain of any ancestry—biological, religious, political, or otherwise—in this melting-pot nation of ours is very unlikely. Surely, the Mexican-American is no exception.

While Mexican-Americans are mostly of Mestizo ancestry (Aztec and Spanish), other strains have resulted from Mexicans combining with Mexican Indian, American Indian, and northern Europeans. These people eventually occupied most of the west and southwestern United States. Without question their history has been that of a people seeking new and better lives, some coming from Mexico to settle new lands, but most fleeing revolution and poverty. While conditions in Mexico are constantly improving, that migration and hopeful search has not ended.

The Mexican-American experience has been disappointing. Dreams of a better life have been realized by a relative few. In the beginning, they were treated and exploited as slaves. Later they were accepted as a necessary evil, segregated into ghettos or barrios and no less exploited. They have always been looked at as a cheap source of labor and been regarded by the majority with all the cruelty of rampant prejudice and discrimination. Some changes have occurred, but Mexican-Americans still face the same problems that have plagued them from the beginning.

MINORITIES—BLAH, BLAH, BLAH

When a person decides to analyze minority groups, the first thing that sets in, if you are not a member of such a group, is boredom. Boredom, because so much of the information reads alike. To paraphrase, if you have looked at one of them, you've looked at 'em all. And, in a very real way this is true, unless of course, you are looking at privileged minorities like the rich and famous. But oppressed, dispossessed, poor minorities are the same in many ways. They all fit the cycle of poverty, and they are all the victims of prejudice and discrimination. Thus the general descriptions and statistics are the same over and over again.

The authors want least of all to bore the reader. Therefore, we shall, here and now, quickly dispense with the description and statistics. Like every minority the Mexican-American is

1. the victim of prejudice and discrimination,
2. alienated from the greater society,
3. segregated and isolated, and
4. generally poor.

What else is new? Not much. The facts of the matter are as follows (Carter, 1989; Hernandez, 1973):

1. Approximately 12 million Mexican-Americans reside in the United States.

2. One-third live in poverty and are disproportionately represented in the low income manual labor occupations.

3. They obtain, on the average, 7.1 years of education.

4. They have a lower educational level than Blacks or Whites and a greater school drop-out rate that either

5. They have the highest illiteracy rate of any group in the U.S.

6. By the 12th grade, 40% have dropped out of school.

7. Only 1% go to college.

8. Many are segregated in schools that are almost all Mexican-American.

9. Many are 2, 3, or even 5 years behind in school.

Sound familiar? Of course, all statistics on oppressed minorities sound like a broken record.

BUT—DIFFERENCES DO EXIST

Now that we have taken care of the statistics, let's go to the focus of this article. That focus is understanding. The writers believe that one of the most important characteristics a counselor must have if he or she is to be successful is empathetic understanding of the client. If the counselor does not understand the unique qualities of the client, he or she cannot help that client. The major purpose of this chapter, then, is to give the reader a better idea of what being a member of the Mexican-American minority is like.

What are some of the factors that make this minority different from others?

Language

Language, of course, is the most obvious problem for the Mexican-American. However, the problem is not the same for all. Some Mexican-Americans speak virtually no English; some speak no Spanish; and others speak every possible state between these extremes. All are, however, members of the same minority group and subject to the same experiences, especially those experiences of a prejudicial nature. The less English spoken, however, the worse the problem.

Little, if anything, is more frightening or will give a person more of a sense of helplessness than being surrounded by people speaking a language one does not understand. Thousands of Mexican-Americans of all ages are in this predicament. Older individuals often find protection by surrounding themselves with other Spanish speaking people, but children are sometimes thrust into the greater society without tools to express even their most basic needs. Youngsters consequently withdraw, become quiet, and hope that they at least do not get in harm's way. Imagine yourself as a nine or ten year old child in a room with twenty or thirty other people and not being able to comprehend a word that is spoken. Of course, those around you are confused and unable to communicate also and behave in ways that are not conducive to growth. They reject, ignore, or aggravate you, the exotic child. In any case, what results is a frightened, confused, isolated, and lonely you—a small child. As time passes, children in conditions similar to this often become more withdrawn and isolated, developing various defenses for protection or reacting with open aggression and hostility.

Migrant Status

Unlike most other minorities, a tremendously disproportionate number of Mexican-Americans is in the migrant labor force. What does this mean? In terms of physical health alone (Hernandez, 1973) the picture is not a pretty one:

1. The infant mortality rate for migrants is 12% higher than the national average.

2. The rate of death from influenza is 200%, from tuberculosis 260%, and from accidents 300% higher than the national average.

3. The life expectancy of the migrant worker is 49 years.

The psycho-social picture is no better. Migrant means moving—constant moving. Many Mexican-Americans remain in one place for only three or four months. They have no roots, no home, no place to belong. Each time they follow the crops they are thrown into a totally new situation with no psychological anchors to grasp. When they arrive at their destination, conditions are disgusting and they are exploited. Little is as depressing as the sight of migrant camps and the abuse to which the migrant is too often subjected. Worst of all, they are in a cycle that offers little hope of being broken. The process keeps adults from being able to improve their skills or positions and offers children small hope of breaking the mold.

Viva Mexico

Mexican-Americans are in a unique situation because they are so close to the country with which they are identified. This causes the larger society to misunderstand the real nature of the Mexican-American and confuse two groups of people which are in some respects very different. Mexican-Americans are not simply displaced Mexican nationals. The problems of Mexicans and the problems of Mexican-Americans are not the same. While many Mexican-Americans can and do take pride in their heritage, it is as Americans and not as Mexicans.

Back to Africa movements have failed because Blacks in this country are native Americans, not Africans. They do not go back to Africa because Africa is not their country. For the same reason, many Mexican-Americans have little or no desire to see, hear, or talk about the old country. When Mexican nationals and Mexican-Americans encounter one another, often no sense of loyalty or brotherhood is felt. In fact, they may well have little in common. Mexicans from Mexico have their problems and Mexicans, who are American and a distinctly different group, have theirs. On occasion one may even detect a degree of hostility between the Mexican nationals and the Mexican-Americans, as though the Nationals regard the Mexican-Americans as being a bit beneath them and perhaps consider them as having deserted the ship. By the same token, those Mexicans who migrated to the U.S. did so because they were unhappy and were escaping a past they did not want following them. Therefore, they can be very uncomfortable when the past interjects itself into their present lives in the form of a Mexican national. The authors, although of Mexican-American heritage, have not particularly identified themselves with Mexico. They have visited there, but when they did the visits were clearly perceived as trips to a foreign country.

This schism will be widened even further by sweeping legislation that has recently been passed in the U.S. affecting the status of illegal aliens in this country. Among other things, the new immigration bill allows millions of these individuals to become American citizens. For most Mexicans this event will likely separate them permanently, both physically and psychologically, from the old country.

Who Am I?

The more a person resembles an Indian, the more prejudice and discrimination he/she will encounter. Mexican-American who do not have these features experience much less discrimination than those who do and have found it much easier to gain access to and integration into the larger society. Those Mexican-Americans who most closely resemble the North American Indian suffer the same kind of nightmarish experiences as the American Indian and African American, while those who do not have these features may go through life relatively untouched by prejudice and discrimination. These conditions have to do with how easily one is identified with a minority and how much different that minority is from the majority. African Americans, as a total group, have suffered the most in this country because they have the most easily identifiable physical characteristic separating them from the majority of Americans—the color of their skin. Mexican-Americans who have distinct Indian features know exactly the kind of prejudicial hell the Blacks have experienced, because Mexican-Americans have experienced and continue to experience the same. The authors have often heard the expression, "Niggers and Spics! They are just alike. Dumb, dirty, lazy, and smelly." The referents were usually talking about Mexican-Americans who "look" Mexican. Hollywood has always know about and taken advantage of this situation. For years Mexicans have been playing Indians and Indians have been playing Mexicans. Yet, not one of either group has ever become a superstar except perhaps Anthony Quinn—but after all, he only looks a tiny bit Indian.

The Mexican-American who does not have the Indian features of his or her brothers and sisters can, with a little trickery, self and social denial, and maybe some transportation, escape nearly all the hazards of prejudice and discrimination. For you see, Mexican is not necessarily Mexican all the time.

When one of the authors was a young boy, he had occasion to mail a package on which was printed the family name, Avila. The postal clerk read the name and brightly asked, "Is that your name?" The author answered that it was; the clerk then asked in a very friendly manner if the name was Spanish. The author in his, then, boyish naivete said, "No, it's Mexican." At that, something happened which the author did not understand until sometime later after he had seen it happen many times. The clerk's entire demeanor changed. He said, "Oh," and was no longer cheery and friendly, but cold and distant. The business was conducted with no further verbal exchanges. The author discovered that people of Mexican and Spanish descent were not the same, and that Spanish was somehow better than Mexican. He also discovered that by simply saying he was Spanish he could be treated much better and have many more doors open for him. (He didn't do this very often though, because when he said he was Mexican and there were no flinches or character changes, he know he was meeting a potential friend. There were times, however, when it was necessary to do so in order to avoid the possible loss of something or someone important to him.)

Thus, "Spanish" people are welcome in many places across this land where Mexicans are not. And many Mexican-Americans have played this game throughout their lives to avoid discrimination. Some, just to be sure, have gone so far as to deny both Mexican and Spanish heritage, passing themselves off as

Italian, Jewish, or some other nationality for which they thought they could be mistakenly identified.

One aspect of this game that would be comical, if it were not so sad, is what the authors call the "Castilian Hussle." Some Mexican nationals as well as Mexican-Americans believe that throughout the history of Mexico a strain of Mexicans dating from the time of Cortes has been able to keep their ancestors pure and untainted by the blood of the natives of the countries they conquered. These true believers refer to themselves as Castilians, and even if they were born in Mexico they will say, "Yes, I am from Mexico, but I am not Mexican; I am Castilian Spanish." And it works!, which probably tells us more about the people it works on, than those who play the game.

The authors' intention is not to make fun of anyone, but to emphasize the desperation that oppressed people can feel and the lengths to which they must go in order to escape injustice. But doing so is sad, because the kind of self-denial we have been discussing must leave terrible psychic scars upon those forced to engage in the process.

In any event, while the Mexican-American is like all other minorities, he or she is different, too.

WHAT'S ALL THAT CRAP ABOUT...

Intelligence

To the authors, one of the most insensitive, damaging and inconceivable pastimes in which academicians engage is the attempt to compare the intelligence of minority groups with that of the majority, particularly if the minority group involved has experienced the consequences of extreme prejudice and discrimination. Individuals who persist in suggesting that the native intelligence of the majority can be compared with that of a minority simply do not have a basic understanding of intelligence measurements and their limitations.

Our most sophisticated intelligence measurements are not culture free and our so-called culture free measurements are notoriously foul with regard to validity and reliability. Intelligence tests do not measure basic capacity. They measure a person's total life experience and cultural milieu. The closer one's life experience is related to the structure and content of an intelligence test, the higher he or she will score; the less related, the lower the score. Intelligence tests in their present form, rather than measuring basic potential, more accurately compare how closely one group's socialization process resembles another group's.

Individuals born into a lower socioeconomic class, shut out of the society, suffering mental and physical deprivations, and having different cultural values are most certainly going to score lower on intelligence measurements constructed by members of groups not fitting this sociocultural mode. Furthermore, until better measurements are developed or a universal indicator of basic intelligence is found, any attempt to compare one group's intelligence with another's is futile, and studying the current research on this topic will tell the reader little about the ability of Mexican-Americans or any other minority group.

Self-concept

The self-concept is one of the most important aspects of behavior. It must be at least mentioned when speaking of any human being. Yet, little time will be spent on the topic because in relation to minorities so little is known about it. The research available on the self-concept of minorities is totally conflicting. Some of these data reveal no difference between the self-concept of minority and majority members; some say that majority members have a higher self-concept than minorities; and some say that minorities have a higher self-concept than majorities. It is confusing just to say it.

The self-concept is probably the most important factor in anyone's life and understanding the self-concept of their clients may be a counselor's most important task. A study of literature, however, will not help the counselor much in trying to do so.

The conflicting data most likely arise from two factors. One is the nature of those groups being sampled and the other is the nature of the instrument used. Minorities cannot be treated as a total group in self-concept studies. If they are, those data are bound to be spurious. Study after study has demonstrated that social class is a much greater base for group differentiation than is minority status. In other words, members of the same social class are more alike and more different from other social classes than are different racial, religious, or national members when compared with one another. Therefore, when one compares a minority group with a majority group, especially when one group has a much larger percentage of its members in lower socioeconomic classes, a higher self-concept reading will be obtained from the group with greater representation from the higher socioeconomic classes. In studying a sample of minority members who are mostly in the higher socioeconomic classes, better self-concept scores may be obtained than in a normally distributed population. Furthermore, instruments may be totally inadequate for reflecting an accurate picture of a particular minority group, especially if class representation is biased. Self-concept instruments are based on middle-class majority values. Examining the self-concepts of groups not representing these values may distort the resultant data.

Mexican-Americans, in particular, have class and social values that not only differ from but also are in direct contradiction with the values of the middle-class majority. The Mexican-American has many conflicts with institutions of the larger society, i.e., educational, legal, and social; but these conflicts do not mean that they do not have a great deal of self-respect and confidence in themselves. These positive feelings simply may not be related to kinds of items one finds on typical self-concept scales. The young Mexican-American male may not feel too competent with regard to reading', ritin', rithmetic', and social skills, but he may experience a great deal of confidence and self-respect in being a member of one of the toughest gangs in a Los Angeles barrio. Suffice it to say that if teachers or counselors approach the Mexican-American expecting a shy, self-depreciating, inadequate individual with no self-respect, the professionals are in trouble. At best they will be fooled; at worst they may be igniting an explosive situation. The authors suggest that Mexican-Americans and all minority groups probably have as good a self-concept and as much self-respect as any member of a majority, which is why many minority groups are refusing to be oppressed any longer.

CASE EXAMPLES

Let's briefly examine some of the experiences typical of those the Mexican-American encounters in the growth and socialization process. The following are real life anecdotes common to the Mexican-American experience.

John

John's real name is Juan, but the school has changed it in order to accelerate the acculturation process. John's father has managed to escape the backbreaking work of the migrant laborer and find a menial, but less demanding job in the city. Unfortunately, only a few other Mexican-American families reside in the area. John and the rest of his family can speak only enough English to satisfy their basic needs.

John is dutifully placed in the local school in the grade appropriate for his cohorts. After two or three days we find his teacher speaking to one of her co-workers:

"May, does anyone on the staff speak Spanish?"

"Not that I know of. Why?"

"Well, I have this little Mexican boy in class and he doesn't understand a word I say. I'm at my wit's end. I can't find any teacher or student who speaks Spanish.

"What are you going to do?"

"I don't know."

"Well, if I think of anything, I'll let you know."

We run into the two colleagues several days later.   May speaks first:

"How are things working out with that little Mexican kid, Julie?"

"Oh, I don't know.   The principal is looking into some possibilities for help, but he says we don't really have a program for kids like that.   He's a quiet kid, and mostly just sits.   He does like to draw, so I let him do that a lot.   If he doesn't cause any trouble, I guess I will just let him be and maybe the problem will take care of itself.   It is tough, though.   The other kids won't play with him because they can't understand him either.   They think he's weird.   So do I."

Mike

Mike finally sorted it all out to his own satisfaction, but it wasn't easy.   Decisions made by others and things happening over which he had no control complicated his life and confused him.   He was the product of a mixed marriage, his mother being Mexican-American and his father a typical American mixture of ancestry.

Mike's parents gave him an Anglo name because they believed he would have an easier time of it.   They also refused to teach him Spanish.   They were afraid he would develop an accent, and they knew children with accents were treated badly in schools.   These two decisions alone caused Mike trouble throughout his life.   His maternal grandparents and assorted aunts and uncles could not speak English; therefore, the only way he was ever able to communicate with them was nonverbally or by having his mother sit beside him and translate the conversations.   Not once in his life had he ever spoken directly to his own grandparents or other relatives.

These things also made it difficult for Mike to relate to his peers.   Living in a multicultural neighborhood, none of the other children was sure what he was or where he belonged, and neither was he.   The Blacks knew he wasn't one of theirs but the Mexicans and Whites weren't sure whether he was one of theirs or not.

"What kinda Mexican can't speak Spanish?", and "What kinda American has a Mexican name and mother?"

As a child, Mike adjusted to this particular problem by being meaner and tougher than all the other kids. In the type of neighborhood in which he lived, that made him a leader. Sometimes he roamed with the Mexican kids and sometimes with the non-Mexican kids, but it was a hard way to go.

Confusion really set in as he would often hear his relatives on his father's side speak about those dirty Mexicans and smelly Niggers. He knew he wasn't Black, but weren't he and his mother Mexican? He would often try to get one of his relatives to explain what they meant, if it meant that they didn't like him and his mother, but he wouldn't get much satisfaction. He would usually get a response like, "Aw, you and your Mom ain't like that. You're not greasers; you're different." This worked out well, however, for he came to the conclusion the whole world was a little crazy. In the end, he grew up almost totally free of prejudice.

Mike's mother probably was right, and his life may have been much more difficult had he been more easily identifiable as a Mexican-American. But he suffered many adjustment problems as he grew up because of the confusion over his identity, and on many occasions wished he could speak his mother's native tongue. He tried in later years to learn Spanish but was unable to do so. Since he had three college degrees, it didn't seem likely that this was due to a lack of intelligence. He concluded, therefore, that not only did he not learn Spanish as a child, but also at some level of awareness he must have developed a mental block to its acquisition.

By his wits and some luck, Mike made it well enough, but he has many scars left from making it as a minority group member; and the making it, itself, was a difficult process. There is no telling what he might have become or contributed had he not been burdened by the evils of prejudice.

Gloria

Maria had just arrived at her friend's house in answer to a tearful phone call from Gloria in which the latter had said she and her boyfriend had broken up.

"What happened," asked Maria.

"It was his parents. He didn't even have the guts to tell me himself. His mother called and told me that she and her husband did not think that different races and religions mix and that they just thought it better if their son did not go around with a Mexican Catholic."

Maria sighed and said, "Oh shit."

"What is it, Maria, this thing about being Mexican? Why does it seem to make everything so hard?"

"I do not know."

"Does it last forever?"

"I think so, Gloria, I think it does."

Friends

Five boys were sitting in a restaurant having lunch. They looked like a group of typical Anglo-Saxon, middle-class American teenagers. One, however, was not. He was a Mexican-American. His name was Henry.

Four members of the group, including Henry, had been friends for some time, and the other three knew Henry was of Mexican descent. The fifth boy was a relatively new member of the group, and the heritage of the others had not crossed his mind.

As they sat, a couple entered the restaurant. The man could have been of Indian or Mexican descent because he had very black, long, straight hair and the physiognomy spoken of earlier that is typical of American Indians and many Mexican-Americans. The lady had blonde hair and fair skin.

The boys all glanced up at the couple as people will do when someone enters a room. At that point the boy who was a newcomer to the group said softly, but so that all at the table clearly heard him:

"God damn! Will you look at that" Nothing pisses me off more."

The other four boys looked up at the fifth, and Henry asked, "What?"

"Seeing a beautiful white woman hunched all up against a greasy spic."

The other four boys froze. Henry's three friends had seen him tear into many another boy for much less. Fortunately, though young, Henry was maturing and beginning to learn the futility of trying to beat prejudice out of people. He let it pass, but you can be assured that the other three friends soon clarified an issue for the fourth, and such an incident, in this group, did not happen again.

A CULTURAL HERITAGE

The Mexican-American experience entails a cultural heritage that often contradicts that of the majority, situational confusion in regard to social adjustment, and negative social attitudes.

Some Mexican-American values place the minority group members at a disadvantage when trying to survive. First, the nature of the Mexican-American cultural heritage is highly socialistic. The family is of primary importance and takes precedence over any outside concerns, be they school, work, or social matters. The family may include neighbors, owners of the small neighborhood grocery store down the street, godparents, grandparents, and close friends. All members may have a say in adopting family rules and solving family problems; thus, the family is often an extended one. Additionally, the ideal family works as a team, encouraging members toward interdependence rather than independence. Many Mexican-Americans enter the competitive society of the majority favoring group rather than individual success. Often these families have a common bond of caring, a deep sense of unqualified caring and protection in which all members are considered equal and accepted unconditionally. They are valued simply for themselves, not because of what they have accomplished or not accomplished. A family member is not usually expelled as a result of unacceptable actions or attitudes (*Reaching Hispanic/Latino audiences*, 1991).

Second, the Mexican-American culture, like all Latin cultures, is highly authoritarian. Children are taught to give unquestioning obedience to the head of the family and to be strongly dependent on that authority for decision making. Thus, partly because of their training to be obedient, partly because they are taught to be polite, and partly as a defensive coping behavior, Mexican-Americans may appear quiet and submissive.

Third, many Mexican-Americans have a present-time orientation that does not stress preparation for the future nor place importance on the acquisition of material goods.

Fourth, the Mexican-American may have a code of honor that emphasizes the "macho" image, where one suffers frustration and disappointment in silence, avoids losing face, and adjusts to problems rather than solves them.

Finally, the status of women is clearly inferior to that of males. Women are expected to be submissive and to overlook the indiscretions of males. For example, there is a certain casual acceptance of men who "play around", but not for women who do so. Virility is measured primarily by a man's sexual potency. Obviously, in American society today, this is not a well received social standard and is the cause for many communication breakdowns with Anglos and others. Torrey (1986) placed the role of Mexican-American female in perspective when he stated:

Girls are valued primarily for their virtue, and an unmarried girl's honor is equated with that of the family. Young women are expected to get married, and the maternal role is very highly valued. Women are late to mature, often because the grandmother lives in the family and competes in maternal care of the grandchildren. There is a concomitant undervaluation of the sexual and companionship roles of women; sex is prudishly accepted by "nice women" only as an obligation (p. 141).

Without question, in our present day American society, any child—brown, black, or white—who is not adamantly achievement and competition oriented; is unquestioning of authority, submissive, and uninterested in material things; is more loyal to a group than to him/herself; and considers females to be inferior-is in trouble. But, let persons engaged in helping professions be forewarned. These characteristics are deeply ingrained and at the core of the Mexican-American character. They are not aspects of the Latin persona to be challenged, attacked, or degraded. To do so is to guarantee that one will not see a helpee again. The best entry into the Mexican-American's confidence is to take the attitude, "I accept you as you are and want only to help you acquire skills that will better enable you to reach your potential." Then if further counseling and guidance temper some of their beliefs, so be it.

Situational Factors

In addition to long-term cultural factors that conflict with the potential development of the Mexican-American, situational factors also make integration difficult. Certain behaviors have grown out of the Mexican-American attempt to adjust to the majority society.

Many Mexican-American parents believe themselves unable to give their children the necessary skills to cope with the larger community. They actually feel inferior to the Anglo members of the society and avoid them, not from lack of concern, but out of this fear. Mothers and fathers will not question their employers and will not go to school or may not even answer the door when some perceived authority comes calling. Fear of making a fool of themselves or embarrassing their children, not a lack of cooperation, causes this behavior. Related to this sense of inadequacy is the fact that parents are sometimes hesitant or refrain altogether from helping their children with school work. They are concerned that they will not know how to help or might do more harm than good if they interfere with their child's studies.

Another consequence of these situational factors is that parents, knowing their values conflict with the majority, refrain from trying to instill them in their children. They hope their children will somehow assimilate the values of the majority, making a better adjustment than they themselves did. This, of course, is no answer. What usually happens is that children reach adolescence without a clear set of values, are more confused, and have more trouble coping. Because of all the conflicts, the Mexican-American family is replete with domestic disharmony—delinquency, hostility, academic difficulty, and the like.

SOCIAL ATTITUDES AND ACTION

The other factor mainly responsible for the failure of our society to adequately integrate the Mexican-American is the attitude and actions of the larger society toward this minority. The most tragic and inexcusable circumstance in the greater society is that where large numbers of Mexican-Americans are found, something very much like a caste system exists. This is similar to the African American situation, but needs to be emphasized because many do not realize that the Mexican-American experience is often no less oppressive or restrictive than that of Blacks. As always, the system results in geographical isolation, job and pay discrimination, restriction of personal interactions, and all of the other deprivations associated with racial prejudice.

Our schools, institutions which should be most responsive to the integration of our minorities, perpetrate some of the worst injustices. Studies have found the following attitudes existing among non-Mexican public school personnel toward the Mexican-American student (Carter, 1989; Hernandez, 1973):

1. inferior

2. lazy

3. unable to learn

4. happy with their lot

5. peculiar

6. hopeless

7. dangerous.

Some of the school practices found to exist are:

1. teachers ignoring students

2. schools making no allowance for the schedule of migrant workers

3. universities not preparing teachers to deal with any minority

4. schools assigning teachers, who do not speak Spanish, to predominantly Mexican-American classes or schools

5. banning of the Spanish language or reference to anything Mexican

6. prohibiting students from speaking Spanish.

RECOMMENDATIONS

The failure of our society to fully integrate the Mexican-American as a first-class citizen is long standing and inexcusable. This integration is not going to be accomplished by the publication of a single chapter in one book. The authors hope, however, that from this reading the counselor will be better able to contribute effectively to that integration. Toward this end we offer some recommendations. The reader may consider them to be no more than common sense. But, we humans are often guilty of not using common sense enough and are more likely to do so if we receive little reminders now and then of just what that commodity is.

Before we enumerate these recommendations we would like to point out what as counselors we are definitely trying to do. Too often the Mexican-American is looked upon as a foreigner who has to be acculturated; this is, taught the characteristics and values of the larger society, usually at the expense of his or her own cultural heritage. Mexican-Americans are not foreigners. They are Americans who have historical roots different from, but not inferior to those of other Americans. Our purpose is not to make them like all other Americans, but to give them the skills and knowledge that enable them to succeed, as they share with us those positive things from their culture. Our task is to integrate, not acculturate the Mexican-American.

Acculturation is an insult. It says that one set of principles, values, beliefs, and behaviors is right while another is wrong. An attempt to acculturate almost always results in an approach where the majority member says, "What you are is bad, and what you have is useless. Leave all that behind and let me show you the way."

The quickest way to failure is to begin our first interaction with other persons by telling them that what they are is bad, wrong, inept, or immoral. If we do so, not only are we doomed to failure, but also we are usually dead wrong! Most often our own house is not in such great order that we can offer it up as a perfect model at the expense of another life-style.

In light of this purpose, recommendations of the authors and of Carter (1989) and Hernandez (1973) when working with Mexican-Americans or any minority are as follows:

1. Always accept clients exactly as they are, accepting their values, beliefs, and behaviors, and go from there. Take the position that what they are is good and that your function is to add to what they are, not to subtract or distract from it. Project an attitude that says, "What you are is good. What I want to do is lend you some things of mine that I think will make life easier for you and give you a better potential for success." If you can't honestly and sincerely do this, we suggest you not be a counselor for the counselee. You're wasting time, or worse.

2. Although you are working with a Mexican-American, recognize and treat that person as an individual. The purpose of this chapter has been to give the reader some insight into Mexican-Americans, not to suggest that they are all alike. They are not. They are like every other group; their members differ from each other in as many ways as they differ from another group. Ascertain those differences before you go blundering in and making a fool of yourself with some kind of generalization.

A word about the term **Chicano** may be in order. It is currently the "in" word and many writers use it to designate the Mexican-American. Militant and poor Mexican-Americans also are using it as a designation of pride or unity. It has not always been so. The exact origin of the term is not known, and it has no exact meaning. To many, especially older members of the minority, it represents a picture of the poor, uneducated, exploited field hand. To many Mexican-Americans it historically has and still does have the same distasteful meaning as the word "nigger" or "spic." These individuals would consider it an insult to be addressed in that way. That is why these authors have used the term Mexican-American. To our knowledge no one is offended by that designation. The term is discussed here in order to emphasize the importance of knowing the individual to whom you are speaking.

3. If you have group counseling skills, use group counseling with the Mexican-American because of their orientation to group cohesiveness. Also, at times it is helpful to form homogeneous groups to foster better group and self-understanding. For better minority-majority group interaction and understanding heterogeneous groups may work best.

4. Initiate programs early and work on them over an extended period of time. Such programs are of an invitational nature, but counselors have found that starting early has a snowballing effect and accomplishes much more than waiting until specific problems arise. Some examples of such programs include:

a. occupational exploration groups,

b. sensitivity groups,

c. college orientation programs that include bringing successful Mexican-American students to the group,

d. role model groups that invite successful Mexican-Americans from all walks of life to discuss their lives and work with the members, and

e. cultural exploration groups.

5. Whenever possible, integrate the values and beliefs of the Mexican-American into your counseling with them by showing the use and place of such values and beliefs.

6. Recognize that the teaching of skills is usually more useful than the teaching of values. Mexican-Americans have most likely already been exposed to any value that might be introduced to them. What they need more are better, more effective academic, social, and vocational skills.

7. Initiate a counseling program early; do not delay the beginning; begin immediately and make subsequent appointments soon and frequently.

8. When counseling is initiated, get to the problems. Do not delay with the accumulation of long case histories or explorations of the past.

9. Be flexible. This client is not likely to be susceptible to "pure line" counseling theory. Get a feel for the client; then select what you believe will be the best process approach to use, whether that be client-centered, behavioristic, rational, or combination.

10. Use standardized tests for individual guidance, not for comparative purposes.

11. Focus on one objective at a time rather than taking a shotgun approach. Sometimes this gives a particular client a greater sense of success and more confidence in the counselor.

12. Be a leader in initiating programs in your community, agency, or school that respond to special needs and problems of this group. Help to accept and include the cultural heritage of the Mexican-American.

13. Don't judge your Mexican-American clients by your own value system. Find out as much as you can about their culture and make your judgments from that frame of reference.

14. Involve the Mexican-American community. The greater the involvement, the more successful a program will be. Every attempt should be made to use the total available Mexican-American population in what you are doing. You will be most successful if you will

a. involve parents;

b. form community groups to achieve language improvement, community counseling, sensitivity to certain issues or concerns, or community orientation to the agencies and facilities available;

c. engage in public relations;

d. encourage the employment of Mexican-Americans in schools, businesses, and community agencies; and

e. include in your program as many successful Mexican-Americans as you can find.

In working with our Mexican-American population a special urgency exists because this minority group is increasing faster than other minorities. For example, the estimate is that the Hispanic population of which Mexican-Americans are by far the greatest number, will be the largest minority in the U.S. by the early 1990s (Long, 1982). Furthermore, because of the new immigration bill mentioned earlier, larger numbers will become American citizens than ever before; and as a result of certain stipulations of the bill that require greater services and protection to aliens, tremendous increases in money and resources will be needed to provide for their needs. Of special importance, then, is the preparation of professionals to work with this growing minority. Cultural sensitivity is a beginning whereby the counselor can enhance effectiveness in addressing the pressing needs of Mexican-Americans.

EXPERIENTIAL ACTIVITIES

Individual Activity

Assume that you are a mental health counselor with a new client who is a Mexican-American male who has just lost his job and is experiencing related family problems. To what cultural variables would you need to be sensitive in order to avoid alienating your client? What stereotypes would you need to avoid?

Group Activity

It can be argued that our society has failed to fully integrate the Mexican-American as a first class citizen. Ask the group to assume that they have been requested to make five recommendations to the United States Congress to assist in accomplishing this integration. What five recommendations would the group make and why?

Outside Class Activity

Attend a Mexican cultural event in your city.

REFERENCES

Carter, T.P. (1989). *Mexican-Americans in schools: A history of educational neglect.* New York: College Entrance Examination Board.

Hernandez, N.G. (1973). Variables affecting achievement of middle school Mexican-American students. *Review of Educational Research, 43,* 1-39.

Long, S.M. (1982). An American profile: Trends and issues in the 80s. *Educational Leadership, 39,* 460-464.

Longstreet, S. (1977). *All star cast: An anecdotal history of Los Angeles.* New York: Thomas Y. Crowell. pp 15-18.

Prescott, W.H. (1934). *The conquest of Mexico.* Garden City, NY: International Collectors Library American Headquarters.

Reaching Hispanic/Latino audiences. (1991, July). *Prevention Review.*

Torrey, E.F. (1986). *Witchdoctors and Psychiatrists.* Northvale, NJ: Jason Aronson.

Chapter 7

THE GAY, LESBIAN, BISEXUAL POPULATIONS

Joseph L. Norton, Ph.D.

Joseph L. Norton, Professor Emeritus of Education at the State University of New York at Albany, has been a counselor and counselor educator since 1949. He has been active in the New York State Association for Counseling and Development, serving as president in 1970-71, and has served in governance of the American Association for Counseling and Development and the SUNY State wide Faculty Senate. He founded the Association for Gay and Lesbian Issues in Counseling and has served on the steering committee of the Association of Lesbian and Gay Psychologists. Co-founder of the Gay, Lesbian, and Bisexual Interest Groups of the American Association of Sex Educators, Counselors, and Therapists and of a similar group in the Society for the Scientific Study of Sex, he has transferred much of his efforts in sex education and work with professional groups to the support of gay/lesbian counseling and liberation. Since retirement in 1983, he has devoted much time to volunteer work with the local AIDS Council and to his favorite recreation, skiing.

AWARENESS INDEX

Directions: Mark each answer true, false, or don't know. Compare your answers with the scoring guide at the end of the test.

T   F   1. Lesbians have not been studied using standard research methods until very recently.

T   F   2. Lesbians comprise a lower proportion of the population than do gay males.

T   F   3. Homosexuals engage in child molestation proportionately more than heterosexuals.

T   F   4. The gay militant is highly susceptible to blackmail.

T   F   5. Those with same-sex behaviors are easily changed through therapy to acquire heterosexual feelings and behaviors.

T   F   6. Male hormones make gay males more active homosexually.

T   F   7. You can be sure a person is not a lesbian or gay male if the person is legally married.

T   F   8. Lesbians may be married to each other in at least five states in the U.S.

T   F   9. Evidence shows that open lesbians and gay males are as well adjusted as non-gays.

T   F   10. The civil rights of gays have never been taken away by law or popular vote.

T   F   11. Bisexuals have been shown to be highly promiscuous.

T   F   12. Most homosexuals have a choice of being "straight" or gay.

T   F   13. Most transsexuals and transvestites are heterosexual.

T F 14. Gay, lesbians, and bisexuals moving to a new city can usually find "the gay scene" by buying a guide to gay bars and groups.

Scoring Guide for Awareness Index

1. T 2. T 3. F 4. F 5. F 6. T 7. F 8. F 9. T 10. F 11. F 12. F 13. T 14. T

FIVE CASES

Three young men and a woman came separately to this counselor's office last month.

Peter

Peter was a tall, all-American boy who had decided he was gay. He told his mother, who accepted it easily, but Peter had little notion of how to go about meeting other gays. He believed he was gay because he fantasized about males while having sex with his girlfriend. He had spoken with her about his inclinations toward males but had never had the "typical adolescent homosexual experiences" and had never had gay sex. He sought ways to get to know other gays.

Anthony

Anthony was less attractive physically, a bit overweight, and, like Peter, a college student. He had been having sex with males for three years, had a lover with whom he was having some hassles, and was bothered about how to tell his parents (if at all) and still have their support through his last year of college and graduate school. Unlike Peter, Anthony had told no one he had homosexual feelings (except those with whom he had sex), but had found his way into the gay scene through overhearing gossip of his (presumed) non-gay acquaintances who mentioned a gay bar.

Ed

Ed's was another situation. Somewhat older, late 20s, Ed was married and had a two-year old son. His work as a salesman took him on the road, and through a chance out-of-town friend he discovered that he enjoyed sex with men as much, maybe more, than with his wife. He did not want to lose his son, whom he loved dearly, nor hurt his wife, but he found himself increasingly seeking out gay locales on his travels. Ed had found a gay guide book which contained information helping him find gays in a new city. Ed wondered if he was likely to bring a sexually transmitted disease, particularly AIDS, home to his wife, and whether he could or should continue to keep his gay leanings from his wife.

Henry

A fourth young man did not come to the counselor. Knowing he was gay from the earliest teens, he fought the feelings and married early to prove he was straight. Three children later, he found himself increasingly turned off sexually by his wife and finally turned again to clandestine, impersonal gay contacts in the local bus station and other public places. Caught by the police, he was unable to face the public humiliation and took his life. This is a true report. However, happy endings have occurred in similar situations where divorce followed and the ex-husband continued happy contacts with the children.

Jane

Jane, too, came for counseling. Forty-six, having trouble both with her lover and her small private business, she sought vocational and relationship counseling. Her lesbianism was not the problem, but she needed someone who would not make it the problem.

These cases are, as in any illustrative cases, only five of hundreds who brought, or should have brought, problems to a counselor. For every Peter, Anthony, Jane, or Ed, there are myriad variations. Some of these stories have ended up in print and can help the counselor get a broader picture of the needs of lesbians, gay men, and bisexuals. Lesbians appear less often in these cases, reflecting the finding that they often are not even thought of when the words homosexual or gay are used. (Adler, Hendrick, & Hendrick, 1986; Biemiller, 1985; Lambda Update, 1992; Norton, 1982; Rickgarn, 1984; Spees, 1987; Wilensky & Myers, 1987).

In an earlier edition of this book, it was said that one of these cases was in a sense insoluble: Ed may be unable to avoid hurting someone sooner or later; but today there is material available to help the bisexual and the spouse (Hutchins & Kaahumanu, 1991; Gochros, 1989). Some decisions are about how to lessen the hurt, how long to postpone it, or how best to balance the counselee's needs with others' needs. Support groups now exist for gay fathers, lesbian mothers, bisexual married men, and wives of these men (Wilson-Glover, 1987; Wolf, 1987; Auerbach, 1987). And for all persons, safer sex guidelines are available.

Different counselors will experience different levels of difficulty in working with gay/lesbian/bisexual clients, depending on their own attitudes and knowledge. Is the counselor's first reaction "Certainly Peter is best off, the easiest to help," or "I wonder if I can help Peter enjoy women more?" Is the first inclination to refer Peter, Anthony, and Ed to psychiatrists to see if they can be cured? Does the counselor know that the latter response flies in the face of current research? Would it be more advantgeous to find out about the local gay scene to help Peter find his way or to discover whether Anthony's dad is homophobic enough to cut off his son's support? How can the counselor facilitate a decision in Ed's dilemma of hiding unhappiness in the closet or "coming out" in the open. Is Jane's problem a long-term one of improving relationships as well as resolving financial problems?

DEFINITIONS

Homosexuality

Varying definitions of homosexuality have been presented (Kennedy, 1977; West, 1977). The simplest is "one who has an affectional and/or sexual orientation to a person of the same sex." This definition seems simple but it leaves room for questions. For example, is an individual with no same-sex experiences, but regular fantasies of such, gay? Does homosexuality require that two people of the same sex achieve climax as a mutual goal? Enough males respond sexually to pressure on the genitals or to other external stimulation that it almost seems as if intent, or at least feelings, should be part of the definition. Evidence clearly shows that a single, or a few, same-sex acts do not necessarily make one gay. In fact, persons with similar sexual histories may label themselves heterosexual, homosexual, or bisexual, depending on environmental factors (Blumenstein & Schwartz, 1977).

As Father Paul Shanley stated, a same-sex act neither defines nor causes a person's sexual orientation. Many youths have same-sex experiences and grow to be adult heterosexuals. For others this experience is not just a phase, and the orientation persists for life. Early experiences simply help the individual verify and substantiate his/her feelings. Thus, for some, extensive behavior leaves no doubt concerning the label; for others it seems to depend on personal beliefs regarding the label (as is the case with many hustlers). The self-labeling, however, has been devastating to hordes of youth in the past. Perhaps some day society will acknowledge simply that humans are sexual beings who can develop a wide range of related behaviors, depending on a myriad of complex factors (Money, 1986).

Many males who have identified themselves as homosexual use the term gay as a self-chosen, nonclinical term. Most homosexual females prefer to be called lesbians, although a few prefer **gay women**. Their point is that the other labels tend to ignore the female. The term gay, not involving "a feigned happiness in spite of it all," came out of the backstage parlance of the theater. The gays say they prefer this term to the outsiders' terms: homo, faggot, dyke, queer, pansy.

Use of the term **same-sex orientation** is more accurate than **same-sex preference** used by some writers, as the word **preference** implies, to some, a choice. The vast majority of lesbians and gay males and bisexuals simply discovered they were wishing for love, affection, and sex from persons of their own or both genders. They did not choose to be gay or lesbian or bisexual; the only choice was whether to act in accordance with their own feelings.

BISEXUALITY

The term **bisexual** refers to persons who respond sexually and affectionately to both genders. It is true that some gay males have never been able to respond to women, but the majority have had successful experiences, thus dispelling the myth that all gay males hate women and have a revulsion toward the female genitals. Many lesbians are mothers and many gays are fathers, indicating at least a literal bisexuality. How they feel, however, is another matter, which is why it is recommended that feelings be part of the definitions in this field.

Homophobia

A term used by George Weinberg (1972), **homophobia** is the state of excessive fear of contact with homosexuals. Since most people with homophobia do not view it as a difficulty, counselors usually will not have the professional opportunity to work with these individuals. Occasionally a gay or lesbian counselee will get her or his parent(s) to come in for counseling. Should that happen, the informed counselor will respond as did one psychiatrist who asked the parents in after talking with their gay son and said, "You have the problem, not he." But counselors should know that negative attitudes toward gays and lesbians function in the dynamics of maintaining traditional sex roles. Fear of being labeled homosexual keeps both men and women within the confines of what society has traditionally defined as sex role appropriate behavior (Morin & Garfinkle, 1978). Furthermore, many gay men and women have internalized society's homophobia and hate themselves.

DIFFERENCES

Identifying differences between homosexuals and the population in general is helpful since these differences are not usually visible. The most crucial difference is the strong affectional and/or sexual attraction toward people of the same gender. Second, the other populations do not fear, or systematically suffer, the lack of family support. Watching parents chortling over voter repeal of a gay rights ordinance makes homosexual less likely to turn to parents for support.

Another difference is that the homosexual can hide. This population is an invisible minority except for a few "flagrant queens," and many have fought their "affliction" alone for years with some even taking it to the grave (Duberman, 1992). Finally, members of the gay/lesbian/bisexual population can be members of any of the other populations discussed in this book. They may be disabled, African-American, Hispanic, or Native American and thus doubly special.

NUMBERS

With such amorphous definitions and ready invisibility, precise figures on the gay/lesbian/bisexual population are difficult to obtain. Kinsey's 50-year-old figures indicated that 37% of males and 33% of females had a climax with another of the same sex after the age of 18 and eight percent lived a primarily homosexual life for a period of at least three years. No one paid much attention to the fact that the 1948 Kinsey scale of 0 (exclusively heterosexual) to 6 (exclusively homosexual) left over 90% in the bisexual category. More recent estimates of four to ten percent of the U. S. population, over 20,000,000 Americans, now have general support. Considering that each gay male and lesbian and bisexual has parents, siblings and/or children, some 50,000,000 Americans have intimate contact with homosexuality. Yet this topic has been virtually ignored in counselor education programs throughout the country.

FURTHER DESCRIPTION OF THE POPULATION

Altogether, generalizing about the gay/lesbian/bisexual population is difficult. Historically, lesbians have been virtually invisible in the research, partially because they appear to be fewer in actual numbers, and probably because men were doing the early research and chauvinism prevailed. Studies of gay men were spotty, and the early ones used subjects involved in therapy. For example, Saghir and Robins' (1973) work demonstrated that gay men had heterosexual experiences earlier than a comparison group of heterosexual men.

Riddle and Morin (1977) reported the average ages when selected events occurred in the lives of 63 lesbian and 138 gay male psychologists. The average ages for the lesbians and gay males, respectively, are shown in Figure 7.1.

Interesting to note is that in the area of awareness of same-sex feelings, males were a year ahead of females, although women usually mature two years ahead of men. The average male was active sexually five years before the average female.

It would seem that the age of coming out as a homosexual is going down. Although definitions vary among studies, in Figure 7.2 are shown results of studies in several countries where reported ages of coming out were studied. Although some people do not come out until their 50s and 60s, it is clear that counselors in schools and colleges should expect many youths to be dealing with this issue.

Initial Occurance of Selected Events	Average Age	
	Lesbians	Gay Males
Aware of homosexual feelings	14	13
First same-sex sexual experience	20	15
Understood the term homosexual	16	17
First homosexual relationship	23	22
Considered self homosexual	23	21
Disclosed identity to parent (Over half had not disclosed)	30	28
Disclosed identity professionally	32	31

Figure 7.1. Average ages when selected events occurred in the lives of 63 lesbian and 138 gay male psychologists. (Riddle & Morin, 1977).

Author	Year of Publication	Average Age
Dank	1971	19.3
Troiden & Goode	1980	16.3
Coleman	1982	15 males, 20 females
Remafedi	1987	14
Ross: Sweden	1989	14.1
Australia	1989	12.5
Finland	1989	13.9
Ireland	1989	15.6
Lynch (suburbans)	1987	30

Figure 7.2. Research studies on ages of coming out.

MYTHS

While some counselors are informed and accepting of homosexuality, many are still misled by the myths or truly believe the following falsehoods:

1. Gays want to be of the opposite gender.

2. Gay males are primarily artists, hairdressers, antique dealers, and interior decorators.

3. All gay males are promiscuous.

4. Gay males are weak, introspective, and inactive physically.

5. Removing laws against homosexuality will increase its frequency.

6. Gays and lesbians hate those of the opposite sex.

7. Gays are a menace to children.

8. Just give a gay male some male hormones and he will want women.

9. Gays in role modeling positions, such as teacher or minister, will turn children into homosexuals.

10. Homosexual partners take on male and female roles.

These myths, when considered rationally, are easily dispelled. No actual research shows gays as a group to be more creative or artistic than others. Furthermore, increasing research on personality characteristics and even sexual responsiveness reflects few differences between hetero- and homosexual people (Masters & Johnson, 1979; Bell, Weinberg, & Hammersmith, 1981; Sakheim, Barlow, Beck, & Abrahamson, 1985; Engel & Saracino, 1986).

Take, for instance, the stereotype that gay men are effeminate. Actually, many young men struggling with their sexual identity say they know they can not be homosexual, despite their strong affection and sexual attraction to other males, because they do not swish, flip their wrists, and cross-dress. Most **transvestites** (cross dressers) are heterosexual. Only 10 to

20% of gay males are **drag queens** (male homosexuals who dress as women), and considerably fewer lesbians dress like men to an extent that would distinguish them from heterosexual women. Many lesbians are very dainty and feminine, quite unlike the bull-dyke (woman homosexual who dresses, acts, and/or talks as a man) stereotype. People who want to be of the opposite gender are properly called **transsexuals**. Lesbians and gay men are happy to be the gender they are; they simply love others of the same gender and prefer them as sex partners. Oddly, our list of misconceptions contains two contradictory myths: one, that guys want to be of the opposite gender and two, that they hate the opposite gender.

Child molestation is primarily a heterosexual phenomenon. Although there was speculation that a couple of notorious mass murderers were gay, they may have been homophobic, rather than gay, since they killed young male prostitutes. There is no evidence that gay teachers molest their students. For example, although New York City schools have numerous records of heterosexual child molestations, there are no recorded incidents of homosexual child molestation (Ellis, Hoffman, & Burke, 1990). Moreover, research on role modeling does not support the fear that gays and lesbians, either as parent or role model, create gay and lesbian children. In fact, gay/lesbian teachers are often "super-teachers" (Smith, 1985).

Besides being faced with stereotypes and myths, gay males and lesbians bring other orientation-related problems to the counselor. For instance, the fear of a lonesome old age is a specter held before gay males, who are led to believe that the gay male subculture is totally youth oriented. In fact, many older gays have lovers or a circle of friends for companionship or sex. While some older gay males have accepted the stereotype, others find it inappropriate. The gay male who is already isolated from his family actually may be better prepared to cope with old age than his heterosexual peers.

CURRENT PROBLEMS

Despite the fact that gays and bisexuals are much like nongays in many aspects of life—career development, intellectual development, and even sexual development—in this society they do have some special concerns, which are elucidated in the following sections.

"I'm Afraid I'm Homosexual"

While fewer clients come to counseling these days expressing this fear, sexual orientation is still a question for some. Going beyond the query "What makes you think you might be?" to "How do you feel about that?" could get at the counselee's issues. Being gay or lesbian is mostly a matter of perception; a few same-sex acts do not make one gay or lesbian (and apparently, for lesbians, most do not act until they are sure of the feeling of identity). Sexual orientation may include fantasy and affection as well as sexual attraction. Knowledge of masturbatory fantasies can give the counselors clues to determining sexual orientation. A review of the person's developing sexuality may still not give a clear answer, in which case keeping all options open seems advisable.

"How Did I Get This Way?"

Experts agree that at this point no one knows the origins of homosexuality. Hormonal influences, family influences, size of parts of the brain, environmental or genetic influences, childhood sexual experiences—any or all of these may be involved. Some know from earliest memories that they are different from their peers, while others do not recognize their orientation until after many years of heterosexual marriage. Not one of the many theories proposed stands up to careful scrutiny (Bell, Weinberg, & Hammersmith, 1981; DeCecco, 1987).

The whole pattern of bisexual emergence into public view raises the question: "Why ask how I got this way?" No one asks, "What made me heterosexual?" Perhaps this helps support the idea that sex is a natural thing that develops variably among individuals (Money, 1986).

"Can I Get Over It?"

Although some gays and lesbians initially desire to change their sexual orientation, most are happy with themselves and their lives. Some psychoanalysts, behavior therapists, Aesthetic Realists, and religious fundamentalists report 20 to 50% success in changing those with strong motivation to change. Most "ex-gays," however, concede they still have the homosexual feelings but have learned not to act on them. Militant gays argue that this "cure" actually forces the person into an asexual life-style. Counselors should carefully consider society's role in client motivation to change, recalling for example the clitorectomies performed even today in societies holding the belief that it is unseemly for women to enjoy sex. Counselors also should know that treating homosexuality with male hormones makes gay men more sexually active rather than changing their sexual preferences.

Another point counselors should make very clear to anyone who seems to have a same-sex orientation is that a heterosexual marriage does not provide a cure or prove heterosexuality. Unfortunately, what is often heard is "All you need is a good woman (or man, for the lesbian) and you'll get over your feelings." After years of marriage some wives are relieved to learn a husband is gay: they had thought themselves to blame for a poor sex life and marriage.

"Should I Come Out to Others?"

This issue of remaining invisible in the closet, "suffering in silence," "carrying this burden," and never fully expressing one's self has no universal solution. Many have lived their entire lives hating themselves. The counselor cannot tell the counselee what to do but can discuss the pros and cons, helping the client weigh the alternatives. Helpful pamphlets and books can be obtained from the National Gay/Lesbian Task Force and the Campaign to End Homophobia (1989). *Reflections of a Rock Lobster* (Fricke,

1981), *Young, Gay and Proud* (Anonymous, 1980), and (Bozett, 1985) are excellent resources.

Sometimes openness leads to hassles from a hostile society: a swishy gay beat up at a local shopping center, "fag" painted on a garage door, urine poured on a dorm room floor. Clear evidence is available to show an increase in gay bashing which began in the late 1980s (National Gay and Lesbian Task Force, 1989). The record by Buju Banton recommending "*Kill a fag*" met with strong opposition from gay activists, as well as others (Pierson, 1992). Yet many gays and lesbians are very open publicly with absolutely no hassles or discrimination. Often openness is met with a shrug: "I couldn't care less." Sometimes the response is "I'm glad you shared this with me: it makes us closer" (sometimes with the added "as long as you don't come on to me").

With such a range of responses from families and the public, it may be difficult for the individual to know what to do. On one hand the open gay can be true to self. He or she has overcome the dissimulation involved in changing pronouns when talking about the weekend or having no picture of a lover on the desk.

But circumstances vary. If Anthony comes out, his father might refuse to pay his tuition. If Anthony decides that to tell is unwise and so far has managed his double life without too much pain, what counselor would override his decision? Many parents must actually know the secret, but appear to want not to bring it out in the open. Many an upset, disappointed, fearful or hostile parent has been won over with patience, by reading relevant material, or by making contact with the group called **P-FLAG** (Federation of Parents and Professionals for Friends of Lesbians and Gays, P.O. Box 24565, Los Angeles, CA 90024). There are incidents of parents who responds "How nice, so am I," and some fathers, gay themselves, who believe that they caused a son's orientation, although research does not support such a possibility.

Finding Others of Like Mind

As pointed out in Peter's case, gay/lesbian invisibility poses another problem for some who are coming out—finding others of like mind. Unfortunately, for too many years meeting places other than the gay or lesbian bar did not exist. It is important to recognize that not all gays fall in love (or bed) the instant they meet another gay of the same sex. Selectivity occurs in the homosexual as well as the heterosexual world. Nor is gay life nor gay sex necessarily more idyllic than heterosexual life or sex. For this population, life with connections to the gay community is simply more satisfying than life with only heterosexual ones.

Gay/lesbian rights groups exist in many college communities. Large cities have groups like New York City's Institute for the Protection of Lesbian and Gay Youth, and Senior Action in a Gay Environment. Church groups also exist: Dignity (Catholic), Integrity (Episcopalian), and the Metropolitan Community Church, a primarily gay and lesbian church. The latter has grown in just a few years to over 100 congregations and 30 affiliated groups. The Unitarian Universalist Association has an Office of Lesbian and Gay Concerns in denominational headquarters which helps congregations welcome gays and lesbians. Counselors can acquire or help their counselees acquire published guides to groups and meetings places, accommodations and social organizations (*Gaia's Guide*, 1992; *Gay Yellow Pages*, 1993).

"Will I Be Blackmailed?"

In the past, blackmail of the homosexual was a prevalent concern. One benefit of gay liberation is that the openly gay or lesbian individual is not subject to such threats. Needless to say, those who believe they must stay in the closet are still fair game. Many find that being "outed" does not seriously change their lives. For others being gay holds the potential for losing one's job. The ban on gays in the military prevented many from revealing their sexual orientation. At this writing court martials are in process against gay military personnel for publicly stating their orientation. The President's removal of the ban in favor of a "don't ask, don't tell" policy is a step in the direction of individual freedom for homosexuals, but a vocal sector of public and congress stands in favor of removing all gays from the military.

Pair Bonding or Not?

Since most gay males and lesbians have been brought up at first with heterosexual expectations, most also have absorbed society's dictate of pair-bonding in monogamous relationships. Without the strictures of a legal marriage, however, many gays find it easy to stray from monogamy. Whether or not to venture into freer patterns of relationship and sex presents a dilemma, especially for the bisexual. Obviously, no one has to be promiscuous, but without question the opportunity is more available for gays and bisexuals than for the rest of society. Some gay and lesbian couples are monogamous for thirty years or more; some are serially monogamous; but the high incidence of sexually transmitted diseases among the homosexual community attests to a fairly extensive exchanging of partners. Certainly any discussion of multiple partners should include safer-sex guidelines.

Although no state recognizes legal marriage among same-sex persons, in recent years several courts and some corporations have recognized registered domestic partnerships. These partnerships help gays and lesbians with legal and domestic matters such as buying communal property and providing health insurance for the partner.

"How Can I Avoid AIDS?"

Acquired Immune Deficiency Syndrome is transmitted by unsafe sexual activity, sharing of contaminated needles (exchange of bodily fluids), and transfusion of contaminated blood. The specter of AIDS has raised much panic and misinformation in the community at large. While anything written about AIDS is out of date by the time it is in print, the first thing a counselor must know is that counseling a client with AIDS presents no danger of the counselor's becoming infected. AIDS is spread only by the exchange of body fluids, and any such close contact is contrary to professional ethical principles. Aside from that, the primary factor involved for people with AIDS is stigma. Both groups that were first affected by AIDS—drug users and homosexuals—were already stigmatized.

Abundant resources exist to help overcome the hysteria and panic that still abound. AIDS is a condition that allows other diseases to run rampant. It has not always been fatal, but the survival rate is not high. As of this writing, there have been exciting developments such as an aerosol spray that prevents the recurrence of the dreaded type of pneumonia, and combinations of anti-viral and T-cell facilitation. For the client, this may involve coping with inability to work or study, loss of family support, need for contact with welfare and Supplemental Security Income staff, or general psychological distress. A counselor can offer support, help the client find other support systems, and deal with the AIDS-infected person as one would with any serious health problem.

Public information concerning AIDS has led to varying reactions in the gay community. Some members relaxed their vigilance in AIDS protection, thinking the battle was won. (Adib & Ostrow, 1991; Gelman, Duignan-Cabrera, Hannah, & Leyden, 1993). Others feared any sexual activity. Certainly counselors can warn clients to avoid overoptimism and reinforce the importance of the protection of condoms rather than the unrealistic option of celibacy. It is still true, however, that non-penetrative sex or abstention and clean needles are the only absolute way to avoid AIDS. Published information and workshops are readily available from schools, health departments, and private gay organizations.

Bisexual Concerns

While most everything said about counseling gays and lesbians also holds for bisexuals, one important point to keep in mind is that open bisexuals have been the brunt of rejection from both gays and nongays for many years. Many a gay has condemned a bisexual for denying his/her gay identity. Some bisexuals may not feel the need to come out at all because they can operate in both gay and nongay circles. With the advent of gay liberation, others feel free to be themselves, allowing both dimensions of their sexual orientation to exist openly and not hide their nongay side. The most important issues for most bisexuals who come for counseling seem to be the issue of spousal relationships and the anxieties and problems related to HIV and AIDS (Auerback, 1987; Myers, 1991; Paradis, 1991; Wolf, 1987).

Ed's situation is typical of bisexuals who come for counseling, and a variety of possibilities can be reviewed with him. Some husbands and wives truly want to make accommodations and maintain the marriage; some may even be willing to join a support group for spouses of gays. Some don't mind infidelity as long as it is with a same-sex partner; others demand monogamy. Some spouses feel so relieved that they are not the cause of the marital problem that, although upset, they can move quickly to making rational decisions about the future. Some bisexual spouses want to be free from marriage but have contact with children, whereas others want to remain in the household with outside gay contacts. Some handle this well; others with great guilt (Gochros, 1978).

OTHER PERSONAL COUNSELING NEEDS

Combating societally dictated sex roles is an issue for many homosexuals, especially women. Lesbians may defy society by asserting they will not be dependent on a male for life or by opting out of motherhood (although, increasingly, lesbians are arranging for pregnancy or adoption and child-rearing). Such defiance of sex role stereotypes creates personal and professional hazards for women. Gay males who are "macho" may fit externally into the expected sex role, but internally their affectional and sexual needs are met differently from those of most men. Because most hostility seems to come from those with a very narrow view of what constitutes a man or a woman and from those with rigid attitudes about sex, counselees may need help clarifying and separating their own feelings from those of other individuals and groups.

One unique problem faced by the gay and lesbian community is lack of security, even in the family. African American children are not rejected by parents because they are Black. Some disabled children are rejected for their status, but often the parents feel guilty. Anecdotal reports indicate that parents who reject gay or lesbian children appear to be more often self-righteous than guilty. Because the prospect of family hostility looms large, referral to support groups and special counseling on the legal aspects of living may be needed. Clear contracts, wills, and joint ownership agreements are important where anger may take the form of legal tangles.

Most personal problems concerned with relationships, loneliness, bashfulness, and so forth are much the same as those of heterosexuals. Unrequited love is unrequited love; yet, falling in love with a straight roommate poses special problems since most heterosexuals are not as closely exposed to their nonresponding loved one nor quite as likely to be met with hostility if feelings are declared.

The lesbian or gay male who comes out will have to deal with the fears of the nongay community. Parents fear the child will have a tortured, promiscuous, or unhappy life, ending up lonely and abandoned. The straight roommate fears that somehow he might be tainted: "What made him think I might be that way?" Parents fear that gay/lesbian teachers will turn their children gay. The counselor can help the counselee see that these fears stem from misinformation and myths and that the task is one of education.

Another important concern involves treatment of the homosexuals in the public schools. If gays are open or happen to be part of the visible, so-called "effeminate" or "butch" groups, they are reviled. One gay was forced to take female-only classes and to eat lunch alone for a year. "Faggot" has not ceased to be a favorite put-down word beginning in elementary school. If one is not gay, such peer put-down can be handled in ordinary ways, but for the gay it is likely to arouse the fearful unspoken response, "Does he/she really know?" So far the schools' sex education of youth has not been very helpful in overcoming hostility. The author can recall local young men screaming "faggot" at him out of school bus windows. The administrator of the school said they did not need sex education. Coaches still brag of their heterosexual success but malign the same-sex successes of others. In a few schools, counselors can still be heard telling and laughing at faggot jokes. Do as many counselors refuse to put up with antigay jokes as reject anti-Semitic ones? While AIDS education has in some schools made a slight dent in ignorance about homosexuality, much of it still reflects homophobia (Campaign to End Homophobia, 1992).

CAREER NEEDS

As a group, homosexuals are as varied as heterosexuals. Gays and lesbians are found in all occupations and all walks of life, although proportionately they have greater representation among the college educated. Gay caucuses found in many professions attest to this variety: The American Psychiatric Association; American Psychological Association; American Counselors Association; American Nurses Association; Modern Language Association; National Council of Teachers of English; American Association of Sex Educators, Counselors and Therapists; Society for the Scientific Study of Sex; American Public Health Association; and National Association of Social Workers. Thus, career counseling needs should not differ much from those of the heterosexual client. Suggestions to consider when making career choices, pointed out long ago by Canon (1973) and Norton (1976), are still pertinent:

1. A large city provides anonymity for those who want it and more gay/lesbian life and support groups than do towns and rural areas.

2. Sexual orientation should be irrelevant to job hiring; however, this is not universally the case.

3. The National Gay and Lesbian Task Force publishes a list of industries which state they do not discriminate against gays. Having a list of communities protecting gay and lesbian civil rights is also reassuring. Little, if any, encouragement can be offered through affirmative action law

4. Although membership in a college gay alliance activity demonstrates leadership ability and a certain amount of courage, some employers may perceive this activity as

dangerous or indicative of social values not held by the company management.

5. While in the past, a gay personnel manager has sometimes been harder on open gays than nongays, since it threatened his/her own exposure, nowadays some business gays are looking for like-minded personnel. A gay bi-weekly publication listed 26 job openings in 1979, but only nine in 1992 (*The Advocate*, 1979, 1992). Another weekly listed 19 in 1987 but only seven in 1992 (*New York Native*, 1987, 1992).

HISTORY OF SERVICES TO GAYS

The history of services to gays and lesbians has been one of oppression—at first punishment, then treatment to cure the "illness." Such treatment has included isolation, incarceration, psychoanalysis, aversive therapy, electric shock, lobotomies, and castration. In years past, many a youth was forced into an insane asylum by parents hostile to same-sex orientation. It was not until 1975 that the American Psychiatric Association removed homosexuality from its list of mental illnesses, and only in 1986 did the word homosexuality vanish completely from the Diagnostic and Statistical Manual III-R with the removal of the term **Ego dystonic homosexuality**.

For many years, laws forbade homosexual acts throughout the United States, although since 1971 some 27 states have decriminalized homosexual acts between consenting adults. In 23 states and the District of Columbia the law still invades the bedroom and labels 10% of the population criminals. For years courts directly punished gays and deprived them of custody of their children and/or visiting rights. Since the 1970s the American Psychological Association has taken the position that affectional and sexual orientation should not be the primary consideration in determining child custody, but despite this stand therapists rate the same hypothetical client as less healthy when the client is presented as homosexual rather than heterosexual.

Quiet efforts at reform have progressed since the 1850s (Lauritsen & Thorstad, 1974), and quiet acceptance of homosexuality grew in some areas of the country such as San Francisco, a comfortable home for many. In 1969, however, during a routine raid of the Stonewall Bar in New York City drag queens rioted in protest of vice statutes. After 1969 the Gay Liberation Front, the Gay Activist Alliance, Street Transvestite Action Revolutionaries (STAR), and the National Gay and Lesbian Task Force rapidly sprang up. Annual marches to celebrate the Stonewall riot spread to cities large and small. In addition to the states and jurisdictions that have passed civil rights ordinances to protect gays and lesbians, local and professional organizations have pressed for education concerning gay and lesbian issues, working to counteract the increased hostility brought about by the AIDS crisis (Berube, 1990).

Despite these advances, homophobia runs rampant. One cannot forget the high school students in Tucson who went downtown to "beat up a queer" and killed a visitor from out of state, but were back on the Student Council within six months. Or the three youths who threw an openly gay male off a bridge to drown in Bangor, Maine; or the lesbian shot in the woods in Pennsylvania; or the sailor murdered on board his ship. Hostility is countrywide, fanned by votes and shrill voices of persons who feel increasingly threatened by a visible gay community.

More than one-half of the population, when polled, said they advocated civil rights of homosexuals. Seven states and over 60 jurisdictions have enacted protections in employment, housing, and public accommodation. The Supreme Court of the United States has ruled that nothing in the U. S. Constitution prevents states from forbidding homosexual behavior, but 27 states have decriminalized it by vote or by judicial decision at the state level. Decisions are beginning to allow visitation rights for the lesbian mother and gay father. Legal organizations such as the Lambda Legal Defense and Education Fund have defended gays and lesbians in court and fought discrimination in a wide variety of situations. Support for gay civil rights also has come from many church groups, including the National Council of Bishops of the Roman Catholic Church (in the United States) and the Central Conference of the American Rabbis of the Reform Movement in

Judaism. Not many groups, however, actually condone same-sex behavior. While the majority of citizens to favor a "live and let live' policy, seemingly they do not understand and accept same-sex orientation, and a very vocal minority actively oppose it, witness the Republican platform in 1992.

In the '90s, despite the loud protests of fundamentalists, society is changing. President Clinton was the first candidate to mention support for gays and lesbians during his campaign and received substantial support from that population. Many national polls show a more accepting attitude, but individual states, cities, and districts are rejecting antigay legislation and overturning civil rights provisions for gays. Thus counselors can be helpful to clients by becoming familiar with local, state, and national trends in gay rights legislation.

THE HELPING PROFESSIONAL'S ROLE

Because most counselors were reared in our heterosexually oriented society, the vast majority have absorbed the misinformation and myths about or even the hostility towards lesbians and gays. The first responsibility of counselors is to reeducate themselves. Meeting and talking to same-sex oriented people helps the individual to discover that they are people, not pariahs. Reading can supplement personal meetings. There are fine books on counseling this special population (Moses & Hawkins, 1982; Dworkin & Gutierrez, 1991), books for parents, and "coming out" pamphlets. In addition, there are now specialized gay and lesbian journals: *Journal of Homosexuality, Women and Therapy, Journal of Gay and Lesbian Psychotherapy, Journal of Gay and Lesbian Social Services*. As part of their reeducation, counselors can learn not only to avoid antigay/lesbian/bisexual jokes, but to avoid heterosexist language. (Committee on Lesbian and Gay Concerns, 1991).

Once counselors have confronted their own personal hostility, doubts or uncertainties, and are able to maintain objectivity, they can counsel the gay male, lesbian, or bisexual just as they would anyone else. Generating a feeling of acceptance and understanding is crucial. Correcting misperceptions, giving appropriate reassurance, evaluating decisions—all regular counseling activities—come into play while working with this population. Counselors must remember that many members of this population go to a counselor because of personal problems and mention sexual orientation only in passing. In the past, some in that situation found the counselor made sexual orientation the problem. Actually, in the past, many homosexuals avoided personal problem counseling just because they were afraid of the reaction they might get if the sexual orientation became known. Counselors have the responsibility to let it be known that they will listen to gays and lesbians as well as to nongays. They can reject antigay jokes; they can put articles about gay civil rights, or gay leaders, on bulletin boards or in school papers; they can make clear that they have discarded, if they ever had, stereotypes about gay males being "effeminate" and lesbians "butch."

Specific suggestions have been scattered throughout the discussion of special problems. Yet the counselor cannot expect to have answers to all problems. Ed's dilemma, for example, has a variety of possible outcomes, The helping professional's role in this and all cases is to know that knowledge of others' behavior will not solve Ed's problem. He alone can make his decision through exploration of his situation, including his concerns for his wife and children. This can be done only in a warm, permissive, nonjudgmental situation. A well-informed, self-aware counselor is what all lesbian, gay male, and bisexual clients desire.

EXPERIENTIAL ACTIVITIES

Individual Activity

Go to the library and ask at the desk for help in finding materials on gays and lesbians. How do you feel about asking for information on this topic? Do you feel the need to explain, for example, that this is a class assignment?

Group Activity

In groups of six to ten, discuss how you would feel if your best friend said to you, "I am gay (lesbian)." Would it make any difference if the discloser were the same or the opposite sex? How would his/her marital status affect your reaction?

Outside Class Activity

Alone, with a friend or a group, visit a gay bar. (There are six listed in the Gay Yellow Pages for Greensboro, North Carolina; five in Albany, New York; all welcome both genders). Finding one is part of the assignment. Do the patrons behave differently from those in singles bars? Did you feel any different in a gay bar than you do in other bars?

REFERENCES

Adib, S.M., & Ostrow, D.G. (1991). Trends in HIV/AIDS behavioral research among homosexual and bisexual men in the United States: 1981-1991. *AIDS Care, 3* (3), 281-287.

Adler, N.L., Hendrick, S., & Hendrick, C. (1986) Male sexual preference and attitudes toward love and sexuality. *Journal of Sex Education & Therapy, 12* (2), 27-30.

The Advocate. (1979, March 22). (1992, Oct. 20). 6922 Hollywood Blvd., 10th floor, Los Angeles, CA 90028.

The Advocate. (1992, Oct. 20). 6922 Hollywood Blvd., 10th floor, Los Angeles, CA 90028.

Anonymous. (1980). *Young, gay & proud.* Boston: Alyson Publications.

Auerbach, S. (1987). Groups for the wives of gay and bisexual men. *Social Work, 32*(4), 321-325.

Bell, A.P., Weinberg, M.S., & Hammersmith, S.K. (1981). *Sexual preference: Its development in men and women.* Bloomington, IN: Indiana University Press.

Berube, A. (1990). *Coming out under fire: The history of gay men and women in World War II.* New York: Free Press (Macmillan).

Biemiller, L. (1985, October 2). AIDS on campus. *Chronicle of Higher Education,* p.1.

Blumenstein, F.W., & Schwartz, P. (1977). Bisexuality: Some social psychological issues. *Journal of Social Issues, 33* (2), 30-45.

Bozett, F.M. (1985). Gay men as fathers. In S.H. Hanson & F.W. Bozett (Eds.). *Dimensions of fathering.* Beverly Hills, CA: Sage.

Campaign to End Homophobia. (1989). I think I might be gay (lesbian). . .Now what do I do? P. O. Box 819, Cambridge, MA 02139: Author.

Campaign to End Homophobia. (1992). Homophobia in HIV Education. P. O. Box 819, Cambridge, MA 02139: Author.

Canon, H.J. (1973). Gay students. *Vocational Guidance Quarterly, 21,* 181-185.

Coleman, E. (1982). Developmental stages in the coming out process. *Journal of Homosexuality, 7 (2/3),* 31-43.

Committee on Lesbian and Gay Concerns. (1991). Avoiding heterosexual bias in language. *American Psychologist, 46,* 973-974.

Dank, B. (1971). Coming out in the gay world. *Psychiatry, 34,* 180-197.

DeCecco, J.P. (1987). Homosexuality's brief recovery: From sickness to health and back again. *Journal of Sex Research, 23* (1), 106-114.

Duberman, M. (1992). *Cures: A gay man's odyssey.* New York: NAL Dutton.

Dworkin, S.H., & Gutierrez, F. (1991). *Counseling gay men and lesbians: Journey to the end of the rainbow.* Washington, DC: American Counselors Association.

Ellis, L., Hoffman, H.F., & Burke, D.M. (1990). Sex, sexual orientation and criminal and violent behavior. *Personality and Individual Differences, ll,* 1207-1212.

Engel, J.W., & Saracino, M. (1986) Love preferences and ideals: A comparison of homosexual, bisexual and heterosexual groups. *Contemporary Family Therapy An International Journal, 8, 241-250.*

Fricke, A. (1981). *Reflections of a rock lobster: A story about growing up gay.* Boston: Alyson Publications.

Gaia's Guide. (1992). Giovanni's Room, 345 South 12th St. NE, Philadelphia, PA 19107.

Gay Yellow Pages. (1993). New York: Renaissance House.

Gelman, D., Duignan-Cabrera, A., Hannah, D., & Leyden, P. (1993, January 11). The young and the reckless. *Newsweek,* pp, 60-61.

Gochros, H.L. (1978). Counseling gay husbands. *Journal of Sex Education and Therapy, 3* (2), 6-10.

Gochros, J.S. (1989). *When husbands come out of the closet.* Binghamton, NY: Harrington Park Press.

Hutchins, L. & Kaahumanu, L. (Eds.). (1991). *Bi any other name: Bisexual people speak out.* Boston: Alyson Publications.

Kennedy, E. (1977). *Sexual counseling.* New York: Seabury Press.

Kinsey, A. (1948). Sexual behavior in the human male. Philadelphia: W.B. Saunders.

Lambda Update. (1992, Fall). New York: Lambda Legal Defense and Education Fund.

Lauritson, J., & Thorstad, D. (1974). *The early homosexual movement.* Albion, CA: Times Change Press.

Lynch, F.R. (1987). Non-ghetto gays: A sociological study of suburban homosexuals. *Journal of Homosexuality, 13*(4), 13-42.

Masters, W., & Johnson, V. (1979). *Homosexuality in perspective.* Boston: Little, Brown & Co.

Money, J. (1986). Homosexual genesis, outcome studies, and a nature/nurture paradigm shift. *American Journal of Social Psychology, 6*(2), 95-98.

Morin, S.F., & Garfinkle, E.M. (1978). Male homophobia. *Journal of Social Issues, 34* (1), 29-47.

Moses, A.E., & Hawkins, R.O. (1982). *Counseling lesbian women and gay men.* St. Louis: C. V. Mosby Co.

Myers, M.F. (1991). Marital therapy with HIV-infected men and their wives. *Psychiatric Annals, 21* (8), 466-470.

National Gay and Lesbian Task Force. (1989). *Anti-gay violence, victimization and defamation in 1988.* Washington, DC: Author.

New York Native. (1987, Apr. 13). P. O. Box 1475, New York, NY 10008.

New York Native. (1992, Dec. 10). P. O. Box 1475, New York, NY 10008.

Norton, J.L. (1976). The homosexual and counseling. *Personnel and Guidance Journal, 54,* 374-377.

Norton, J.L. (1982). Integrating gay issues into counselor education. *Counselor Education and Supervision, 21*, 208-212.

Paradis, B.A. (1991). Seeking intimacy and integration: Gay men in the era of AIDS. *Smith College Studies in Social Work, 61*, 260-274.

Pierson, R. (1992, Oct.). "Kill gays" hit song stirs fury. *New York Post.*

Remafedi, G. (1987). Male homosexuality: The adolescent's perspective. *Pediatrics, 79*, 326-330.

Rickgarn, R.L. (1984). Developing support systems for gay and lesbian staff members. *Journal of College & University Student Housing, 14*, 32-36.

Riddle, D.I., & Morin, S.F. (1977, November). Removing the stigma: Data from individuals. *APA Monitor*, pp. 16;28.

Ross, M.W. (1989). Gay youth in four cultures: A comparative study. In G. Herdt (Ed.), *Gay and lesbian youth* (PP. 299-314). Binghamton, NY: Haworth Press.

Sakheim, D.K., Barlow, D.H., Beck, J.G., & Abrahamson, D.J. (1985). A comparison of male heterosexual and male homosexual patterns of sexual arousal. *Journal of Sex Research, 212* (2), 183-198.

Saghir, M.T., & Robins, E. (1973). Male and female homosexuality: A comprehensive investigation. Baltimore: Williams and Wilkins.

Smith, D. (1985). An ethnographic interview study of homosexual teachers' perspectives. Unpublished doctoral dissertation, SUNY at Albany, NY.

Spees, E. (1987). College students' sexual attitudes and behaviors, 1974-85: A review of the literature. *Journal of College Student Personnel, 28*, 135-140.

Troiden, R.R., & Goode, E. (1980). Variables related to acquisition of gay identity. *Journal of Homosexuality, 5,* 383-392.

Weinberg, G. (1972). *Society and the healthy homosexual.* New York: Anchor/Doubleday.

West, D.J. (1977). *Homosexuality re-examined.* Minneapolis: University of Minnesota Press.

Wilensky, M., & Myers, M.F. (1987). Retarded ejaculation in homosexual patients: A report of nine cases. *Journal of Sex Research, 23* (1), 85-91.

Wilson-Glover, R. (1987, March 2). *Married men, double lives.* Rochester (NY) Times Union.

Wolf, T.J. (1987). Group psychotherapy for bisexual men and their wives. *Journal of Homosexuality, 14,* 191-199.

Chapter 8

ON THE RESERVATION

Marilyn Jemison Anderson, B.A. and Robert Ellis, Ph.D.

Marilyn Anderson is currently the Human Services Administrator of the Seneca Nation Health Department, which includes Social Services, Mental Health and Substance Abuse, Community Outreach, and Medical Transportation. She has been actively involved in the delivery of health services on the Cattaraugus Reservation, where she has lived with her husband and two children, since 1973. Mrs. Anderson received her Bachelor's Degree in Sociology from D'Youville College, Buffalo, in 1969. Mrs. Anderson has served as editor of Si Wong Geh, the reservation newsletter. In addition she served on the advisory boards for a number of local mental health institutions and the National Indian Food and Nutrition Resource Center. In 1974, Mrs. Anderson was named an outstanding young woman of America from New York State.

Robert Ellis is the Senior Psychologist at the Resource Center in Jamestown, NY, a community-based rehabilitation program that works with 600+ mentally disabled adults and preschool children. He also maintains a private practice in Fredonia, NY. He completed the Bachelor's and Master's Degree in

*Psychology at San Diego State University in 1968 and
1970, respectively. He was awarded the Ph.D. in
Educational Psychology by the University of California
at Santa Barbara in 1974. Prior to his present position,
he taught at Idaho State University in Pocatello, Idaho,
and the State University of New York, College at
Fredonia. Besides his interest in the structure of the
tribal culture and its impact on the clash between Native
Americans and western culture, he also has investigated
the development of tribal-like behaviors in abusive
families. Dr. Ellis is a member of the American
Association of Applied and Preventive Psychology and
the National Academy of Neuropsychology.*

AWARENESS INDEX

Directions: These questions are to help you to evaluate your
understanding of the Indian and Indian culture. Mark each item
as true or false. Compute your score from the scoring guide at
the end of this Awareness Index.

T F 1. The Native American behaves differently from
non-Native Americans because of the poverty in
which the great majority of Native Americans live.

T F 2. The non-Native American counselor is at such a
severe disadvantage when working with Native
American clients that the attempt should not be
made.

T F 3. Native Americans are at a disadvantage because
their social consciousness has not yet developed to
the point that they can enjoy the advantages of the
Native American life.

T F 4. Because of their different culture, Native Americans
do not have the Western concepts of right and
wrong, truth and falsehood.

T F 5. Relatively more alcoholics live on the reservation than in the dominant non-Native American society.

T F 6. The notion of change to a Native American is negative because of its implication that the present order of things is inadequate.

T F 7. A Native American can live off the reservation without compromising any basic cultural value

T F 8. Because of their sense of tribal integration, Native American student may cheat on a test when asked to do so by another member of the tribe.

T F 9. Native Americans are not punctual because they do not respect non-Native American peoples.

T F 10. The Native American culture could be classified as primitive.

T F 11. In terms of perceived confidentiality, a non-Native American counselor has an advantage over Native American counselor when working with Native American clients.

Scoring Guide for Awareness Index

1. F   2. F   3. F   4. F   5. F   6. T   7. F   8. T   9. F   10. F   11. T

"The use of ardent spirits amongst the Indians, and the attempts which have been made to civilize and Christianize them by the white people, has [SIC] constantly made them worse and worse; increased their vices, and robbed them of many of their virtues; and will ultimately produce their extermination." Mary Jemison (Seaver, 1925, p. 48)

Mary Jemison, a White woman, had been living with the Seneca Indians in upstate New York for over 60 years when she wrote the preceding statement. Although the description was written more than 160 years ago, it appears as valid now for this group of Native Americans as it was then. Her remarks eloquently and succinctly illustrate the Native American's two major problems in American society today: (1) the attempt by members of the dominant culture to interpret Native American behavior in terms of norms and expectations not shared by the tribal culture, and (2) the continuing attempt to convert the Native American to a "better" culture. This chapter offers several suggestions for helpers who might provide counseling services to the Native American client, suggestions that will assist counselors in avoiding common errors that may alienate a client in trouble and damage the counselor's credibility as a helping professional.

Too often, non-Native Americans are admonished to be sensitive to cultural differences when dealing with Native Americans, but one can look far and wide before finding a list or specific statement of those differences. The usual suggestion is for the individual to go and live among Native Americans for a while. But, as many workers in the Bureau of Indian Affairs will attest, mere association is not enough. What is needed is a point of view, a new perspective from which to observe problems. To help you, the reader, develop this perspective, two areas will be discussed:

1. the general relationship between the Native American and the tribe, noting some of the implications of that relationship that have proved confusing and foreign to the great majority of non-Native American observers, and

2. the specific problem of alcohol abuse, which is identified quite closely with the Native American, differentiating the problem from alcoholism in the dominant, non-Native American culture.

The authors recognize the danger of treading in these extremely sensitive territories, especially because a great diversity exists among tribes and individuals both on and off the reservation. The interests, needs, and culture of the reservation Native American may vary greatly from those of the urban Native American. A similar difference may be found between Native Americans living in the eastern, midwestern, and western parts of the United States. However, the difficulties caused by well-meaning helpers justify the risk. We ask, therefore, that the following be read with the recognition that our comments, based on the experiences of Seneca reservation Native Americans, are offered as suggestions to heighten awareness and not as the final word on the subject.

Several basic assumptions must be understood and accepted before one can begin working with a Native American clientele. The Native American has a culture, a cultural heritage, and a right to that culture as inalienable as any other basic human right. Accordingly, any discussion or suggestion with regard to assimilation—i.e., the suggestion, implication or otherwise, that an "inferior" culture be abandoned for a "superior" culture—will be viewed, rightly so, as a direct insult and slur.

Most Native Americans, especially those who remain on or return to the reservation, do not prefer assimilation and may not want all of the "advantages" of the non-Native American life. For this reason, the counselor must not take the position that a Native American's problems are merely cultural. The themes of cultural disadvantage and cultural poverty have been popular in the social services literature and suggest that one culture is richer or better than another. Although a Native American may be having difficulty in resolving expectations based on apparently incompatible cultural values, to suggest that the conflict can be consistently resolved in favor of one of those systems, especially if it is the Native American culture, is blatant cultural arrogance.

Native Americans do have problems and do require help. Like everyone else, they are best served by a helper who considers them and their problems individually and with sensitivity to their context. No one is helped when a problem is dismissed by saying, "Oh, it's just cultural"; nor can the individual be helped when his or her basic value system is dismissed casually.

The point that we would like to make is that the dynamics of problems faced by the Native American are no different from those faced by any other human being; that is, a temporary inability to resolve conflicting pressures in a successful and satisfying way. The difference between Native Americans and others, however, is found in the kinds of pressure with which they have to contend given their particular culture and the dominant society in which they live.

The following preparatory steps are very important for human services counselors working with Native Americans:

1. Recognize that Native Americans approach life with a different set of expectations, values, and interpretations of events, and that their approach can be as satisfying and as rich to them as any other culture is to any other person.

2. Become familiar with those specific cultural values so that one can begin to understand and appreciate the pressures being faced by Native American clients.

3. Resist the temptation to interpret a particular behavior or problem as if it emerged in a manner typical of that problem in a non-Native American, middle-class society.

4. Appreciate that Native Americans, like everyone else, want minimal stress and aggravation in their lives.

5. Consider Native Americans with an attitude of respect rather than paternalism.

THE TRIBE

The first step in understanding the Native American's cultural differences is appreciating that the relationship between the Native American and the tribe is different from the relationship between the non-Native American middle-class person and society. The Native American sees self as an extension of the tribe in the sense that he or she is a part of a whole, and that wholeness of the tribe is what gives meaning to the part. For example, a flower petal has little beauty by itself, but when it is put together with the other parts of the flower, the whole is a thing of great beauty. This relationship stands in contrast to the non-Native American middle-class position where society operates primarily as a set of rules to promote individual accomplishment. Stated somewhat differently, the tribe provides the meaning and justification of existence for the individual from the Native American's point of view, while the individual provides the justification for society from the non-Native American Western perspective. As a consequence, Native Americans judge their worth primarily in terms of whether their behavior contributes to the harmonious functioning of the tribe. In contrast, White, middle-class America judges worth primarily in terms of individual accomplishment, individual prestige, individual power, and/or individual values. While these generalizations are clearly too simple, they do serve to illustrate that the Native American uses a value system that is fundamentally different from that of the dominant culture; basic worth is judged in terms of tribal enhancement and not individual enhancement. On the other hand, the Native American is not against individual accomplishment; for example, in craft work or sport, when it reflects positively on the tribe. In short, one would make a mistake to assume, as so many have, that the concept of tribe to the Native American is synonymous with the concept of society to the non-Native American.

At this time, approximately 650,000 of the one million Native Americans still live on or close to a reservation. Many pressures, however, exist for the Native American to leave the reservation. The main culprits are the public school system with its main-street value system and the television set with its fantasy-consumption value system. Pressures to leave the reservation also may be more direct. The explicit termination policy of the Eisenhower Administration was to "assimilate" the Native American by providing social services support only if the Native American left the reservation (Some have said that the actual goal was to acquire the now valuable reservation property). The reservation, however, is the physical embodiment of the tribe and for an individual to leave the reservation that individual must, in a sense, reject the tribe and the values it represents. Such a separation for a Native American, if it is not complete (i.e., accompanied by the adoption of an "individual" point of view), will be traumatic and leave the potential for psychological insecurities and conflicts unfamiliar to the great majority of human-service counselors.

A non-Native American has difficulty appreciating the trauma of Native Americans leaving the reservation. Leaving means that they must abandon behind a value system that has provided nurturance all of their lives and adopt a system of being independent and alone for which they have neither preparation nor relevant role-models. An additional point is that one's family tribe does not extend beyond the reservation. While support and social groups on the outside are made up of individuals from different tribes, these provide little satisfaction for they are no substitute for the tribe. In order to leave the reservation, a Native American has to adopt one or more of the values of the non-reservation world and, in so doing, lays the groundwork for potential future problems. Conflicts arise when values from basically incompatible cultures are mixed, and, unless resolved, the resulting anxiety and stress interferes with the performance of day-to-day tasks. As can be seen, the non-reservation Native American presents a complex and difficult therapy situation. Accordingly, we have chosen to restrict our comments, to the Native American who has chosen to remain. Because of the ubiquity of the dominant culture, however, even those who choose to stay are not immune to the pressures of the individual ethic. As a consequence, the reservation counselor can expect to face many situations requiring a surgeon's skill to disentangle the themes of Harmony (tribal culture) and Individuality (Western culture) in conflict.

HARMONY

Differences among tribes and among individuals are enormous, a fact that must be recognized by counselors. On the other hand, the authors believe that common sets of values are shared to various degrees by the great majority of Native Americans and can be identified and discussed as a family of characteristics without suggesting a stereotyped Native America image. Furthermore, the fact that these values are discussed within the context of problems that may bring a Native American into contact with a counselor or human services provider is not meant to suggest that these values are negative or in any way inferior to other values. As a matter of fact, these values many times contribute to the Native American's problems only because helpers fail to recognize that the Native American has a different, yet legitimate, way of approaching the world. The following, then, is an attempt to clarify some of the ramifications of a tribal society without suggesting either that they are shared in the same degree by all Native Americans or that they reflect negatively on the tribal culture.

As can be imagined, the tribal culture places a high value on the harmonious relationship between an individual and his or her peers, that is, all the other members of the tribe. A high value is placed on behavior that advances harmony and cooperation in the tribe: to not cooperate would be to assert one's individuality and suggest that one is better than the tribe. To be a member of the tribe, then, means that the individual is honor bound to defer to the wishes of others, to be polite, to be unassertive, and to work hard to prevent discord. Because of this value of promoting harmony above all, many counselors have falsely concluded that because Native American clients fail to disagree, they must agree with the counselor. Then, when the client behaves in a way out of keeping with this agreement, the counselor jumps to the conclusion that the Native American lied.

The tribal culture, however, does not support lying, and regardless of myth or stereotype the Native American is not a liar. He or she will, however, go to great lengths to develop misdirection and ambiguities to avoid disagreement or contradiction. From the Western point of view, such behavior is synonymous with telling untruths (lying) because it does not clarify the truth. Of more value to the Native American is the fact that contradiction and disagreement are disharmonious and are to be avoided whenever possible. Furthermore, to disagree with someone is in one sense an assertion of ego and individuality and, for that reason also, the Native American works hard to appear to be in agreement.

As a variation of the same phenomenon, consider the dilemma of the Native American student who is called upon to answer a question in front of a group in a class with other Native American students and a non-Native American teacher. To answer it correctly would be an act of individuality and apparent superiority while to answer it incorrectly or to stand mute in indecision would bring humiliation to the individual and to the tribe—a classic no-win situation brought on by the cultural insensitivity of a non-Native American.

By the same token, a Native American student cannot refuse to show a test paper to another Native American student when requested to do so. To refuse would be to violate the mutual dependence, cooperation, and politeness held valuable by the tribal culture. To anticipate somewhat, the Native American is put in rather the same dilemma when asked to have a couple of beers; to refuse would be again an assertion of individuality and a social *faux pas*.

Other deeply misunderstood consequences of the tribal culture are the Native American's apparent disregard for punctuality, planning for the future, and the concept of time in general. The Native American's disregard for time has given rise to the stereotype of the Native American as shiftless, lazy, and undependable. Time is a fairly recent invention on the part of the Western civilization and is necessary only in a culture that values change. If no change occurs, time to measure that change is unnecessary. Change exists only within the context of time, and for a culture that values stability and actively discourages change, as the tribal culture does, time becomes an unimportant consideration. Therefore, no support exists for future plans because such plans imply that the individual is trying to better himself or herself at the expense of the tribe.

Accordingly, most Native Americans live in the here and now with little concern for long-term projects that require delayed gratification and sacrifice, such as education or vocational training. In a sense, Einstein's conceptualization of time as a relative phenomenon that is affected by other events is much closer to the Native American idea of time than the Western notion of an absolute, quantifiable, and linear quantity. The same holds for the Western concept of punctuality: Why would one do something solely for the sake of finishing at a certain point in time? Is not something that is worth doing, worth doing well regardless of how long it takes? In short, when a conflict exists between quality and punctuality, punctuality is sacrificed.

The counselor also must recognize that a tribal culture is inherently conservative and resistant to change. From a Western perspective, then, the tribe generates a tremendous amount of social and peer pressure for conforming to tribal custom and tradition. A way to appreciate this pressure is to remember that all behavior is evaluated in the here and now and in terms of how it contributes to the present welfare of the tribe. This concept is changing slowly, but long-term plans such as going to college, which also involves leaving the reservation, are seen as acts of egoism and individuality and suggest that the tribe is inadequate and that things should be done differently. In very general terms, to suggest doing something different is to suggest that you as an individual may know more and may be better than the tribe as a whole. This is not to say that tribes do not change, rather that they do not value and promote change as inherently valuable. As noted previously, behavior that does not contribute to harmony and to the tribe, is frowned upon and censured. As a consequence, the Native American client is very sensitive to the expectations of the tribal peer group, and the counselor must recognize and accommodate those sensitivities in work with a Native American if cooperation and a trusting relationship are to develop.

Another consideration is the relationship of the Native American to personal wealth. The Native American tends not to cultivate a life-style directed toward either conspicuous consumption or the accumulation of personal property. By now the reader may anticipate why the Native American does not subscribe to those behaviors which are fundamental to the economy of the dominant culture; conspicuous consumption clearly smacks of individual egoism and a means of communicating superior individual worth. The accumulation of personal wealth requires, as well, both delayed gratification—saving for tomorrow what you could consume today—and active future planning, behaviors that are as foreign to the tribal culture as the cut-throat competition that generally accompanies the struggle to accumulate wealth and power.

The cultural characteristics of harmony and tribal tradition have been interpreted negatively by the dominant culture and, as a consequence, have resulted in many subtle prejudices against the Native American. The primary reason for this interpretation, as far as the authors can determine, is that non-Native Americans tend to assume that the tribal behaviors developed out of an individual-oriented culture. That is, Native American behavior has been and continues to be evaluated in terms of standards held by the evaluator and not by the tribe. The consequence is that the tribal behaviors are viewed as manifestation of individual pathology or cultural inferiority. For example, counselors are taught that breakdowns in ego functions are key symptoms of impending mental illness, e.g., schizophrenia. This interpretation is often true for individuals reared within a Western culture, but a so-called "weak-ego" is normal within the dynamics of a strong tribal system and therefore is not necessarily a symptom of mental illness for its members. If a counselor confused common tribal phenomena, nonassertiveness and disregard for punctuality, with symptoms of Western individual pathology such as time disorientation and loss of the concept of *I*, a Native American client would likely receive inappropriate therapy.

ALCOHOL ABUSE

One way to illustrate the problem of evaluating behavior in one culture by standards derived from another culture is to look at the problem of the Native American and alcohol. The misuse of alcohol may occur in one cultural setting for reasons completely different from those of another culture. Likewise, techniques developed to deal with alcohol abuse for one situation may be inappropriate in a different cultural context.

Such is the case with the Native American and alcoholism. Alcohol abuse in the dominant culture quite often operates to insulate the individual drinker from both personal responsibility and a stressful environment. As the counselor examines alcohol use and abuse among Native Americans, it becomes apparent that such an abuse syndrome is considerably less common among reservation Native Americans, although its incidence increases dramatically as the Native American becomes isolated from the tribe. Rather, the Native American who drinks to the extent that health is endangered drinks in binges and in groups. The Native American does not drink to get through the day but rather to have a good time with his tribal brothers and sisters.

In developing a treatment program, the counselor should not expect a program designed for non-Native American alcoholics to be useful with the Native American problem drinker; rather, the counselor should begin to look at the personal/social mechanisms that maintain the behavior. For example, drinking among men, even to the point of stupefication and unconsciousness, is usually not frowned on by the tribe. In fact, for some Native Americans, a certain degree of social approval is associated with an ability to tolerate large quantities of beer. The notion that Native Americans have a lower tolerance for alcohol has never been demonstrated physiologically or psychologically.

For the Native American, drinking is often a social event performed in groups where it acts as a social facilitator. Many Native Americans are shy and withdrawn as one would expect in a culture where prescribed social behavior is a key component of an individual's self-worth. As a consequence, the Native American may use alcohol to overcome the reticence to socialize. Furthermore, the sociability caused by the first few drinks also heightens the sense of tribe and brotherhood, both of which then operate as powerful reinforcers to maintain group drinking behavior. Also, because many Native Americans believe that to disagree with or contradict another person is bad form, to turn down proffered beer would be socially difficult to do.

One also must remember that without a concern for the future and with an orientation more to the here and now, an individual Native American may be unconcerned about some future, long-term consequence that may result from too much drinking. In addition, excessive drinking may not interfere with the Native American's life-style if he or she generally does not work at a job where punctuality is paramount. When the binge is over, the person can return to work with no problems whatsoever. Within that context one can easily understand how alcohol abuse and, increasingly, drug abuse can become widespread health hazards. The counselor must recognize that whatever helping process is chosen, it must be suited to the social context within which the abuse pattern was developed and maintained.

PERSONAL AND CAREER GUIDANCE NEEDS
OF THIS SPECIAL POPULATION

Clearly, the Native American has special personal and career-guidance needs. Native Americans are rarely career oriented because of the necessary long-term planning implied, past oppression by non-Native Americans, and the fact that, in many areas, few career options are open on or near the reservation. In addition, most careers require some college training. This in turn requires long-term planning and an early off-reservation move, further implying personal betterment and egoism. These perceptions or biases against personal development are changing, but the counselor can help by explaining how the tribe can protect its special values and environment if its members are trained to deal directly with the non-Native American world rather than relying on missionaries and the Bureau of Indian-Affairs (BIA).

The career guidance counselor also should be aware that many college-bound reservation Native American students may not stay a full month on campus. Their first trip away from their home is shock enough, but the apparent individual coldness can be too much for the adolescent Native American. What is necessary is that the career guidance counselor make an effort to identify those colleges with a significant Native American population so that the environment will not be too alien and hostile.

If one primary career and/or personal guidance need of the reservation Native American exists in either the schools or society, it is to feel a part of the tribe. Given that the individual Native American may evaluate personal worth in terms of how contributions can be made to the tribe, decisions, suggestions, and recommendations must be made in like fashion.

The following is a list of what might be described as cultural barriers that must be recognized and accommodated by the helper in order to be effective. Again, these items and characteristics are not universal; they do not characterize all Native Americans nor do they characterize even Native Americans from the same tribe. They do, however, provide a list of cultural differences that should be kept in mind and used to evaluate behavior.

1. The Native American client will most likely be shy, unassertive, passive, and very sensitive to the opinion and attitude of peers.

2. The Native American client may actively avoid disagreement or contradiction and, if allowed, will appear to agree or conform even though the person has no intention of behaving in that way. Note that the best response in this situation is not to try to outwit the client but to ask questions directly so that no opportunity is available to be evasive.

3. Many Native Americans do not like being singled out and made to perform, especially when peers or Native Americans from other tribes are present. The exception is an athletic competition where the tribe as a whole will benefit.

4. Respect must be earned by the helper. Degrees, experience, and reputation carry no weight on the reservation; counselors must demonstrate their respect and sensitivity to the needs of their Native American clients before respect will be returned. Given the passivity and nonassertiveness of many Native Americans, one has difficulty knowing when that respect has been earned. One indication may be the care the client takes in preparing for the meeting; the more he or she prepares, wearing neat and clean clothes (regardless of the "dressiness" of those clothes), or making the effort to brush hair, the more likely that the client respects the counselor.

5. Most Native American clients have little tolerance for long-range planning and delayed gratification. The counselor, therefore, must not become impatient nor expect a major commitment to a complex treatment plan. Taking things one step at a time, demonstrating personal commitment to planning, and emphasizing direction at every opportunity are key factors.

6. The Native American client may not view time as a linear, ordered process. Patience and recognition that punctuality is not a highly valued behavior are absolutely essential.

7. Property and possessions are most often valued only to the extent that they can be used in the present. Possessions are not used in the sense of reflecting personal worth, nor as a protection against some future calamity.

8. Alcohol plays a positive role in the social functioning of the tribal society but is easily abused because of its social acceptability.

HISTORY OF COUNSELING
AND OTHER SERVICES AVAILABLE

Historically, counseling services have not been available to the Native American client on the reservation; however, since the early 1980s tribes have begun to provide a wide variety of human service programs. The primary experience of the Native American with help services has been in the form of either missionaries or bureaucrats (euphemism for BIA workers) whose philosophy of counseling has been to tell the Native Americans that they are uncivilized savages and that they must change. The attitude that Native Americans are and must be treated as children (paternalism) is not yet history, and potential counselors must avoid behaving paternalistically if they hope to be accepted and effective on the reservation.

THE HELPING PROFESSIONAL'S ROLE

The authors would like to suggest that despite all of the previous warnings and traps to avoid, the non-Native American counselor has certain advantages over Native American counselors in working with reservation clientele and, given sensitivity to that potential, can provide effective help. Because of the close social relationship inherent in the tribal culture, these clients may not, in fact, be as open with their own counselors as with non-tribal ones. They often fear that whatever they say will be broadcast over the whole reservation (via the very effective "tribal telegraph"). Although a professional counselor, regardless of background, would not break confidentiality in so blatant a way, the client knows only that on the reservation everyone seems to know everything about everyone else and therefore would be extremely reluctant to discuss personal problems with another Native American. Accordingly, a counselor from another cultural group has the advantage of not being considered part of the reservation social communication system and should take advantage of that perception immediately by emphasizing that all communications will be held in confidence. The Native American counselor, by the same token, is put at a decided disadvantage and must demonstrate over quite an extended time period that confidences are respected. A new Native American counselor may find the job very trying because tribe members will be suspicious of the counselor who has just returned to the reservation. The best advice to all counselors is to keep a low profile and demonstrate trustworthiness through action. With trust, respect will grow.

Given the advantage on confidentiality, non-Native American counselors must nevertheless recognize that they will be approached with suspicion and distrust by Native American clients. Of course, suspicion and distrust are not unique to Native American clientele. All counselors are familiar with it, but the non-Native American counselor must be prepared to undergo testing by clients who resist counseling assistance and who will use the fact of the counselor's non-tribal status as an excuse to avoid or prevent change. The testing may be used to intimidate to a certain extent, but testing primarily will be used to probe the counselor's understanding of the Native American culture with the purpose of finding and exploiting ignorance as a defense against effective counseling. How does the non-Native American respond to the direct challenge, "You're not one of us; you don't understand us. You can't help us. Leave me alone!"? Inform the client that you are not there to help Native Americans but to help an individual help himself or herself and, furthermore, that the burden of responsibility for change lies with the client, not the counselor.

An effective tact is to make sure that clients assume as much responsibility for change as they are capable. In working with Native American clients, that goal is difficult to achieve because of the Native American's general nonassertiveness, uncommunicativeness, and tendency to promote harmony through apparent agreement. A strategy that we have found effective in overcoming this agreeable passivity is to ask questions that allow the client to assume some authority in the situation. For example, a noncommital or ambiguous statement can be challenged by indicating a lack of understanding and asking for further explanation. The client is thus encouraged to assume the role of teacher and take the responsibility of providing a clear communication. In this way the counselor encourages autonomy and responsibility in the client while simultaneously demonstrating respect for the individual and the culture.

On that note, we conclude with an observation made by a Chief of the Six Nations (of New York) as written in Benjamin Franklin's *Remarks Concerning Savages of North America* (Smyth, 1970):

> You who are wise, must know that different nations have different conceptions of things; and you will not therefore take it amiss, if our ideas of this kind of education happen not to be the same with yours. We have had some experience of it; several of our young people were formerly brought up at the Colleges of the northern provinces; they were instructed in all your sciences; but when they came back to us, they were bad runners, ignorant of every means of living in the woods, unable to bear either cold or hunger, knew neither how to build a cabin, take a deer, nor kill an enemy, spoke our language imperfectly, were therefore neither fit for hunters, warriors, nor counselors; they were totally good for nothing. (p. 99, Vol. X)

EXPERIMENTAL ACTIVITIES

Individual Activity

Many students in cross-cultural counseling classes have attempted to contact Native American groups for information interviews but have been unsuccessful. They are not told "No" but no one returns their calls. Students often become angry and sad over this lack of response to their overtures. How would you explain the dynamics of this situation?

Group Activity

Discuss the concept of tribal behavior. Are there tribal counterparts to be found in mainstream American society? What are the strengths of a tribal system? The weaknesses? As a counselor, what difficulties might you experience when counseling on a reservation?

Outside Activity

Read *Bury My Heart At Wounded Knee*. Keep a journal of your thoughts and feelings as you read each segment. Toward the end of the course, bring your reactions to the class for discussion.

REFERENCES

Seaver, J.E. (1925). *A narrative of the life of Mary Jemison: The white woman of the Genesee* (22nd ed.). New York: The American Science and Historic Preservation Society.

Smyth, A.H. (1970). *The writings of Benjamin Franklin: Volume X, 1789-1790*. New York: Haskell House Publishers.

Chapter **9**

SINGLE PARENTS

Susan B. DeVaney, Ed.D..

Susan DeVaney is an assistant professor in the Department of Educational Leadership at Western Kentucky University. She teaches a variety of counseling courses, including Social and Cultural Diversity in Counseling and Techniques of counseling. She and her former husband share parenting responsibilities for their two sons, who are now in their early twenties.

AWARENESS INDEX

Directions: Mark each answer true or false. Compare your answers with the scoring guide at the end of the test.

T F 1. Fifty percent of all babies born out of wedlock are put up for adoption.

T F 2. Many school personnel assume single-parent children will have difficulties in the classroom.

T F 3. Both widowed and divorced persons suffer a period of mourning for the loss of a spouse.

T F 4. Public policy has traditionally supported the dual-parent family.

T F 5. For black children today, living with one parent is more common than living with two.

T F 6. Twenty-five percent of all children from divorced families now live under joint custody arrangements.

T F 7. When counseling single parents it is best to consider only the custodial parent and the children.

T F 8. Children living in single parent households often take on the role of a substitute spouse.

T F 9. Property distribution, followed by issues of fidelity, are the greatest factors contributint to hostility among divorcing parents.

T F 10. Equitable property distribution by the courts has virtually eliminated financial difficulties experienced by single parent females.

Scoring Guide for Awareness Index

1. F   2. T   3. T   4. T   5. T   6. F   7. F   8. T   9. F
10. F

SITUATIONAL EXAMPLES

Situation 1

Myra is a 32 year old woman with two children: Annetta (18) and Samuel (14). Myra and her children live with Myra's brother (35), mother (50), grandmother (65), and Annetta's 18 month old baby. Myra has never married but occasionally sees Samuel's father on a social basis. She does not know the whereabouts of Annetta's father. Myra's mother has been divorced for 12 years. Her grandmother is a recent widow. Annetta and the baby's father, James (22), have continued their relationship.

Situation 2

Tyrone (42) and Sandra (38) were married 16 years when Sandra asked for a separation. Tyrone, a moderately successful businessman, kept the house and primary custody of the children: Horatio (7) and Alex (12). Their separation agreement calls for Tyrone to buy a condominium for Sandra and to pay for her college tuition. Saundra carries a full course load and works part-time at an insurance agency. She has difficultly paying her basic expenses. Recently Tyron's 19-year-old girlfriend, Virginia, moved into the house. Saundra is unhappy with the settlement, the custody arrangement, and Virginia's presence and influence on the boys. Tyrone resents Saundra's increasingly hostile comments and desire to argue in front of the children.

SINGLE PARENTS, THE POPULATION

According to the 1990 U.S. Census, 25% of all households with children under the age of 18 are headed by single parents. Nearly 7 million households with children were headed by single women and 1.6 million by single men. Asian Americans with children reported 156,000 single heads of households, 73% of which were female. Four-fifths of the 5.1 million single White households with children were headed by women. Among African Americans the figures rose to nearly 90% of 2.6 million families. For black children today, living with one parent is actually more common than living with two (Anthony, Weidemann, & Chin, 1990).

Women are most likely to become single parents through divorce, but may also become parents outside of marriage, through spousal abandonment or absence, separation, or widowhood (Anthony, Weidemann, & Chin, 1990). For men the most prevalent paths to single parenthood are divorce, spousal absence, never having been married, and widowhood. While marital separation leading to eventual divorce is clearly the greatest contributing factor to single parenthood, the number of births among teens continues to increase and more unmarried adult women are choosing to bear children outside of marriage

(Pakizegi, 1990). Of the 4.1 million children born in 1990, 1.1. million had unmarried mothers. Of these 67% were African American, 20% hispanic, and 20% caucasian ("Unmarried moms," 1993).

Single parent families compare unfavorably with two-parent families both socially and economically (Norton & Glick, 1986). Family incomes in single parent situations are less than one-half that of other families. Government figures in 1985 revealed that 34.6% of households headed by a single women fell below the poverty line (Rich, 1987). This figure is a function of the facts that women in general earn only 74 cents for every dollar earned by men in comparable positions, that women's financial positions drop precipitously upon separation and divorce while men's rise, and that large numbers of women entitled to child support never receive it (Wallerstein & Blakeslee, 1989, U.S. Census Bureau, 1992). Perhaps because the economic and social handicaps are so great, children from single parent homes are at increased risk of poor school performance and psychiatric disorder (Blum, Boyle, & Offord, 1988).

CURRENT PROBLEMS

In discussing problems associated with single parent families, one should remember that each family member is an individual with an array of strengths, failures, beliefs, and characteristic behaviors. Not all difficulties discussed here will be problems for every family or every individual. In considering a family system, however, the presumption exists that what affects one person will affect the others. Whatever particular manifestations of these general problems are present within a family will to some extent affect total family functioning.

The Stigma of Singlehood

In today's America to be a single parent is to contend with a variety of negative stereotypes and prejudices. Television idealizes the two-parent family (think "Huxtable"). Single women are portrayed as sirens with expensive wardrobes, impeccable make-up, and perfect bodies. Single men are presented as devilish rakes, rarely encumbered with children. Widows are portrayed as pathetic and naïve or hard-nosed business women. Even our language reflects the prejudice against singles. Unmarried women are "old maids" or "spinsters." Children of divorced parents are said to come from "broken homes". Single mothers who have not married are "unwed" or "welfare mothers".

Clearly, marriage is considered to be the ideal. Being single, whether by choice or circumstance, carries with it connotations of deviance. Singles are encouraged to "find a nice man (woman) and settle down"—even if they do not wish to. Married persons often shun their newly single friends. Divorced persons are often considered, both by themselves and others, as failures at their life's work. Widows and divorcees are thought to be threats to the sanctity of their former friends' marriages. Gay and lesbians parents are widely regarded as threats to society and to the children they rear. Whether the reaction is pity, fear, or disapproval, single parent families are, in our social milieu, aberrations of the "ideal" nuclear family.

Overcoming Loss

Persons recently separated, divorced, or widowed suffer acute difficulties in coming to terms with the loss of a spouse. A period of mourning typically occurs wherein the person experiences a mixture of conflicting emotions: regret, guilt, depression, sadness, relief, excitement, loneliness, optimism, and confusion (Wallerstein & Blakeslee, 1989). The severity and duration of this emotional upheaval depend in part on the factors surrounding the loss. The length of a deceased spouse's illness and the quality of the marital relationship among widows, the presence of infidelity, the amount of social disapproval experienced, the children's current reaction to the situation, the degree of mutuality in deciding to divorce, and the presence or absence of a satisfactory social life all influence an individual's ability to say goodbye to what once held great promise.

Wallerstein and Blakeslee also describe the tasks of divorce as ending the marriage, mourning the loss, finding one's personal identity, resolving passions, and rebuilding one's life. Lingering attachment to former spouses, however, often inhibits this adjustment. Intense emotional connections, typically anger, may be present 10 years after the formal break (Pett, 1982) The same may be said for the widowed. In general, the longer an individual has been married, the greater the distress experienced in parting. Loss of appetite, concentration, and energy; excessive smoking and drinking; promiscuity; and general self neglect are common during the first year of loss. Headaches, chest and stomach pains, and other somatic complaints also are typically present (Kitson & Raschke, 1981).

Loss or absence of a partner also opens questions of whether, when, and how to resume dating or other social interaction. Years of physical intimacy with one person, growing older and adding a few extra pounds, fear of sexually transmitted diseases, concern for the children's disapproval, and personal moral standards may prevent a newly single parent from forming new, healthy cross-gender relationships. Fear of managing without a partner may bring a newly single person quickly into another marriage. For others, issues of trust prohibit forming more than superficial or sexual relationships. In addition, public policy often makes single parent status more profitable than employment or marriage, thus encouraging couples to remain single and live apart.

Restructuring the Household

With the establishment of a new single-parent family, parents, children, relatives, and friends take on new roles - some welcome, others difficult. Newly single fathers may be ill-prepared for child rearing tasks and household chores formerly left to their spouses. Women may be inexperienced at managing auto maintenance, family finances, and other traditionally male occupations. Both males and females, accustomed to sharing duties and obligations with an adult partner, may chafe under the burden of attending to family needs alone. In addition, reduced income often forces strict cutbacks in leisure activities, meals out, housing, and other amenities formerly taken for granted. Moreover, with many single mothers entering the workplace, child care may become a problem for the first time.

Children, too, may be counted on to assume a larger place in household functioning. In addition to cleaning and cooking, older children may babysit for their younger siblings. Many children, even those under the age of 10, often are responsible for their own care, staying unattended for long periods of time. With the family in upheaval following divorce or death of a parent, it is not uncommon for a child to take on a parental role, becoming a substitute spouse. Lonely and confused, the parent may come to rely on the child as a helper and confidant. In extreme cases of prolonged role reversal the child may miss out on important aspects of childhood and teenaged years. Seeing that the child has missed a "normal" life by taking care of a needy parent, the parent is often faced with feelings of guilt and depression. In other situations where the child does not assume extra duties, the harried parent feels anger toward the child -and guilt at feeling the anger (Morawetz & Walker, 1984).

In the case of divorce, custody arrangements often exacerbate hostility among parents and children. With the advent of equitable distribution and communal property laws, child custody has replaced property distribution as the primary source of divorce hostilities. More fathers now have sole custody, joint custody, or extensive visitation privileges than at any other time during this century. After two years, two-thirds of non-custodial fathers see their children at least every other week (Hodges, Buchsbaum, & Tierney, 1983). These circumstances set up opportunities for missed or late appointments, scheduling conflicts, and differing parental expectations. "But Mom lets me do it at her house" becomes a battle cry arousing a wealth of conflicting emotions in a parent who may believe his or her authority is threatened. In anger, parents may subtly encourage children to ally with them and misbehave with the other parent.

Hostility, bitterness, and anger often arise from the loss of financial status experienced by many single parents. When desired support is not forthcoming, the mother may retaliate, denying child access to the father and leaving him angry and resentful. Expensive legal costs, which have traditionally been born by the individual, have prevented many women from seeking greater financial support. "Extras" such as braces, camps, and college tuition may become subjects for argument between ex-spouses.

Thus, despite the fact that all family members do not live together, the absent parent has an abiding effect on family decisions and behavior. Many persons who are not married consult each other on matters of finance, child-rearing, and social life. For ex-spouses to date, provide assistance in home maintenance, or otherwise maintain close contact for a number of years is not unusual. These adaptations of former living patterns, even if amicably implemented, may serve as sources of confusion, anger, bitterness, and hostility. Adjustment may be further complicated by the presence of relatives or new opposite-sex companions who presume to take a role in decision-making. The emotional tenor of this "extended" family is what most affects the psychosocial adjustment of children. Hostility among parties perpetuates emotional distress and confusion while close cooperation is more likely to convince children that their emotional bonds are not severed entirely. In the long run, discord is more damaging to the child than divorce (McLanaham, 1985; Wallerstein & Blakeslee, 1989).

Parenting

Parenting is a difficult business for which most persons are poorly prepared. Few individuals have received formal training in child development, learning strategies, and methods of consistent discipline. The single parent, however, may be at an added disadvantage in successful child rearing for a variety of reasons. First, successful parenting takes time and money, often short commodities in single-parent homes. Second, the single parent may be in emotional turmoil, suffering the effects of an unplanned pregnancy, marital separation, or death of a spouse—events that often require a two or three year adjustment period. Moreover, any stressors present in the family also will affect the children. Both parent and child will respond in characteristic ways to those stressors; acting out, withdrawal, temper tantrums, or nurturing family members. Single parents may express tremendous concern for their children's welfare and development and at the same time have little time or energy to spend on it. Having few resources themselves, they may hand these responsibilities to school personnel and become irate when they observe learning or behavior problems manifesting at school. School personnel, themselves overwhelmed with responsibilities, may hold perceptions of single parents as uninvolved in their children's education. Although generalizations are dangerous, it is important to remember that single parents are more likely to fall below the poverty line and thus not have ready access to a telephone or means of transportation through which to contact the school. In addition, these persons may themselves have been unsuccessful in school, have low expectations for the success of their own children, and thus be unlikely to initiate contact with learning professionals.

Career Needs

Becoming a single parent necessitates reevaluating one's current employment situation. Displaced homemakers may be in need of job training or schooling in order to be employable at a reasonable wage. Young mothers and fathers may not hold high school diplomas nor possess the desire or skill to find a job. Women and minorities in general have low career aspirations; those holding jobs are concentrated in a restricted, low-paying range of occupations. Supporting a family on a minimum wage job or what was once a second income may not be possible.

Every employed single parent has special need of negotiation skills in order to obtain time off for care of sick children, teacher's conferences, and errands that can only be accomplished during the day. Finding child care during irregular work hours or periods of travel is a difficult matter in the best of circumstances. In addition, opportunities for relocation often meet with angry resistance from family members or former spouses.

Public Policy and Special Services

Until the 1970s services for single parents were virtually non-existent. The sole exception was Parents Without Partners, a private organization providing workshops, discussion groups, and social activities for both parents and children. Recognizing the need, women's organizations, themselves newly established, sponsored support groups for women reentering the workforce and lobbied for child care legislation. Community organizations and churches followed suit creating day care facilities and classes for single adults. Under pressure from these groups, local governments funded crisis intervention centers, hot lines, referral services, and spouse abuse programs through mental health agencies. Interest in changes in American family structure has resulted in the adoption and growth of the American Association of Marriage and Family Therapy (AAMFT) as a specialty area among counselors. Requiring special training for certification, AAMFT tracks are being developed by counselor education departments throughout the country. More recently the International Association of Marriage and Family Counselors has formed as a specialty division of the American Counseling Association.

Public policy has historically endorsed the two-parent family primarily through tax laws and social legislation. For years property was divided between divorced spouses on the basis of income (So much for the value of the homemaker). Enforcement of child support decrees is still notably lax. Alimony has been virtually abandoned by the courts in favor of equitable distribution of property.

Poor single women have felt the brunt of legislation affecting Aid for Dependent Children (AFDC) and the availability of job training and day care. Legal aid for divorce and separation proceedings was denied in the Reagan Family Protection Act. The Job Training Partnership Act eliminated funds for child care and transportation, effectively excluding poor single parents from those programs. Cuts in public housing and supplemental feeding programs and the elimination of CETA and WIN further restricted opportunities for single parents to break the poverty-unemployment-welfare cycle.

In the late 1980s the Bush administration continued to cut social and education programs. The recession of the early 1990s swelled the unemployment roles and necessitated extension of unemployment benefits. The presidential election of 1992 focused largely on public policy issues with Bill Clinton's platform of job creation, national health care, and child advocacy deemed responsible for his election. On the state and local levels, greater efforts have been made to enforce child support decrees and to protect women and children caught in situations of violence and neglect.

THE HELPING PROFESSIONAL'S ROLE

In today's society a helping professional may not encounter members of some special populations discussed in this book (Asian refugees, Amish, or even hispanics), but each and every one will have many dealings with single parents. Single parenthood is a fact of life; no counselor, social worker, friend, or parent can escape the impact of the changing structure of the American family. Of particular importance, then, is a thorough understanding of issues, problems, and circumstances common to single parents as well as adequate preparation for working with this group. In the interest of space the following recommendations for helping professions will be listed rather than discussed in detail. For a fuller discussion, consult the references at the end of the chapter.

1. The counselor should examine personal prejudices and stereotypes concerning marriage, divorce, and single life-styles that may stand in the way of personal growth and adjustment for the client. While most counselors are careful not to condemn, other attitudes such as pity or acceptance of an untenable situation can create barriers to client problem solving.

The mental pictures you formed when you read the Case of Myra at the beginning of the chapter can provide a clue to your personal biases concerning marriage, divorce, and family life. The students to whom I give this case often image the family to be poor, black or hispanic, and poorly educated. In reality, this case describes a white, middle class family with which I worked in counseling.

2. Even if single parenthood is not the presenting problem, the myriad of conflicting feelings, life changes, and responsibilities faced by an unmarried person will influence the goals and mode of treatment. The effective counselor will be attune to these concerns and integrate them into the total therapeutic picture.

3. Referrals to vocational rehabilitation, Social Services, child care centers, community organizations, and support groups are part and parcel of work with single parents. Encouraging stable community and social ties, the counselor serves as a liaison between clients and organizations providing help with parenting, social life, finances, education, and job training. Maintaining a list of written materials appropriate for the single parent is a helpful adjunct to agency and organizational referral.

4. Being a single parent does not necessarily mean that parents have no significant partners in the parenting process. The counselor considers who is involved in the family—ex-spouses, friends, relatives, or lovers whose attitudes influence child rearing practices and family life-styles.

5. Many single parents believe something is wrong with them because they are not married. The counselor can help liberate parents from excessive self criticism and develop client confidence in self.

6. The single parent may be ambivalent about accepting advice from yet another helping professional. Having sensed disapproval in past interactions with pastors, teachers, agency personnel, or employers, the parent may need the counselor's help in overcoming the fear of being blamed for what are perceived as "past mistakes".

7. Counselors should remember that behavior which may appear pathological (depression, promiscuity, fits of temper) may be normal reactions to a particular stage of separation or loss. One role of the counselor is helping the client work through maladaptive behavior patterns in favor of more successful ones.

8. Many clients will attempt to use the counselor as an ally against the absent partner. The thoughtful counselor will avoid this trap by remaining emphatic but objective and refusing to take sides.

9. The counselor may serve as a mediator between ex-spouses or between client and family members. The myth that divorced persons cannot cooperate is detrimental to the adjustment of both parents and children and can be expunged with appropriate help.

10. Initial crises such as a separation, out-of-wedlock birth, or family death may change the family organization. Thorough assessment of the family system as it exists currently and as it existed prior to trauma is essential to anticipating and managing conflicts.

11. Family members may actively or subtly oppose therapy or job placement. Happy for their newfound influence, relatives and companions may enjoy the single parent's dependence on them and resist the client's attempts to develop self sufficiency.

12. Many single parents blame others for their difficulties. A primary task of the counselor is to help the client develop responsibility, self confidence, and an identity apart from a spouse.

13. The experienced counselor recognizes that in crisis situations a parent may be incapable of attending to parenting responsibilities. The counselor encourages examination of client attitudes toward children and parenthood, reduced access to the children, and parental expectations.

14. A single parent may benefit from help in recognizing disfunctional strategies used to maintain emotional balance in the family. Excessive focus on the child's needs, adoption of a child as a substitute parent, or refusal to set appropriate limits may inhibit healthy family functioning.

15. The counselor can teach a parent to establish a healthy relationship with the child by allowing the child some control over his or her life. The parent learns to afford the child privacy, respect, a listening ear, and opportunities to work through feelings.

16. Many single parents deal with a child's misbehavior by either punishing or ignoring it. The counselor can train the parent to use more appropriate response parenting strategies.

Some of these strategies include:

a. beginning calmly and using affectionate language,

b. describing appropriate behavior,

c. describing inappropriate behavior,

d. demonstrating new behavior,

e. giving a rationale for new behavior,

f. asking for acknowledgement,

g. actively involving the child in practice,

h. giving feedback on the practice, and

i. encouraging the child through praise and reward.

17. Single parents may have low self esteem, few career aspirations, or little sense of what is required to find and maintain a satisfactory job. Thorough assessment of the client's family and life stressors and a grasp of occupational information is essential to successful career counseling. The counselor should be familiar with the services of the National Occupational Information Coordinating Committee (NOICC) and its state branches (SOICC) which coordinate the development of occupational information systems, publish career information, and provide training to counselors (Isaacson & Brown, 1993).

18. The wise counselor will anticipate scheduling and payment problems and maintain flexibility in order to avoid premature termination. In short, nothing is inherently undesirable about being a single parent. However, the role brings with it vicissitudes above and beyond those of two-parent families. Counselor sensitivity to the myriad of conflicting pressures and attitudes facing a single parent provides a base on which to build client independence, confidence, and positive self-image. The role of the counselor, then, is to liberate the single parent from any negative beliefs or stereotypes that hinder full adjustment and to open the door to new and happier possibilities for living.

EXPERIENTIAL ACTIVITIES

Individual Activity

Use the situations at the beginning of the chapter. Choose a character and define him or her using the following criteria.

What is it like to be _____ ?

If you were put in _____'s position, what thoughts and feelings might you experience regarding the following matters? Consider these matters for yourself or for significant others in your family.

1. Marriage

2. Separation and divorce

3. Dating and live-in arrangements

4. Parenting

5. Family finances

6. Your role in the family

7. The family's importance in your life

8. The role of government/public policy

9. Your personal goals and expectations

10. What the family expects of you.

Group Activity

Have each person in the group choose a character from one of the situations and perform the Individual Activity detailed above. Each person speaks to the group, explaining the character's perspective on the family situation. Finally, the characters discuss their points of view with their respective family members using "I" statements.

"I'm real lucky to have found Melinda; she's great about keeping things in order. I'm gone on business so much of the time."

Outside Class Activity

Attend a meeting of Parents without Partners or other support group for single parents. Note which of the issues (or any other issues) discussed in this chapter take precedence in the meeting. If no such group is available, interview a single parent using five or six open-ended questions pertaining to the issues discussed in the chapter.

REFERENCES

Anthony, K.H., Weidemann, S. & Chin, Y. (1990). Housing perceptions of low-income single parents. *Environment and Behavior, 22,* 147-182.

Blum, H.M., Boyle, M.H., & Offord, D.R. (1988). Single-parent families: Child psychiatric disorder and school performance. *Journal of the American Academy of Child and Adolescent Psychiatry, 27,* 214-219.

Hodges, W.F., Bachsbaum, H.K., & Tierney, C.W. (1983). Parent-child relationships and adjustment in preschool children in divorced and intact families. *Journal of Divorce, 7,* 43-58.

Isaacson, L.E., & Brown, D. (1993). *Career information, career counseling, & career development* (5th Ed.). Boston: Allyn & Bacon.

Kitson, G.C., & Raschke, H.J. (1981). Divorce research: What we know: What we need to know. *Journal of Divorce, 4,* 1-37.

McLanahan, S.S. (1985). Single mothers and psychological well-being: A test of the stress and vulnerability hypotheses. *Research in Community and Mental Health, 5,* 253-266.

Morawetz, A., & Walker, G. (1984). *Brief therapy with single-parent families.* New York: Brunner/Mazel.

Norton, A.J., & Glick, P.C. (1986). One parent families: A social and economic profile. *Family Relations Journal of Applied Family and Child Studies, 35,* 9-17.

Pakizegi, B. (1990). Emerging family forms: Single mothers by choice: Demographic and social variables. *Maternal-Child-Nursing Journal, 19(1),* 1-19.

Pett, M.G. (1982). Correlates of children's social adjustment following divorce. *Journal of Divorce, 5,* 25-39.

Rich, S. (1987, July 31). Proportion of poverty-level families drops. *Greensboro News and Record,* p. 2A.

Unmarried moms (1993, February 26). *USA Today,* p. 1.

U.S. Census Bureau. (1992). Census of Population and Housing. Summary Tape File 1C United States (C.D. Rom version), Race of Householder by Household Type.

Wallerstein, J.S., & Blakeslee, S. (1989). *Second chances: Men, women, and children a decade after divorce.* New York: Ticknor and Fields.

Chapter 10

COUNSELING AFRICAN AMERICANS

Roderick J. McDavis, Ph.D., Woodrow M. Parker, Ph.D., and W.J. Parker, M.S.

*A native of Dayton, Ohio, **Roderick J. McDavis** received a B.S. in Social Sciences in Secondary Education from Ohio University in 1970, a M.S. degree in Student Personnel Administration from the University of Dayton in 1971, and a Ph.D. degree in Counselor Education from the University of Toledo in 1974. He is currently Dean of the College of Education and Professor of Counselor Education at the University of Arkansas, Fayetteville. Dr. McDavis also serves as the Director of the Arkansas Academy for Leadership Training and School-Based Management.*

Dr. McDavis served as Associate Dean of the Graduate School and Minority Programs from 1984-89 and Professor of Education in the Department of Counselor Education from 1974-89 at the University of Florida. He also was a co-host of The Black Family, a program aired on public television in Jacksonville, Florida, from 1977-89. Dr. McDavis served as the first President of the Florida Association for Multicultural

Counseling and Development and as a member of the Editorial Board of the Journal of Multicultural Counseling and Development.

His primary interests and publications focus on restructuring teacher education programs, improving public education, counseling ethnic minorities, recruiting and retaining minority students and faculty, and evaluating student personnel programs. He has authored or co-authored 4 chapters in books, 23 articles in refereed journals, and 14 articles in other publications.

*A native of Atmore, Alabama, **Woodrow M. Parker** received his B.S. degree from Stillman College in 1963, his M.S. degree from the University of South Florida in 1971, and his Ph.D. degree in Counselor Education from the University of Florida in 1975. He served as University Counseling Psychologist in the University Counseling Centers at both the University of South Florida and the University of Florida from 1971 through 1977. Currently he holds the rank of Professor in the Department of Counselor Education at the University of Florida, and is an affiliate member of the staff in the Psychological and Vocational Counseling Center. He is a licensed mental health counselor.*

Dr. Parker has served as the President of the Florida Association for Multicultural Counseling and Development, has served on a task force for developing competencies for preparing culturally skilled counselors, teaches a course in multicultural counseling, and has recently been cited as one of the most prolific contributors to the Journal of Multicultural Counseling and Development. His books include Consciousness Raising: A Primer for Multicultural Counseling (1988) and Multicultural Relations on Campus: A Personal Growth Approach (1992).

Willie James Parker, M.S., is an Associate *Professor of Education in the Department of Health, Physical Education and Recreation and serves as Facility Director of the Joe L. Reed Academy at Alabama State University. In these capacities he teaches courses, conducts research and counsels students at this predominantly Black institution. Before entering the field of higher education, Mr. Parker spent 26 years in the coaching profession. He was head coach at two Division 1 universities, and served as an assistant coach at the University of Cincinnati and the University of Florida. He has been named three times to the Board of Directors of the Community Action Agency in Montgomery, AL, and was the first Executive Director of the National Black Coaches Association. The father of three children, he lives in Montgomery, with his wife.*

AFRICAN AMERICAN COMPONENT OF THE ETHNIC MINORITY CULTURAL AWARENESS TEST (EMCAT)

INSTRUCTIONS: The following test is designed to measure your level of cultural knowledge about African Americans. Please read each question carefully and choose the answer that, in your opinion, is correct, and mark the corresponding letter.

1. The number of African Americans is
   a. 10-20 million.
   b. 20-30 million.
   c. 30-40 million.
   d. 40-50 million.

2. Thurgood Marshall was the first African American to be
   a. Governor.
   b. Mayor.
   c. Supreme Court Justice.
   d. Astronaut.

3. Who was the African American woman who sparked the Civil Rights Movement in 1955 by refusing to give up her seat on a city bus to a White man?

a. Angela Davis
b. Fannie Lou Hammer
c. Maya Angelou
d. Rosa Parks

4. In 1896, *Plessy vs. Ferguson* upheld the 1883 Supreme Court educational decision of

a. integration in schools.
b. segregation in schools.
c. Separate but equal schools.
d. increased funding for African American schools.

5. Most people convicted of welfare cheating are

a. African Americans.
b. White Americans.
c. Hispanic Americans.
d. Asian Americans.

6. A person who is "African American" is one who

a. was born in Africa, but lives in America.
b. was born in America, but lives in Africa.
c. has a cultural heritage in Africa, but lives in America.
d. is a Black American.

7. In 1863, President Lincoln issued the Emancipation Proclamation. This Proclamation declared

a. slaves were 3/5 of a person.
b. Missouri was a slave state and Maine a free state.
c. women could legally vote.
d. all slaves under the Confederacy were free people.

8. Which constitutional amendment abolished slavery?

a. 21st
b. 13th
c. 1st
d. 5th

9. In the primaries of 1984 and 1988, which African American civil rights leader successfully campaigned to receive millions of votes in the bid for the presidency of the United States?

   a. Jesse Jackson
   b. Barbara Jordon
   c. Mike Dukakis
   d. Paul Jackson

10. The first African American scientist who gained national prominence, aiding the economy of the South through developing multiple uses for crops such as the peanut was

   a. Louis Pasteur.
   b. J. Oppenheimer.
   c. George Washington Carver.
   d. Clarence Darrow.

(Adapted from Parker, in press)

Scoring Guide for Awareness Test

1. B 2. C 3. D 4. C 5. B 6. C 7. D 8. B 9. A 10. C

CASE EXAMPLE

When Derick was very young, his parents told him that he was a good person, intelligent, and capable of achieving anything if he was willing to work hard. Derick believed his parents and, when he started school, was eager to learn as much as he could about science since he wanted to become a medical doctor. During his elementary school days Derick did very well in his studies, but his scores were low on standardized aptitude tests. His White classmates made jokes about how dumb Derick was and started telling him that their parents said that African American people could never do as well on these tests as Whites. Derick did not believe his classmates but he was disturbed by their comments. When he discussed his concern with his teachers and counselors, they avoided telling him some of the negative effects that standardized tests have for many African American students.

One day when Derick was walking home from elementary school, a car passed him and he heard someone yell, "Hey nigger, you and your kind should go back to Africa!" When he got home, Derick asked his parents what the person in the car meant. They told Derick that some White people are prejudiced and say unkind things to show their dislike for people of other races. Derick's parents also said that he should not worry too much about being called bad names by White people. Since this was Derick's first encounter with being called a nigger, he did not know whether he should ignore it, get mad about it, or worry about it at all.

Derick completed elementary school with a B average in his studies, but he continued to score poorly on standardized aptitude and achievement tests in high school. He began to think about what his classmates in elementary school had said to him. Perhaps they were right — African American people could not score as well as White people on standardized tests. His counselor suggested to him that he might consider a career in some area other than medicine because his scores were so low, but Derick continued to make Bs in most of his courses and did particularly well in science classes.

During his junior year, Derick decided to try out for the school baseball team. He had played Little League baseball, been on the All-star team, and played summer league baseball for three years. On the first day of tryouts, Derick noticed he was the only African American competing for a position on the team. The manager asked the candidates to catch fly balls and grounders and to practice throwing. Derick was the only one who caught every ball hit to him, and he made accurate throws to the proper people. The next day, however, Derick was cut from the team. That summer, Derick played baseball on the same summer league team as a White student who had played and started on the high school team. Derick started in every game for this team while his fellow classmate sat on the bench. His experience in the summer league confirmed his suspicion that he was cut from high school team because he was African American.

Upon graduation Derick went to college. His parents told him that if he continued to work hard, he would achieve his dream of becoming a doctor. Majoring in pre-med, he maintained a B+ average in his courses. In most of his classes after his sophomore year, Derick was the only African American student. This situation did not concern him until he enrolled in an advanced zoology course during his junior year. He noticed that although his hand was raised the White professor never called on him to answer questions in class. Several times he attempted to make an appointment to talk about this avoidance, but the professor was always too busy. At the end of the term, he received a C grade in the course despite having received Bs on his tests and projects. Again, Derick tried to arrange a meeting with the professor, but he was never available. He thought about appealing the grade but was afraid he would create more problems for himself. Through this experience Derick became more aware that some people will harm, ignore, and/or avoid helping when a person's skin is black. He began to realize that he would probably be discriminated against at various times throughout his life.

Derick received a low score on the standardized test required for entrance to medical school but was admitted anyway because of his good grades. He worked hard, finishing in the top third of his class. Ironically, some of his White classmates told him that the only reason he was admitted to medical school was because he was African American. Derick had encountered many trials and tribulations in his quest to become a physician, and yet he knew to some people he would always be "just a nigger." As Derick began to plan the rest of his life, he wondered if he would ever live long enough to see the day when he and other African American people would be fully accepted by White Americans.

THE AFRICAN AMERICAN POPULATION

In 1991, the nearly 30 million African American people living in the United States comprised the largest ethnic minority group in America and 12% of the total population (U.S. Department of Commerce, 1992). Forty-eight percent of African American households were husband-wife families while 46% were headed by a single female.

With regard to education, 66.7% of the African American adults 25 years of age and over were high school graduates, and 11.5% had completed four or more years of college. Among Whites 79.9% completed high school and 22.2% had four years of college. Of the 13.5 million African American people eligible to work, 7.8% were unemployed in 1991. The median income of African American families was $21,423 with 25.6% of African American families earning less than $10,000 annually, 11.3% earning between $10,000 and $14,999, 19.5% earning between $15,000 and $25,000 and 43.5% earning over $25,000.

HISTORICAL BACKGROUND

African American people were first brought to the United States in 1619 when a Dutch ship landed at Jamestown, Virginia, with 20 slaves of African descent (Sloan, 1971). During the first 244 years of their presence in America, African people were used exclusively as slaves in most parts of the country, especially the South. Most slaves lived on plantations and worked in the fields or houses of Whites without receiving wages. On January 1, 1863, President Lincoln signed the Emancipation Proclamation which freed all African American people from the bondage of slavery. The thirteenth amendment abolished slavery, the fourteenth amendment gave African American people citizenship, and the fifteenth amendment gave men the right to vote.

Since the 1860s the history of African Americans in the United States has been affected significantly by court decisions and congressional legislation. In *Plessy versus Ferguson* in 1896 the Supreme Court upheld the doctrine of *separate but equal* educational facilities for African Americans, a decision which resulted in over 50 years of segregated education in the South and contributed to the migration of many African Americans to the North in the early 1900s.

Another outcome of *Plessy vs. Ferguson* was the development of predominantly African American colleges and universities. During this period African Americans were influenced by two significant figures in African American history, Booker T. Washington and W.E.B. DuBois. Washington's contention was that African Americans could be more progressive if they learned skills or trades in agricultural and mechanical fields while continuing to live and work in rural areas of the South. DuBois, on the other hand, believed that African Americans should pursue education in professional fields and become leaders of their race. Both men inspired African Americans to acquire more education in a wide variety of occupations during the period between 1900-1950.

Segregated school systems lasted until 1954 when the Supreme Court declared racial segregation in public schools to be unconstitutional in *Brown versus Board of Education*. For the first time in 335 years, African American students were permitted to attend the same schools as Whites. This integration led to a larger number of African Americans being educated in such professional fields as law, medicine, business, and engineering. The Civil Rights Act of 1964 provided African Americans with basic human rights that had been previously denied. African Americans were able to eat in any public restaurant and stay in any public motel. In 1965, through the Voting Rights Act, Congress removed barriers in the South that had effectively denied African Americans the right to vote. With the Bakke decision of 1978, the Supreme Court ruled that race could be used as a factor in admitting students to colleges and universities. Institutions were permitted to use affirmative action measures to increase the number of African American students admitted to undergraduate and graduate programs.

Court decisions and congressional acts have had both positive and negative effects on African Americans. The plight of

African Americans in 1993 is far better than it was in 1619. Increasingly more citizens perceive themselves as equal under the law. Still, many find themselves in a society that does not fully accept them. Some majority group members have not accepted Supreme Court decisions and congressional acts and view African Americans as inferior. The real tragedy is that many African Americans have internalized this racial inferiority, thus limiting their potential and resulting in mistrust and dislike of themselves and of many majority group members.

CHARACTERISTICS OF AFRICAN AMERICANS

In order to provide effective counseling for African American clients, counselors need to know what characteristics, behavior patterns, and values distinguish African American people as a group. Such group characterization, however, reinforces and perpetuates stereotyping, a limiting and destructive force in the struggle for human understanding. In addition, African Americans are almost impossible to describe owing to the broad spectrum of racial and cultural variations within the group culture as well as within the African American race. Even among slaves, diverse subgroups existed. Blassingame (1972) identified three kinds of slaves during the years of slavery in the United States: Nats—the militant fighters (Harriet Tubman, Nat Turner, and Frederick Douglas); Jacks—slaves who accepted life as it was, did not work, but ran away if the opportunity existed; and Sambos—shuffling, grinning, happy slaves who used their image as a mask to help other slaves escape.

Cross Model of Nigrescence

Cross (1991) made a monumental contribution toward understanding African Americans through the development of the Nigrescence Model. This model describes attitudes and behaviors African Americans may demonstrate and responses to persons from the White majority. These stages or phases of nigrescence are important because they help the counselor to

1. understand within group differences,

2. understand how African Americans view themselves,

3. understand how African Americans view other ethnic minority groups,

4. understand how African Americans feel about the White majority populations.

5. predict counselor preferences for African American clients

6. diagnose problems and

7. select appropriate counselor interventions.

The following five stages are a brief summary of the characteristics of the Cross model.

Stage 1: Pre-encounter. In this stage the African American denies that racism exists and believes that his/her life conditions have nothing to do with race. In general, this individual is more eurocentric than afrocentric. Being anti-African American, this person internalizes the intellectual inferiority of African Americans and intellectual superiority of White people.

Stage 2: Encounter. African Americans often experience racial encounters that cause them to become more aware of racial differences. Such encounters may be positive or negative but often leave individuals with feelings of anger, guilt, or shame. In this stage a very slight tendency toward afrocentricity exits.

Stage 3: Immersion-emersion. In this phase individuals become deeply involved in the African American world, developing a dichotomous world view where White is evil and African American is good. Often a deep love for African Americans develops and an uncontrolled rage toward White people exists. Individuals functioning in this stage of development are not shocked or surprised by any negative action of Whites toward African Americans.

Stage 4: Internalization. In Stage 4, African Americans achieve inner peace. The individuals are more realistic in their understanding of the racist system and less defensive about their blackness. They develop a solid defense against racism by developing their own ego strength. A strong self-concept as an African American is what gives the individual purpose in life. Finally, the individual is an advocate of harmony between African Americans and Whites.

Stage 5: Internalization-commitment. Cross's latest addition to the nigrescence model is a stage of internalization-commitment in which the individual moves from theory to practice in terms of commitment to societal change. One's concept of blackness here is much more realistic and mature than in some of the earlier stages.

While the case has been made that differences exist within African American people as a group, certain characteristics nevertheless distinguish African American people from White people. An exhaustive discussion of characteristics, values, and behaviors of African Americans is beyond the scope of this chapter. The authors, however, would like to provide enough information to help counselors gain a better understanding of people by detailing two primary distinguishing features of the African American population: the family and the church.

The African American Family

The African American family has been generally described in social science literature from a deficit perspective. While negative aspects of the African American family are indeed present, the present authors choose to focus on the positive qualities and values that have facilitated the survival of the 30 million African Americans living in America today. Some of the qualities include reliance on the extended family, filial piety, respect for elders, and socialization of children.

The extended African American family often consists of many members including the mother and father, children, grandparents, aunts and uncles, nieces, nephews, and cousins. There appears to be a willingness on the part of African American family members to accept all relatives regardless of their circumstances. For example, a common practice is for a mother and her children to live with relatives when life circumstance, death, divorce, or pregnancy warrant it. Generally, they are permitted to live in a given home until their situation improves.

Filial piety refers to African American children's devotion to their parents. In many families children are taught early to take care of their parents and to be genuinely devoted to them. African American children know that making a negative comment about another's parents, known as "playing the dozens", is an invitation to a serious confrontation. African American children, especially males, may become angry to the point of fighting anyone who questions the honor of their mothers.

Another aspect of filial piety is the devotion of the children to one another. Many well known African Americans have reported that they owe their success to an older brother or sister who helped them along the way. Usually, older siblings are responsible for the younger ones. A female graduate student told the authors that her sister came from another state to keep her children while she did an internship in another part of the state. The willingness of African American family members to help one another has been a major contributing factor to the survival of the community in America.

Elderly persons are a prized commodity in the African American family. Elderly African Americans play key roles in the family, church, and community. Younger family members who experience difficulty in their development are often referred to their grandparents for counsel. Many grandparents accept the responsibility for rearing their grandchildren while the parents of those children work or acquire education.

In addition, elderly African American family members play a significant role in passing on cultural values, customs, and traditions to the children. One of the authors, whose grandparents lived in his home, remembers the stories they told about the family history. The author's recollection of these stories helped him understand his family and himself as he grew to manhood. Partly because of the large measure of respect accorded them, the elderly in the African American community are placed in nursing homes only as a last resort.

While socialization of children is one of the most important functions in African American families, parents encounter challenges and difficulties in the process. A recent study (Coleman, 1987) showed that feelings of racial inferiority among young African Americans children were as strong in 1987 as they were 40 years previous when the original study was conducted. Coleman recommended that African American children be helped to develop self-esteem through the efforts of teachers and parents and by changing the ways that African Americans are portrayed in the media. The African American family in general, and African American parents in particular, have the responsibility of teaching their children that it is as honorable for a child to be African American as it is for a White child to be White. It is important that parents first be secure in and accepting of their own blackness in order to model self-esteem for their children.

Another socialization process for African American parents is teaching their children how to survive in the White society. African American children can be taught how to respond when they are the only African American persons in the presence of Whites, how to respond to name-calling, or what to do when they are stereotyped or labeled. Education is another value that African American parents often instill deeply in their children. Unfortunately, many African American children do not take advantage of the educational opportunities available to them. They are not taking the courses needed in math and science to prepare them for the technological world in which they will live and work. Acquiring an education is critical for African Americans because it is often the only vehicle through which they can achieve upward mobility.

The African American Church

Douthis (1985) described the African American church as "A rock in a weary land" and a "shelter in a time of storm." According to Douthis, the early African American church was not only concerned with the spiritual needs of its people, it also played a major role in their education, politics, economics, and social welfare. He reported that early African American church groups formed and supported schools and colleges, mutual aid societies, and banks. It served as a meeting place for spiritual leaders and community workers in the fight against slavery and again during the civil rights movement. Well known leaders such as Dr. Martin Luther King, Jr., Dr. Ralph David Abernathy, and Reverend Jesse Jackson used the church as a launching pad for social and political reform.

Today, the church remains the cornerstone of the African American community. Since the elimination of African American neighborhood schools, the church has assumed even greater responsibility for spiritual renewal, educational development, political awareness, and social and psychological support in the community. One church's slogan typifies the character of most African American churches: "Our church is the church where everybody is somebody." The membership of most African American churches represents people from various occupations and economic levels. A janitor, therefore, might as easily serve as a church officer as would a judge or medical doctor. Church may be the only place in society where some African Americans feel accepted and worthwhile. The church allows each member to participate in the worship service in some meaningful way, which might explain why some African American church services last nearly three hours.

Finally, an important point for counselors to note is that the church is viewed by many African American clients as their major support system. Simply going to church helps them feel rejuvenated, less depressed, and less anxious. Because many African Americans seek ministers for psychological help, the authors suggest that counselors build rapport and working relations with African American clients through ministers from selected churches in their communities.

PROBLEMS CONFRONTING AFRICAN AMERICANS

The Minority Label

Skin color, texture of hair, and facial features vary among African Americans and influence their lives politically, economically, socially, and psychologically. While some may argue that differences in people's skin color have not mattered since the 1960s, results from recent studies have shown that African American people with lighter complexions are preferred over those with darker skin (Gaines-Carter, 1985). If this is true, then skin color is still a variable by which African Americans are labeled in society.

Simply being labeled a minority group member is a problem that all African Americans face. While the word *minority* is not necessarily negative, the term causes many African American people to wonder if they are perceived as equals by majority group members. As African American children grow older, they soon realize that they are labeled as minorities by majority group members. Some students begin to believe that being a member of a minority group means being unable to achieve as successfully as majority group students. A second effect is a growing mistrust of majority group members. As African American children learn the history of their people, they may doubt that White people will ever understand, accept, and respect them. When persons are perceived to be untrustworthy, healthy interpersonal relations are difficult to establish.

Discrimination

Another problem that faces all African Americans is discrimination. In spite of all the legislation and court decisions that have provided legal rights to African Americans, they are still discriminated against in society and schools. In the area of housing, the vast majority of communities in urban centers are still segregated or minimally integrated. In other words, most African Americans live in one part of the city and most White people in another. Many Whites do not want African Americans living in their neighborhoods and when they do move into these communities, White flight occurs. Further, although the practice is illegal, some real estate companies will not show homes in some White neighborhoods to African Americans.

Discrimination in our society also affects the employment rate among African Americans. While many factors contribute to higher unemployment and underemployment among African

Americans, one of those factors is racial discrimination. Many African Americans have the experience of applying for jobs, being told they are not qualified, and discovering that the only difference between them and the person who received the job is the color of their skin.

Discrimination in schools is reflected in the attitudes of many administrators, teachers, and counselors toward African American students. In order to perform well in school, students must believe that those responsible for their education are genuinely interested and concerned about them. Unfortunately, many educators have negative attitudes toward African Americans and are unable or unwilling to work effectively with these students.

Standardized and competency tests are other examples of discrimination in schools. Research indicates that African American students score lower on these tests than their White counterparts. When African American students learn this fact, they begin to doubt their intelligence and potential. Many of these students lose interest in their school work and begin to look for other ways to become successful. While many educators are aware that these tests are biased against African American students, they continue to use them to judge their knowledge and aptitude. Students have difficulty in being motivated or believing in themselves when they know they are being tested unfairly in school.

Lack of Role Models

A third problem that faces all African Americans is the lack of role models in traditional and nontraditional careers. As of this writing there is one African American Senator, no significant number of African Americans in chief executive positions of major corporations or television networks, few administrators in predominantly White colleges and universities, and a relatively small percentage of African Americans in medicine, dentistry, law, college teaching, engineering, pharmacy, architecture, or aeronautics. Without appropriate role models, many African American students perceive these and other technical professions as career areas that African American people do not enter.

Likewise, many African American parents, educators, and counselors tend not to encourage children to seek careers in nontraditional areas. Labeling, discrimination, and lack of career role models will continue as pressing problems and sources of disillusionment until a concerted societal effort is mustered to dispel them.

PERSONAL AND CAREER GUIDANCE NEEDS OF AFRICAN AMERICANS

Personal Needs

African Americans, like all human beings, *need to be understood, accepted, and respected.* Many White people have had limited contact with African American people as individuals and minimal involvement in activities sponsored by African American organizations. Hence, White people have not been exposed to some of the differences in the culture, life-style, and communication patterns of African Americans. For example, some White people criticize African Americans for using dialect although this style of communication is accepted in the home and community. Denigration of their very speech leaves many African Americans feeling ignored and rejected by White people. In the end that mistrust and hatred are fostered, leading to further separation of the groups.

Negative stereotypes about African American people have existed since Africans were brought to America as slaves. Many White people learn these stereotypes at an early age, believe them, and never challenge them. Sensitive to negative stereotypes, some African American people may consent to the attitudinal and behavioral expectations of White people and assume certain roles for survival. Others may learn to rationalize or deny the existence of negative stereotypes, while still others may absorb them as part of a negative self-concept. Thus, a second personal need of African Americans is *to be perceived as individuals who are judged by character rather than color.* In other words, African American people do not want White people to have expectations of them that are based on stereotypes; they want to be seen as individuals who have different as well as similar needs to those of White people.

A third personal need of African Americans is *to be treated equally*. As African American people become aware of history in America, they learn that their ancestors have been treated as second class citizens. The effect has been an expectation of unfair treatment in their associations with majority group members. African American children learn from their parents at an early age that they should be very cautious about trusting Whites. Most of these parents can share personal experiences of their unfair treatment by White people. Many African American parents have stories to tell about having to drink from separate water fountains, sitting in the balconies of movie theaters, not being able to stay in certain hotels, and not being able to obtain commercial loans.

A fourth personal need of African Americans, one that perhaps encompasses the others, is *to be included in the mainstream of society*. African Americans rarely feel an integral part of society. The effect of this is that they have learned to live in two worlds, one African American, the other White. African American parents teach their children that they must learn to function in White society as well as they function in African American society. Developing a "dual personality" is necessary for African American children in order to survive in both worlds. They must learn to function within the White system to avoid isolation and segregation in society. African Americans want to be included in society's mainstream without having to sacrifice the qualities that make them different. They want to be themselves and to be perceived by majority group members as having something to offer society.

Career Needs

African American students need to be provided with information about nontraditional careers, including examples of African American males and females who currently work in engineering, architecture, mathematics, basic sciences, computer science, and medicine. Through the provision of culturally relevant career guidance materials including slide/tape presentations, career scrapbooks, and African American speakers, students can be made aware that African Americans have entered these career areas and experienced success.

Since African American students may perceive nontraditional career areas as unrealistic for them, counselors should encourage active career planning to help students identify career alternatives, develop strategies, complete appropriate course work, and seek career information. Thus, a person can better understand the education necessary and the skills needed to do the job, the amount of time involved in preparing for this career, and the options available within an area of interest. Counselors should not be afraid to encourage African Americans to explore and enter nontraditional as well as traditional career areas. Challenging these students to enter nontraditional careers communicates in a positive way that counselors believe they can succeed in their endeavors.

COUNSELING SERVICES FOR AFRICAN AMERICANS

Underutilization

Being generally unaware of the services that counselors provide, many African American adults do not utilize the available community counseling services nor do they encourage their children to seek the help of school counselors. Most African American students, however, have become familiar with counseling and counselors during their tenure at public schools. African Americans who have not had positive experiences with counselors in schools are likely not to seek the help of counselors in the community. Based on these observations, one can understand why counseling services in the community are underutilized by African Americans. Moreover, many African Americans assume that significant others (ministers, relatives, friends) in the community are more interested and qualified to help them than are professional counselors.

Moreover, African Americans have not utilized counseling services because many counseling agencies expect clients to come and ask for help, the traditional way that counseling has been made available to all people. In African American communities, however, this system does not work well because African Americans are not accustomed to sharing their personal problems with strangers.

When compared to Whites of similar educational levels, African Americans are less likely to self-disclose in counseling. When gender is considered, both White and African American females disclose more readily than males (Jourard & Lasakow, 1958). Ridley (1984) offered a plausible explanation for the African American's reluctance to self-disclose. He reported that they have been socialized to "play it cool" or to exhibit "healthy cultural paranoia." That is, they have been taught to view every White person as a potential enemy. African Americans must guard themselves from pain and hurt from White people using mistrust as a defense mechanism.

Availability

During the 1980s a significant decrease occurred in the availability of counseling services in the African American community. Federal budget cutbacks coupled with the lack of new legislative domestic programs discouraged many African Americans from seeking mental health services. At a time when the need was growing for more counseling services. Few politicians championed programs to alleviate the growing social problems.

Recently, some community mental health agencies have been established directly within the African American community, a circumstance which has improved the availability of counseling services to African Americans. Since these agencies are highly visible, African Americans may eventually begin to perceive them as a part of their community and make better use of them. Because a stigma has been attached to them in the past, it may be a long time before these agencies are fully accepted by African American communities. In terms of increasing availability, awareness, and use of counseling services, however, community centers are a step in the right direction.

Experiential Training for Counselors

One problem that faces many helping professionals in their attempt to provide better counseling services is their lack of experience in working with African Americans. Not having lived among or developed friendships with African Americans, many helping professionals leave preparation programs unsure of how to approach and counsel African American clients. Frequently, these inexperienced professionals refer African American clients to African American counselors. While this practice may seem plausible, it is nonetheless limiting. The competent counselor learns to work with many different clients.

A question that might be posed is, "Are helping professionals responsible for being able to counsel African American clients effectively?" Without hesitation, the answer is yes. A necessary first step is fostering awareness of how one thinks and feels about African Americans. Awareness of attitudes can help individuals determine if they as counselors need to increase experiences with African Americans to learn more about their culture, life-style, and communication patterns. Experiences with African Americans also can serve as a vehicle for counselors to dispel myths or stereotypes that they may hold. Clients have a way of knowing whether a counselor is genuine. We do not fool any of our clients, any of the time. They know if we are just talking to them because it is our job. If a client is racially, ethnically, or culturally different, helping professionals must find ways to appreciate those differences, as opposed to believing something is wrong with clients who are different. Neither can it be assumed that because helping professionals have received graduate training, they are well equipped to work with all clients who come into their offices, regardless of the race, culture, or language.

The most effective method of increasing knowledge and awareness is to place oneself in situations which enable a feeling of differentness. Attending social affairs sponsored by African American organizations, such as dances, parties, and picnics is one way to better understand how it feels to be a member of a minority group. By eating meals and talking informally with African Americans at restaurants in their community, helping professionals can begin to learn the culture, life-style and language of African Americans. The aim is to become helping professionals who believe that all people have an inherent right to retain their identities, make their own choices, and be self-directed individuals.

Neither of these tasks is easy. Changing attitudes requires commitment. Acquiring knowledge of African Americans places us in strange environments. We may feel uneasy, uncomfortable, and even insecure. These are the same feelings African Americans experience when they visit helping professionals. It is incumbent on the helping professional to take the same risks they ask of their clients. Competent helping professionals may stumble and fall in their attempts to learn more about African Americans, but they stand up and try again.

An Eclectic Counseling Approach

All of life centers around our constant struggle to become better persons, to develop better self-concepts, and to become all that we can be. When African American clients have problems, and they bring those problems to us in counseling relationships, what they are really saying is, "I'm stuck, I cannot move, and I need you to help me learn how to move from this point to a better point in life." We have to say, "Yes, I can help you, and this is how I can help you." Therein lies the essence of counseling: the ability to help somebody. Counseling is not for counselors; counseling is for clients. Clients' needs are the most important ingredients in the entire counseling relationship.

During the past 20 years much has been written about counseling African American clients. Most authors suggest that counselors use a counseling approach based on one of the directive-cognitive theories, such as reality therapy. Others recommend that counselors use a counseling approach based on one of the nondirective-affective theories, such as client-centered therapy. Our view is that an eclectic approach with an existential philosophical base can be used effectively with African American clients. Existentialism is a school of thought that is concerned with individuals and their attempt to develop personal identities, make their own choices, and provide self-direction. An existentialist approach views racially, ethnically, or culturally different clients as individuals. It also means understanding that we all have different physical and mental characteristics and that we all have an inherent right to be who we are; thus, the role of the counselor is to understand clients as they exist in their worlds. Counselors who imagine what African American clients are experiencing better understand their meaning, values, life-styles, concerns and choices. We advocate an existential philosophy for counseling African American clients because it places emphasis on existence, humanity, and individual differences.

The seven phases of the counseling process include building rapport, identifying the problem, setting goals, working, planning action, following-up, and terminating. The first step is ***building rapport***. At the beginning of the counseling relationship the helper takes time to establish a *personal* relationship. Building rapport communicates to African American clients that we care about them as persons and that we want to know more about them. An important part of promoting trust is shaking hands. It is one quick way of saying, I do not mind touching you. Counselors also may share some personal information about themselves, thus inviting African American clients to share similar information. In addition, providing an orientation to counseling (i.e., telling African American clients what happens in counseling relationships) lets clients know what to expect, prevents confusion and misunderstanding, and helps build the relationship.

The second step is ***identifying the problem***. African American clients must be allowed opportunities to indicate in their own words why they are seeking help. Counselors help explore the problem by asking probing questions, clarifying, and sharing hunches. They search with the client within the client's world to discover the nature of the concern.

Having identified the client's difficulty, the third step is *setting realistic goals*. Setting goals that are outcome-oriented is important with African American clients because it helps them understand the purpose of counseling. Counselors should designate the outcomes of the counseling relationship in clear, simple language, indicating that help is available to solve the problem.

The fourth step in the counseling process is *working*. Working involves both clients and counselors in a mutual enterprise. By investing in the partnership, the counselor challenges clients' irrational beliefs and negative self-concepts. The counselor must remember that African American clients have their own experiences, and it is within this framework of experience that they are sharing their problems and concerns. While accepting what clients say is very important, doing so does not mean that the counselor should not debate what they say, or discourage irrational thinking patterns. Counselors have to be able to respond to African American clients in a way that says, *I understand what you are saying; I'm trying to understand what you are feeling; and I want to struggle with you.*

The fifth step in the process is *action planning*. Here the focus is on what African American clients can do to help themselves and what counselors can do to help them help themselves. A practice instrument in action planning is the use of *homework* assignments, specific actions that counselors and clients will perform between the counseling sessions. Counselors and clients both need to make a commitment to the plan of action, facilitating the counseling process by becoming *we* and *us*. Thus both the client and the counselor are involved in the formulation and the implementation of the plan.

The sixth phase is *following-up*. Counselors must find out whether the action plan worked and for what reasons. How effective was the action plan? Is there a need to create another plan or modify the existing one? What blocks exist to effective implementation?

The seventh and last step is *terminating* the counseling relationship. Here counselors become teachers by explaining what was done, why it was done, and how clients can use similar techniques to help themselves in the future. Moreover, there is time for counselors to offer encouragement to African American clients, to communicate that whether or not we walk with them, when they leave us, we will be with them in spirit, and that we believe in them. So often the difference between effective and ineffective counseling relationships lies in whether clients leave believing they can solve their problems. In other words, we can make a difference in the lives of African American clients by simply believing that they can become better persons.

An eclectic approach following these seven steps is a viable one for counseling African American clients. The authors no longer believe that counselors can afford to debate which counseling theory or approach is more effective with African American clients. All counseling approaches can be effective with African American clients if used properly. The most important element in counseling relationships is that counselors meet the needs of their clients. If that means needing to be directive, then we should be directive. If it means needing to be nondirective, we should be nondirective. If it means needing to listen, we should listen. If it means needing to talk, we should talk. The eclectic approach provides a process through which counselors enter African American clients' worlds, enter their struggles, and together create alternatives and plans for action.

Culturally Specific Therapy

Recently, many African American social scientists have advocated culturally specific counseling or therapy for African Americans. Culturally specific therapy takes race and culture into consideration in work with clients (Locke, 1990; Parham, 1989; Parker, 1988; Pinkney, 1993). This therapy involves the exploration of issues of race and how race affects the client's life. Other aspects of this therapy also may involve conversation or experiences where African ancestors are celebrated.

Pinkney (1993) suggested that culturally specific therapy could mean seeing a therapist who is African American, one who, having experienced some of the same things, can better understand the client's experience. Most of these therapists weave African values into their therapy with African American clients. One African value is the emphasis on the family, community and connectedness rather than on the single individual or the self. Others focus on closeness with clients rather than distance, making the client a part of the extended family.

Some culturally sensitive therapists, according to Pinkney (1993), involve the entire family as part of treatment. This practice is similar to an African practice where the entire community becomes involved when an individual has a problem. One of the authors himself recalls a similar practice in his home community in Alabama. He remembers being a member of a community group which spent several days and nights with a young African American man who had attempted to commit suicide by drinking lye. The whole community prayed for him, offered moral support, and provided food and other needs for his family. In addition, many parents wanted their young children to see and remember the horrible condition of a mouth burned by lye.

During the last 20 years much has occurred in the area of counseling African American clients. Many articles and books have been published on the subject. Conferences and workshops on counseling African American clients have been sponsored by many helping professional organizations. Counselor education and psychology departments now offer courses and other academic experiences in an effort to better prepare helping professionals to work with African American clients. Indeed, counseling African American clients has become a legitimate area of scholarly thought and research in the helping professions. As we move closer to the 21st century, counseling African American clients is becoming an integral part of all helping professions. Our challenge is to equip ourselves and future helping professionals with the necessary skills to respond effectively to the needs of African American clients. The authors believe that counselors can meet this challenge. It is our hope that the ideas presented in this chapter represent steps in that direction.

EXPERIENTIAL ACTIVITIES

Individual Activity, Number 10.1

What stereotypes do people still hold concerning African Americans? From your perspective, create a list of ten such stereotypes and briefly indicate the "reason" or "roots" of each. How might these stereotypes affect communication?

Individual Activity, Number 10.2

The title of this activity is "Literary Sharing for Understanding African Americans." The objectives of this activity are

1. to help you understand the relationship between Cross's Nigrescence Model of Identity Development and literary characters, and

2. to help you expand your knowledge and awareness of racial/cultural identity development through literature and art.

Directions for the participant

Review the summary of Cross' Nigrescence Model discussed in this chapter, then think about how racial identity attitudes and behaviors are manifested in characters you have read about in novels, poetry, or history or characters you have seen in movies.

Now, trace the racial identity development of one selected African American character based on the Nigrescence Model. For example, you might follow the evolution of Malcolm X's racial identity development from his pre-encounter period (idealizing White people) through his stage of internalization (building bridges between African American people and White people).

Question for Discussion

How might your understanding of the Nigrescence Model assist you in understanding and counseling African Americans?

Group Activity, Number 10.3

Divide the participants into small groups of five or six. Ask each group to select a discussion leader. Give the group about 10 minutes, during which time each person describes a leader. Give the group about 10 minutes, during which time each person describes a "typical" African American communication style and their own communication style. How do the two differ? How might these differences affect your communication with one another?

Group Activity, Number 10.4

Divide the participants into groups of five-seven members each. Select group leaders and ask each group member to read the African American Case (allow about 10 minutes to read the case). Then conduct a small group discussion based on the questions listed under the heading *Case Conceptualization*. After allowing at least one hour for group discussion, you might select two group members to role-play a counselor/client interaction based on the African American vignette. Other members may take turns in playing the role of counselor or client. This role-play should be followed by additional discussion.

African American Case

Anthony (Tony) is a tall, handsome, 17 year old African American male who is a graduating senior from a predominantly White high school in suburban Washington, DC. Tony's parents are middle-class professional people. One works for the Federal Government and the other teaches school in the public school system. While Tony was once a model student, his behavior has taken an unexpected turn characterized by skipping classes, disrespectful behavior toward his teachers, withdrawal, and discontentment.

Within the past few months there have been many discussions regarding Tony's college plans. Tony's parents believe that he should attend a predominantly African American college similar to the one they attended. To familiarize him with these colleges, Tony's parents planned their vacation around visitations to African American colleges in the South. In addition, Tony's father has taken him to several lectures focusing on supporting historically African American colleges. He often explained to Tony that the African American college was the place where African Americans can best understand who they are and where they are going. His father quoted statistics indicating that the majority of African American leaders today graduated from these institutions.

Tony has lived most of his life in the presence of White individuals or groups. He wonders how he would feel if he were suddenly thrust into an African American college campus? Would African American students enjoy tossing the frisbee as his White friends do? Would African American students appreciate music by Brian Adams or the Grateful Dead? Thoughts of being around so many African Americans cause him to shudder and to grow somewhat sick at heart. His closest friends are White whether his parents like it or not.

Tony's older sister is somewhat different from Tony. She decided to attend Tuskegee (an African American college in Alabama) a year ago, and she really likes it. She has always encouraged her parents to move to inner city DC, which is mostly African American. She made it her business to associate with the few African American students in her high school, and she always stayed in tune with issues related to the African American community. She believes that the quality of life of most African Americans demonstrates that they are victims of an insensitive and racist society. She feels guilty that she lives so comfortably in suburbia while other African Americans undergo so much suffering, pain, and hardship.

On the other hand, Tony believes that segregation is past history and African American colleges are relics of history. Further, he believes that African Americans need to take advantage of opportunities and stop using race as a crutch.

Frankly, he thinks that greater educational opportunities for all people exist in White institutions. They have broader course offerings, have greater possibilities for networking, and are generally the places most suitable for preparing students for a future that will be more scientifically and technologically advanced than any other period of American history.

Case Conceptualization

Assume Tony comes to you, the counselor, for help with the issues outlined in the case. Role-play a brief counselor/client interaction relative to the case.

What is the presenting problem?

What is your assessment of the problem?

Describe the historical and sociological context in which this client's experience can be placed.

What values do Tony and his family members demonstrate? Where are the value conflicts? Contrast the client's values with your own.

What stage of nigrescence does the client seem to be in at this time? Explain.

What are some potential cross-cultural counseling issues in this case?

Outline at least three different possible interventions you would consider with this client. Describe each intervention (or type of response in session) and state your reasons for using it.

What additional information would you want to know in order to work effectively with this client?

What sort of follow-up would you want to do?

Outside Class Activity, Number 10.5

Attend a cultural event with another person whose ethnic or cultural background differs from yours.

Outside Class Activity, Number 10.6

One general objective in multicultural counselor training is for trainees to become more aware of their and others' attitudes toward racially and culturally different individuals. Trainees are also expected to gain knowledge and skill to help them work more effectively with culturally different clients. Outline a three-level action plan designed to achieve these goals.

As these action plans are formulated and carried out, allot time for small group discussion for the purpose of brainstorming, processing fears or difficulties, and describing experiences and personal reactions.

Action Plan One should be observational (observe African Americans from a distance through viewing movies, reading novels, or by touring African American neighborhoods. *Action Plan Two* should be investigative (collect information) about African Americans by interviewing African American leaders concerning their needs, problems, and concerns. *Action Plan Three* should be personal involvement (being involved with an African American on a more personal social level). These activities are especially important for individuals who have had limited contact with African Americans throughout their lives.

REFERENCES

Blassingame, J. (1972). *The slave community: Plantation life in the ante-bellum south.* New York: Oxford University Press.

Coleman, D. (1987, September 1). Study finds feelings of inferiority among Black children. *Gainesville Sun,* p. 1D.

Cross, W.E. (1991). Shades of Black: Diversity in African-American identity., Philadelphia: Temple University Press.

Douthis, J. (1985). Black churches provide more than spiritual needs (Report No. 44). Washington, DC: Smithsonian Institution Research Reports.

Gaines-Carter, P. (1985, September). Is my "post-integration" daughter Black enough? *Ebony*, pp. 54-56.

Jourard, S., & Lasakow, P. (1958). Some factors in self-disclosure. *Journal of Abnormal and Social Psychology, 56,* 91-98.

Locke, D.C. (1990). A not so provincial view of multicultural counseling. *Counselor Education and Supervision, 30,* 18-25.

Parham, T.A. (1989). Cycles of psychological nigrescence. *Counseling Psychologist, 17,* 187-226.

Parker, W.M. (In Press) Ethnic minority cultural awareness test.

Parker, W.M. (1988). Consciousness raising through minority identity development. In W.M. Parker, *Consciousness raising: A primer for multicultural counseling.* (pp. 61-77). Springfield: Charles C. Thomas.

Parker, W.M., Archer, J., & Scott, J. (1992). *Multicultural relations on campus: A personal growth approach.* Muncie, IN: Accelerated Development.

Pinkney, D.S. (1993, March). Healing with therapy. *Essence,* pp.45, 46, 152, 154.

Ridley, C.R. (1984). Clinical treatment of the nondisclosing Black client. *American Psychologist, 38,* 1234-1244.

Sloan, I. (1971). *Blacks in America 1492-1970.* Dobbs Ferry, NW: Oceana.

U.S. Department of Commerce, Bureau of the Census. (1992). Statistical abstract of the United States. Washington, DC: U.S. Government Printing Office.

Chapter 11

INDIVIDUALS WITH A PHYSICAL DISABILITY

Nicholas A. Vacc, Ed.D., Kerry Clifford, Ed.S.

Dr. Nicholas A. Vacc is Professor and Chairperson of the Department of Counseling and Educational Development at the University of North Carolina, Greensboro. He received his degrees from Western Reserve University, Syracuse University, and State University of New York. He has been a public school teacher and counselor, school psychologist, Veterans Administration Counselor, and Director of a University Counseling Center. Dr. Vacc has served on community health boards and is past chairman of a county subcommittee on mental retardation. He was a member of the Board of Visitors of a state residential unit for the developmentally disabled. In addition, he has served as a consultant to programs and agencies serving diverse populations.

__Kerry F. Clifford__ has been a Clinic Coordinator and Counselor for Union County of the Bradford-Union Guidance Clinic, Florida. He received his bachelor's degree in Mechanical Engineering at Kansas State University where he was a scholarship athlete. In 1967, *as the result of an industrial accident, he became paraplegic. He received a Master's of Rehabilitation Counseling at the University of Florida in 1971 and has served as an instructor at Santa Fe Community College in the Work Exploration Unit and in the CETA program Vocation Preparation Class. He is past chairman of a chapter of Florida's Governor's Committee on the Employment of the Handicapped. He also served on the Handicapped Advisory Committee for the North Central Florida Regional Planning Council. Mr. Clifford has been involved in the development of and has participated in wheel chair athletics, has served as a volunteer consultant on architectural barriers, and designed his own home. A major hobby has been CB radio with which he has assisted in the promotion and organization of a local REACT team.*

AWARENESS INDEX

Directions: These questions are to help you to evaluate your understanding of individuals with a disability. Mark each item as true or false and then compute your score from the scoring guide at the end of the Awareness Index.

T F 1. The term "wheelies" refers to a common expression used for individuals who need to use a wheel chair for mobility.

T F 2. Individuals who have a disability like to be recognized as an example for "normal" individuals.

T F 3. Fund raisers have been very helpful in assisting individuals with a disability to change the attitudes of others.

T F 4. Generally speaking, society places a high premium on physical perfection.

T F 5. The paraplegic personality can be summarized or characterized by the word angry or hostile.

T F 6. Society is increasingly recognizing the capability of individuals with a disability to assume competitive employment.

T F 7. Counselors as helpers need to focus attention on advocacy for helping individuals with a disability.

T F 8. As helpers, we must recognize aspects of our behavior and society that provide limits on individuals with a disability.

Scoring Guide for Awareness Index

1. T 2. F 3. F 4. T 5. F 6. T 7. T 8. T

REFLECTIONS

The authors of this chapter care deeply for the welfare and productive existence of all individuals. Their interest, however, evolved from two very different sets of events. Very early in his professional career the first author became conscious of inequities in our educational system for children with handicapping conditions and has been involved since then with the education and welfare of individuals with disabilities. The second author experienced an accident on the job that resulted in a severed spinal cord and a disability that immeasurably affected both his professional and personal life. Although a paraplegic and a "wheelie", he does not view himself nor does he wish others to view him as a disabled person. Yet, during the years that have passed since his injury, he has had many experiences which have conveyed to him that the majority of people regard him as disabled. The first person accounts included in italics in this chapter convey some of his personal experiences and feelings.

To speak of individuals who have disabilities, who differ from the nondisabled in physical, emotional, and/or mental ability, is to speak of a minority group. As with any minority group, this one is and will continue to be faced with hostility, lack of understanding, indifference, and prejudice.

Many wheelies believe that they cannot condemn members of the general public for their attitude towards a disabled individual because "walkies" (people other than wheelies) have limited exposure to disabled individuals. Some nondisabled think that the wheelie and other individuals who have a disability should stay at home, while other nondisabled individuals believe that those with disabilities should be protected from the rough and tumble world. Thus, attitudes of the general public range from one of complete ignorance and lack of understanding to that of being over-sympathetic and protective.

Many individuals cannot camouflage their disability because a wheelchair or prosthetic device is not easily concealed. The wheelie is literally looked down upon. However, while they cannot "stand tall" in a wheelchair, wheelies are not less than a full-grown person.

> One day when I had on my braces and was just about to stand up, a neighbor woman dropped in. She had never seen me standing, only sitting in the chair. I stood up, moved out into the room and stopped. She sort of stared at me with a "funny" look on her face. I immediately checked the air by nose to see if, as often happens when I get up in braces, I had done a "no-no." There were no signs. I then quickly looked to see if my "plumbing" was in order. Everything was all right, but she was still looking at me the same way. Suddenly she smiled, ran over and put her arms around me and said, "Man! You are a big one aren't you." I didn't ask her, "A 'big one' of what?" but after that event, a subtle change was made in her attitude towards me.

CURRENT PROBLEMS

Even in this enlightened age, a stigma is often attached to a disability. Some paraplegics have expressed their concern that people tend to think they are paralyzed from the neck up as well as the waist down. Some people have difficulty talking directly to people in wheelchairs: they may talk over their heads or discuss them as if they are not present. Many years ago, Martin (1974) accurately characterized the public's response to the handicapped by saying, "They are different, they trouble us in deep, unexplainable, irrational ways, and we would like them somewhere else, not cruelly treated, of course, but out of sight and mind" (p.150). Many nonhandicapped individuals appear to be uncomfortable in the presence of anyone with a disability, and some try to hide their feelings by over-attention, over-kindness, or maudlin sympathy.

It is difficult for many paraplegics to accept the attitudes of some people towards them. At first they resent the people who, meeting them for the first time say, "You poor thing, what is wrong with you?" Or, the more common situation of manner and tone of voice when they say, "Boy! You can sure handle that thing! How do you do that?" These same people would never dream of saying to Carlos Alvarez, "Man! You sure can catch that ball! How do you do it?"

Historically, society has not expected people with a disability to function as normal people and, therefore, has been somewhat hesitant to accept the achievements of individuals with disabilities. As a result people may cover up their feelings by being over-lavish in their praise, with some being patronizing as if praising a child or someone from whom such a standard of achievement is not expected. These people may look on an achievement by the disabled in the same way that Dr. Samuel Johnston did a dog walking on two legs. As Dr. Johnston stated, "It is not the fact that he does it well, but the fact that he is able to do it at all that brings praise."

Persons with a disability want to be recognized as individuals, not as statistics or wonderfully courageous persons—examples for the world. And many do not enjoy being objects used to stimulate fund raising such as a campaign picture of a child on crutches, standing in the shadows with a woeful look as he or she gazes into the distance where other boys and girls are playing. A more desirable image would be to have the same child mixing with playmates and sharing in the fun, even if he or she is only sitting in the sandpile making roads while the rest run and play.

Sometimes the mass media negatively stereotypes individuals with disabilities. For example, in many plays and novels, a disabled male has been portrayed as a miserable tyrant who is often very wealthy and makes life unbearable for all who come in contact with him, an evil villain who seeks revenge for his disability by committing horrible crimes, or a meek pitiful creature who suffers greatly and tries to smile but must spend the rest of his life wrapped in a blanket and sipping hot milk. Fortunately, current literary works are beginning to portray these people as believable human beings. The television series, "Ironside," was a good attempt to show a paraplegic in realistic terms. Ironside, however, generally did not propel his chair by himself as much as he might have. This consistent negative portrayal of individuals with a disability only serves to stigmatize individuals and constrict them from normalization.

One of the myths about well-adjusted persons who have a disability is that they are always supposed to be happy or at least pretend to be. However, individuals with disabilities have feelings that parallel those of nondisabled individuals including, happiness, loneliness, fear, and anger. For wheelies, the latter often accompanies problems with architectural barriers, such as lack of access to building facilities.

If you would like to see and hear a display of anger by a paraplegic, come to the hospital parking lot with me some day. I have upon several occasions arrived early enough to have a pick of parking spaces. I always choose one so that the door on the passenger side of the car is free to swing open wide for easy egress and ingress of the car. However, several times upon returning to the car, a small car has been parked next to the passenger side of my car with two wheels up on the grass and the other two almost in my car's fender wells. Of course, I have passed about fifteen empty spaces on the way to the car. The temperature of the air rises about five degrees centigrade and the tar in the road melts under my wheelchair.

An injury that confines one to a wheelchair, does not change a person's personality. However, some feelings such as fear, anger, and sex drive may be lessened. Yet, if these feelings are indeed lowered, their manifestation is not. The shy, retiring person will still be shy though confined to a chair, the complainer will still complain, and the aggressive person will still be aggressive. There is no paraplegic personality; each wheelie is an individual. Physically disabled people do not want to be viewed as handicapped or disabled. Rather they are individuals with a disability, who can become well adjusted if they receive love, understanding, and tactful help in meeting problems. They want to be judged competitively in their community, on what they can do being emphasized rather than what they cannot do.

More than ever before, recognition is growing of the potential capability of individuals with a disabilities to assume independent living and competitive employment. With this recognition, change is occurring in the direction of a more comprehensive attack on the problem of providing resources, facilities, and services to help integrate these individuals into the community as evidenced by The Americans with Disabilities Act of 1990. The following verse by an unknown, presumably paraplegic author aptly conveys the frustration of being separated from society:

I burn the rubber off my wheels; I can hardly wait. My wheelchair's 30 inches wide, the john is 28. Some plead for civil justice when they are set upon. I ask for just one freedom the right to use the john. I've thought about reforming and changing my evil ways; To be a model of deportment for the remainder of my days. But when I get to heaven and face the Pearly Gates, St. Peter will say, "You're 30 inches wide. Our gates are 28."   Unknown

NORMALIZATION

Normalization is usually defined as enabling people to participate in the normal range of societal activities as much as independently possible. With legislative requirements of normalization principles (sometimes referred to as least restrictive environment), it has become increasingly important that schools and other agencies of society find ways of working with and helping individuals with disabilities who may differ from the "normal" population in emotional stability, learning capability, and/or physical capability.

Helping persons to cope with problems in their natural environment so that the handicapping aspects of their disabilities are minimized and their level of life functioning is maximized, has produced a need for a change in counseling services to include advocacy. At this time, however, the response appears to be inadequate to this need for extended and strengthened services. As with any diverse population, helpers must be conscious of the present inequities for individuals with disabilities and strive to adjust the "system" to allow for maximum personal achievement. As Tennyson so capably put it:

How dull it is to pause to make an end, to rest unburnished, not to shine in use.

A disability represents a massive assault on an individual, and how he or she acts will depend on environmental experiences. These experiences are influenced by the nature of the disability, the realistic problem(s) it creates, the person's attitude, material resources, and the attitude of family members, people in the immediate environment, and/or society in general. Helpers should be sensitive to developing an understanding of these factors and their manifestations relative to the individual.

The importance of helpers striving to "adjust the system" can be dramatically illustrated by the case of a Vietnam War veteran whom the second author was requested to assist. This pleasant, good-looking young man, who will be referred to as Joe, had attempted suicide two times within a three-month period.

We talked initially of the things that two "paras" usually discuss, especially in a hospital setting with one person being a relatively novice wheelie and the other a more experienced one. The topic included incidence of injury, medical/surgical course, hospitals and care, bowel/bladder control, decubitus ulcers, types of chairs, and operations. After a while it became evident that Joe had two major concerns. The most important by far was sexual function; the other was mobility, especially operating an automobile without assistance. That these subjects were important to Joe was not surprising. What was surprising was that he had not been offered counseling and information concerning them. According to Joe, his inquiries about the subjects had elicited vague, confusing, and unsatisfying responses.

Counseling after two suicide attempts had never touched upon these two main concerns. The question is whether individuals without a disability view as important those activities which they take for granted, or whether they view individuals with a disability as having no needs except those directly related to the disability.

Joe's ignorance of whether or not he could obtain a reflex penile erection paralleled my own previous experience. A few suggestions on procedures plus health and safety precautions were offered on determining whether an erection, plus its degree, could be obtained. With this, the two-hour visit with Joe terminated. His smile and demeanor during my visit the next day answered the question of whether he had been successful. During the ensuing months with Joe, sexual-function education and possible procedures were presented and discussed. At the same time, Joe obtained an automobile with hand controls and received instruction and training on how to use them. Subsequently, Joe became very busy in living. Times for the unofficial counseling visits became increasingly short and finally ceased. When Joe was discharged from the hospital, he rented an apartment which had been made architecturally adequate, set up independent living, and started classes at the nearby community college.

Sad but true Joe did not continue to "live happily ever after." He had other handicaps with which to contend in addition to his physical disability. He was young and had experienced a rather protected earlier life. As a result, he was psychologically and emotionally immature, lacing experience in coping with the demands of independent living. He developed behaviors indicative of arrogance and pride, spurning further counseling and even friendship. Alcohol and other drugs became increasingly part of his life-style. He quit school, wrecked his car several times, and finally, due to improperly caring for himself, developed a chronic urinary tract infection as well as a decubitus ulcer of his buttock. He became rather desperate and his parents took him back to the home area. I have not heard from Joe since that time.

In the case of Joe, the system was eventually adjusted so he could function independently in society—he was helped in learning how to function adequately with his disability. In the past, many individuals like Joe, in addition to not receiving the type of assistance they desired, would have been separated from their natural environment based on the rationale that their removal would eliminate the problems and frustrations they might encounter in their everyday life. School-age children with disabilities often have been removed from the public classroom and/or placed in special care facilities. Fortunately, a change has taken place via the significant movement toward improving educational programs for school-age individuals with handicapping conditions, a movement which resulted from the enactment of Public Law 94-142 (now referred to as IDEA). Perhaps schools may be the place where bridges can be built between the past and the future. Old policies of separation and passive service are being replaced with programs that encourage involvement and aggressive action. The goal is a full relationship with society for all individuals.

CHANGES IN EDUCATIONAL PROGRAMS AND RELATED SERVICES

Even people not immediately affiliated with the educational profession seem to be aware of the law which acknowledges equal educational opportunities for all children. Public Law 94-142 resulted from the work of parents and other individuals who brought public attention to the handicapped through policy victories won in the nation's courts and state legislatures. This legislation was designed to insure that all public education agencies provide an appropriate educational program for a child with a disability or handicap.

The Education for All Handicapped Children Act applies to all persons aged 3 to 21, who require special education and related services. As defined by this Act, handicapped children are those who are mentally retarded, hard of hearing, deaf, orthopedically impaired, other health impaired, speech impaired, visually handicapped, or seriously emotionally disturbed. Also included are children with specific learning disabilities who by reason thereof require special education and related services.

The major purposes of Public Law 94-142, as summarized by Ballard and Zettel (1977), were to

guarantee the availability of special education programming to handicapped children and youth who require it.

assure fair and appropriateness in decision making with regard to providing special education services for handicapped children and youth. Establish clear management and auditing requirements and procedures regarding special education at all levels of government.

financially assist the efforts of state and local government through the use of federal funds.

Section 504 which was enacted through the Vocational Rehabilitation Act Amendments of 1973, applies to all Americans with a handicap or disability but has special meaning for school-age children because it guarantees them access, when appropriate, to regular education programs. As the statute reads:

> No other qualified handicapped individual in the United States shall, solely by reason of his (sic) handicap, be excluded from participation in, be denied the benefits of, or be subjected to discrimination under any program or activity receiving Federal financial assistance. (Ballard & Zettel, 1977, p. 178)

In 1990, the Education of the Handicapped Act was renamed the Individuals with Disabilities Education Act (IDEA) (PL 101-476). The new law expanded the definition of special education to include instruction in all settings such as the work place and training centers. As was true with PL 94-142, IDEA also stipulated that students with disabilities had to receive services that are necessary to ensure that they benefitted from their educational experience. The law also increased the number of disability conditions eligible for services to include autism and traumatic brain injury. IDEA also continued to provide for nondiscriminatory and multidisciplinary assessment of educational needs, parental involvement in the development of their child's educational program, education in the least restrictive environment, and an individualized education program (IEP). (Hardmen, Drew, Egan, & Wolf, 1993). Added, however, were provisions to include instructions in the workplace and training centers, and transition services for students 16 or younger, when appropriate. Transition services include special transportation and other support services such as rehabilitation counseling and social work assistance.

Another important and precedent-setting law for individuals with disabilities is PL 101-336, the Americans with Disabilities Act (ADA) of 1990 (1988). Initiated almost 30 years after the Civil Rights Act of 1964, ADA provides the constitutional guarantee of access to services and jobs, for people with disabilities. This law provides civil rights protection to people with disabilities for private-sector employment, all public services, and public accommodations, transportation, and telecommunications. Access to such places as public rest rooms, restaurants, businesses, and corporate America have not been necessarily available to those with disabilities because of architectural and "attitudinal" barriers. Some physical changes required as a result of ADA include making curb cuts in sidewalks, widening entrances, doorways, repositioning shelves and telephones, and convenient alternatives to turnstiles. Under ADA, employers are required to make "reasonable efforts" to hire people with disabilities. ADA has the promise to provide 43 million Americans with disabilities with the bases for lawsuits when they believe they wrongfully have been denied employment or access to services because of their disability. Much as the Civil Rights Act of 1964 gave clout to ethnic minorities struggling for equality, the ADA has promised to be equally helpful to those with disabilities. Of particular interest to professional counselors are the barriers removed in public and private employment by ADA. Under ADA, employers

cannot discriminate against an individual with a disability during employment or promotion if the person is otherwise qualified.

can ask about someone's ability to perform a job but cannot inquire if he or she has a disability or has had prior medical treatments.

need to provide reasonable accommodations to people with disabilities, such as modification of equipment or job restructuring.

cannot use tests that tend to screen out an applicant or worker due to his or her disability.

cannot deny access to employment or advancement to someone living with or involved in a relationship with a person who has a disability.

These changes in the law will assist persons with disabilities in getting jobs and reversing the situation of high unemployment among individuals with disabilities.

Schools in particular have the potential for providing intervention for children with a disability because they are a major part of children's natural environment. Accordingly, the next section of this chapter will focus on the school as an agency that is potentially capable of providing important assistance with helping students with a disability achieve preparation for employment.

Because children and youth with disabilities have greater contact with the school than any other agency, personnel should be in schools who are adequately trained to work with these children concerning their career, personal, and social problems. The goal for significant adults, who work with these children, should be to develop a milieu that prescribes normative behavior and ways of problem solving that can be followed when facing dilemmas in their lives.

HISTORY OF COUNSELING SERVICES FOR CHILDREN WITH DISABILITIES

Relatively speaking, only in recent years have children with disabilities been provided for in the public schools. Even then, it has been done mainly through special education classes. Counseling for the handicapped was first mentioned after 1950 with the formation of the National Association of Retarded Children (NARC), the organization that brought pressures to provide services for the mentally retarded in areas previously neglected. Yet, more than four decades later, little progress appears to have been made in this area. The literature concerning counseling children with disabilities remains limited.

Counseling assistance in schools for children with disabilities has often been limited to practical information—providing or advice-giving efforts. Most counselors are aware of students in their schools who have a disability and are concerned about providing appropriate services for them. Yet, it seems fair to conclude that incomplete services are provided. Counselors' inadequate involvement may be attributed to lack of time and/or apprehension caused mainly by limited knowledge of and experience with such children. Consequently, it appears that many counselors are not meeting the career development, social, and personal adjustment needs of children with a disability. There needs to be an operational awareness that the career and personal-social needs are inextricably bound. Children with a disability, no matter how well trained in academic skills, cannot hold a job if, for example, they cannot get along with their fellow workers or have limited knowledge of career opportunities.

In order to meet the needs of children with any disability, an urgent change must be made in the traditional behaviors of school counselors. They must assume appropriate counseling responsibilities with children having disabilities.

HELPING PROFESSIONAL'S ROLE

Helpers need to examine and realistically appraise their own attitudes when working with an individual with a disability. They need to be cognizant of not over simplifying problems as being directly related to the disability alone. Mental, emotional, and career problems of individuals with a disability are likely to originate from as wide a spectrum as do those of non-disabled individuals. The individual with a disability is likely to have not only diverse career goals and leisure interests but also limitations concerning life management. Accordingly, it is important that we as helpers do not categorize individuals and limit our involvement with them to concerns that are only directly related to their disabilities.

Essential Facts

Helpers need to be fully cognizant of three facts in order to assist a person with a disability:

1. Functional limitations among individuals classified as possessing a particular type of disability vary as much within the group as they do between diverse population groups.

2. Modern technological changes have created vast new possibilities for minimizing physical limitations.

3. An individual's attitude, approach to life, and will to achieve can bring about achievement that may seem impossible with a given disability.

Basic Assumptions

Four basic assumptions should be underscored.

1. Each individual with a disability is a unique person whose wish to receive and respond to life's experiences can vary significantly from that of other individuals with a disability.

2. Elements of a helping relation that are advocated for individuals without a disability are equally applicable to individuals who have a disability.

3. Individuals with a disability are limited by having to function in a world with architectural obstacles, debilitating attitudes, and assumptions which until recently, separated these individuals from the nondisabled world.

4. Because an individual with a disability has more than the usual amount of contact with helping professionals, a helper must necessarily become involved with a number of other helping professionals such as physicians, rehabilitation counselors, and staff members of community agencies.

Important Daily Functions to Address

Helpers working toward possible solutions for individuals who have a disability must gain an understanding of four areas of daily life functioning that are affected by the handicapping aspects of a disability: mobility, time, physical or body requirements, and personal and social disposition. These areas provide a point of departure for helping individuals seek solutions to problems in their environment. Although these daily life functions are interrelated, they are separated in the following discussions to highlight their importance to an individual with a disability.

Mobility. Mobility means being able to move freely in one's environment. Each of us, from infancy to adulthood, desires being as physically independent as possible. We hold dear the ability to be able to go wherever we want whenever we want. Individuals with a disability are no exception to this desired goal.

Time. In general, we are not concerned with time per se, but rather with its utilization. Yet, it is this utilization of time concerning daily living that affects some individuals with a disability. Common functions such as getting dressed, preparing a meal, or other tasks that are taken for granted by individuals without a disability, may occupy a place of major importance in the daily routine of an individual with a disability. Time is finite; if daily living requirements involve longer time frames, a person's choice of activities becomes restricted.

Physical or Body Requirements. Physical or body requirements of an individual with a disability may vary from those of persons without a disability, depending on the nature of the disability. Conditions that are most important include additional safety requirements, avoidance of activities that risk creating injury to the body, and assistance with physical or body care.

Personal and Social Disposition. Personal and social attitudinal disposition starts at the most basic point of an individual's commitment to growth and desire to set goals in the search for an improved quality of life. Personal and social attitude is the desire to command one's physical environment and to acquire social knowledge of self. The attitudinal disposition for individuals with a disability is to treat the disability as a challenge, another life problem to be solved. As such, helpers need to teach new skills to individuals with a disability for the purpose of assisting them in adapting to their environment.

SERVICES HELPERS CAN PROVIDE

Services, which helpers can provide to individuals with a disability, can be divided into two areas: direct service and advocacy. Each are outlined below:

Direct Services

1. Providing career, personal, and social counseling on an individual and group bases.

2. Assisting individuals to obtain appropriate in-school placement or employment, secure admission for appropriate training, and/or participate in leisure and/or extra-curricular activities.

3. Consulting regularly with employers and/or appropriate school personnel.

4. Assisting in arranging the transition of an individual with a disability from one setting to another.

5. Identifying needs of family members.

6. Evaluating the efficacy of the counseling program.

Advocacy

1. Sensitizing other staff members to practices and materials which may be prejudicial to individuals with a disability.

2. Informing family members of mandates and regulations concerning the rights and opportunities of individuals with a disability and their families.

3. Assisting individuals in seeking and using school/community resources.

4. Participating in identifying the needs of individuals with disabilities at all developmental levels.

LAST WORDS

Certain issues should be addressed in order to provide more and better services for individuals with a disability. Research needs to be conducted in the area of counseling services for these persons, and our training programs need to be improved to include the development of skills for working with individuals with a disability. Also, inservice training programs need to be included for helpers in all agencies to improve their skills for direct-service roles.

Assistance can be provided with some immediacy by focusing attention on self-appraisal of existing services. Consideration should be given to whether each of the following important services for individuals with a disability is incorporated into the program:

1. providing information to an individual concerning his or her legal rights and opportunities;

2. using assessment materials to assist individuals in understanding themselves in relation to educational and career opportunities and requirements;

3. cooperating with significant others of individuals with a disability to develop or review and revise programs and plans; and

4. conducting workshops on topics such as careers, human relationships, and decision making for individuals with a disability as well as significant others in their environment.

In earlier sections of this chapter, emphasis was placed on the importance of recognizing aspects of our behavior and society that impose limits on individuals with a disability. Public Law 94-142 (IDEA), Section 504 of the Rehabilitation Act of 1973, Public Law 101-476, and Public Law 101-336 (ADA) have increased public awareness of the right of every individual to have a productive and meaningful life. It is up to helpers to assist individuals with a disability and their families to expand control over their own life-styles. Passiveness on our part is a compromise of our professionalism. Continual evaluation of both our attitudes and our services is necessary to improve the total milieu for all individuals in society. We should keep in mind the words of Szasz (1961) which were spoken in another context, but are applicable to this situation... "although there are certain biological invariants in behavior, the precise pattern of human actions is determined largely by roles and rules" (p. 13). Individuals without a disability need to understand that their perceptions and anticipations of behavior curtail the freedom of individuals with a disability to a greater extent than do their respective physical limitations. Meeting this need is a step toward full humanity for all people.

EXPERIENTIAL ACTIVITIES

Individual Activity

Please read the following information and then respond to the questions.

You are to imagine that this coming Monday you will experience an accident which will result in a physical disability. Close your eyes and imagine your physical condition after Monday—firmly establish the disability in your mind before proceeding.

1. List four ways your life would change following your release from the hospital.

2. Comment briefly on your feelings with regard to adjusting to each change listed in item 2.

3. List two ways you could be helped to cope with your difficulties resulting from the disability.

Group Activity

In a small group discuss (a) the architectural, attitudinal, and emotional barriers you might face as an individual with a disability in a school setting or (b) the effects of PL 94-142, PL 101-476, and PL 101-336 on individuals with a disability.

How has their situation improved?

What have been some specific effects on education?

What are some of the remaining challenges for individuals with a disability?

Outside Class Activity

Become an individual with a disability for a few hours and go to a public place such as a shopping mall. Use such items as a wheelchair, ear plugs, a cane, or crutches in order to create a more realistic experience. Include a friend and use caution.

How did people react to you?

What physical challenges did you face?

REFERENCES

Americans with Disability Act of 1990, 42 U.S.C. S 12101 et seq. (1988).

Ballard, J., & Zettel, J. (1977). Public Law 94-142 and Section 504: What they say about rights and protections. *Exceptional Children, 44*, 177-184.

Hardmen, M.L., Drew, C.J., Egan, M.W., & Wolf, B. (1993). *Human Exceptionality: Society, School, and Family.* Newton, MA: Allyn and Bacon.

Martin, E.W. (1974). Some thoughts on mainstreaming. *Exceptional Children, 41*, 150-153.

Szasz, T.S. (1961). *The myth of mental illness.* New York: Dell Pub.

Chapter 12

SOUTHEAST ASIAN REFUGEES

Rhonda L. Rosser, Ph.D. and Joseph Nguyen

Rhonda L. Rosser began her interest in multicultural counseling when working with the Lutheran Family Services Montagnard Refugee Resettlement Project from 1984-1988. Upon obtaining her Ph.D. from the University of North Carolina, Greensboro, in 1991 she opened a private counseling practice in Greensboro, North Carolina where she currently maintains an ethnically diverse clientele. Publications by her related to Southeast Asian persons have appeared in the Journal for Counseling and Development, the American Journal of Psychiatry, the American Journal of Orthopsychiatry, the Journal of Traumatic Stress, and the Journal of Reality Therapy.

Joseph Nguyen learned English in a Malaysian refugee camp called Pulautanga where he arrived as a Vietnamese boat person. In 1980 at the age of 15 Nguyen and his family settled in the U.S. He has attended North Carolina State University as a Caldwell Scholar and a North Carolina Fellow and has served as the Chairperson, Board of Directors, North Carolina State Legal Defense Corporation.

AWARENESS INDEX

T F   1. The biggest barrier to Indochinese refugees in seeking professional counseling is their lack of fluency in English.

T F   2. Socioeconomic and psychological characteristics of Indochinese students are virtually indistinguishable from those of Asian students in general.

T F   3. For the Indochinese refugee with family members left behind in transit, life is often full of guilt.

T F   4. The Indochinese are relative newcomers, with most of them arriving in the U.S. after 1975.

T F   5. There are tremendous diversities within the small Indochinese community.

T F   6. Because of the Indochinese's strong attachment to their families, the basic family unit and power structure has remained unchanged over time.

T F   7. The Indochinese community is almost always the greatest source of support for the Indochinese refugee in time of mental distress.

T F   8. The overwhelming need to gain command of the English language compels most Indochinese refugees to encourage their youngsters to practice English at home.

T F   9. Among newcomers from Asia in the past two decades, the Indochinese are the only true refugees.

T F 10. As a group, the Indochinese tend to be at least as affluent and educated as other Asian-American groups.

T F 11. Vietnamese and Cambodians, because of their emphasis on hard work and family orientation, have a lower than average rate of depression and marital discord.

T F 12. Most Indochinese share Confucian or Buddhist values with other Asian-Americans.

Scoring Guide for Awareness Index

1. F 2. F 3. T 4. T 5. T 6. F 7. F 8. F 9. T 10. F 11. F 12. T

THE SADNESS IN GREENSBORO

Written in Rhade by Y Sung Ding Plai. Translated into English by Rmah Dock.

This deserted evening I am very sad to be alone.

This deserted evening I alone contemplate the East, all of the mountains, I look towards the West. I only see the brook and stare at the trees. I only see the red leaves are falling down to make me sadder, this is my dream.

How miserable is my lonesome life now.

My mother is already quite old. My people are already too far from me. My life is as sad as the running river that does not return.

I am already very far from you, my beautiful highland. I am already very far from you, my beautiful highland, days and nights I never forget you.

Oh, Sadness! Who may give me a consolation?

Contemplating the sky, I only see the flying cloud. How sad my life is, when will I be able to get the happy chance?

Y Sung Plai was born in 1959 in Darlac Province of Vietnam. He fled his country during the war and came to the United States in November of 1986. Y Sung is a Montagnard refugee from the central highlands of Vietnam.

A CASE EXAMPLE

Y Nie Eban came to this country with his young wife, H'Bel, and his two preschool-aged children, Dethai and Uno. He and his family escaped the communists by hiding in the jungle for many years before fleeing to a refugee camp on the border of Thailand and Kampuchea. He witnessed the death of his two older children, one from starvation and the other from the brutal hands of the Khmer Rouge. He prefers not to talk about his two deceased children or the atrocities and persecution he and his family have suffered.

Life in the United States is perplexing to Y Nie Eban. The smells; the language; the sounds; the customs; the big, rich American people; and, the many automobiles are strange to him. He has come to accept and understand that Americans are always in "the big rush," as he puts it, but he wonders why it is necessary for Americans to move so very fast in all of their pursuits.

Y Nie Eban is struggling to keep his family self-sufficient. Although he was a chief administrator in his own country, his past experience and degrees are of no use in America. He is only beginning to really understand or speak English as a second language. He finds it hard to concentrate on learning English after working as many as ten or eleven hours a day.

After working long hours and trying hard to understand his American co-workers, some of whom resent him and harbor deep prejudice, Y Nie Eban arrives home to his family. He knows his wife is lonely and longs for her family and friends, whom they both know she will never see again. Y Nie Eban tries to be cheerful upon his arrival, but it is very hard for him. He thinks to himself that the suffering in this life is sometimes too hard to bear, but he knows he must be strong for his family. Late in the evening, when the children are asleep, he and H'Bel soothe the aches of their homesickness by softly talking about the days before the Communists, the days when their lives were not so full of pain and sorrow, the days when they had a country to call their own.

Each and every day here in this strange land of America, Y Nie Eban prays for strength and patience to deal with the many frustrations that he and his family experience. Other refugees who have lived in this new land remind him that with time his life will become easier. He can only hope this is true. For now, the disturbing dreams of the brutality and hardships his family endured are haunting, and this new culture of America is overwhelming.

THE SOUTHEAST ASIAN REFUGEE POPULATION

The Southeast Asian or Indochinese refugee population is comprised of three nationalities: the Vietnamese, Laotians, and Cambodians. The population also includes Vietnamese of Chinese ethnicity, tribal groups from the central highlands of South Vietnam, and various tribal groups from the mountains of Laos. Since the fall of Saigon in 1975 over 800,000 of these refugees have arrived in the United States (U.S. Immigration and Naturalization Service, 1990). These refugees all share one main characteristic. They have fled their country to escape persecution. They have among them tremendous diversity in background and education. The Vietnamese are by far the most educated, averaging nearly ten years of formal education, while the Hmong and Khmer of rural Laos and Cambodia have an extremely low educational level, averaging only 1.5 to 5 years of schooling (McLeod, 1986).

Within each nationality are vast differences in background. Among the Vietnamese, particularly those arriving immediately after the evacuation of Saigon, were academicians, bureaucratic workers, and governmental officials as well as merchants, laborers, and maids. The Vietnamese arriving after the "first wave" (termed "boat people" because of their method of escape) tended to be less educated and, consequently, less affluent than the first group. The Cambodians or Khmer came primarily from rural backgrounds influenced by the past purging of academics under Pol Pot. Khmer children were virtually unexposed to formal schooling after 1975. The Hmong people of Loas perhaps have had the most difficult time adjusting to their new culture as they come from an agrarian culture where no written language existed until 30 years ago (Doerner, 1985).

The most recent refugee group to come to the United States is the Montagnards, or "mountain people," which represent tribal groups from the central highlands of Vietnam. This ethnically distinct group of Indochinese refugees are diverse in formal education within their own group. They are Christian, both Catholic and Protestant, unlike other Indochinese refugee populations that are predominantly Buddhist or Confucian. Since 1975 they have spent their years hiding in remote jungle areas of Southeast Asia.

The Indochinese refugees have all lived through extensive and brutal civil wars and have endured incredible suffering both in their country and during their escape. They have lived under oppressive governments. Almost all Indochinese refugees have experienced the death of one or more family members, and many have witnessed these deaths. The mass killings and forced relocations of the Pol Pot regime have caused 80% of Khmer refugees to be completely cut off from family members, while this percentage is 30% for the Hmong, 21% for the Chinese, and 5% for the Vietnamese (McLeod, 1986).

Indochinese refugees have lost their country, their occupational status, and their family and friends. Many have lived through the horror of forced labor camps. Upon arrival in the United States, the refugee must learn a new language and culture, find employment, and learn to attend to totally new daily tasks of living in America: paying rent, buying groceries, opening a checking account. A great tribute is due these refugees because despite the many stresses and frustrations, they are coping and succeeding in America.

PROBLEMS CONFRONTING INDOCHINESE REFUGEE

Stereotypes

MYTH #1: The "Super Achiever" Myth. The media have recently given a great deal of publicity to the super achievements of Asian American immigrants. This has given rise to false perceptions of and expectations for Southeast Asian refugees. Among Indochinese refugees with their distinct nationalities of Vietnamese, Cambodians, and Laotians are great ethnic diversity. Racial and physical characteristics are not frequently recognized by other Asian immigrant groups and the majority of Americans. In reality, Indochinese are less affluent and educated than similar Asian groups, such as the Japanese or Koreans, with whom they are confused.

Contrary to common perceptions that Asian students are over-achievers in school, professional high school counselors have noted that the majority of Indochinese are not college material. Hmong and Khmer students are particularly ill-prepared for academic success because of extensive warfare and unfortunate economic conditions in their homeland. One high school counselor commented that to keep these students for a few semesters and teach them the rudiments of language and cultural skills before they drop out is a major accomplishment.

An undeniable fact is that some Indochinese do excel academically. These students generally tend to be from educated families in their native country. Because of their success they are the focus of media attention. Consequently, they innocently perpetuate the myth of super achievement. The fact remains, however, that most Indochinese refugee students arrive at their American schools with no language skills and must go through language training such as "English as a Second Language" (ESL) courses. The brighter few who move out of ESL classes into remedial courses tend to possess better study skills than the American children in these remedial classes. Because of their language deficiency, they do not move to regular classes but do make high marks where they are, thus perpetuating the super achiever myth.

For those students unexposed to academics in their native country and those unable to live up to the super achiever myth, they often have guilt and intense family pressure. Indochinese refugee students often report that they are "shaming" their ethnic group. They try to live up to their teachers' and peers' expectations (both ethnic and American) to do well.

The Buddhist/Confucian cultural values of hard work and education are extremely important in Indochinese families. Often, well-meaning refugee parents equate poor grades with laziness, and refugee students are compared to superior Indochinese peers. At a time when refugee children are in great need of support because of "loss of face," these students remove themselves from their two most valuable assets, their ethnic peer group and family. The result is withdrawal for these Indochinese refugee students who are already conditioned by their culture to be obedient and quiet.

MYTH #2: The Indochinese as a whole are less likely to seek professional mental health counseling and are therefore adjusting well. While true Indochinese refugees are less likely to seek professional counseling than their American counterparts, they are far from being problem-free. The first obstacle in obtaining professional help is often financial. Although mental health centers have available free services, few refugees are aware of these services or can afford a private professional counselor.

The reluctance to enlist professional help is also rooted in their culture. All refugees suffered material and family losses during the war and in transit. However, being unfamiliar with the treatment of psychological problems, refugees choose not to receive help. Furthermore, the Asian culture attributes sorrow and grief to the "natural" course of one's life and does not label such mental states as "sickness" or mental distress.

The family is the basic social unit in Asian culture and individual family members rely on one another for support in times of distress. However, they are faced with a dilemma. In a culture that discourages outward expressions of emotion, family members are found needing support but being unable or unwilling to ask for it. In these cases the ethnic community is helpful if someone is present in whom they can confide. However, the ethnic community in general discourages individuals from seeking professional treatment for fear that once they are discovered, "the individual may cause the family to lose face." Many refugees with whom the authors have worked reported that they either tried to internalize their stresses or rationalize their grief rather than risk losing face for themselves and their families.

Prejudice

One major problem Indochinese refugees face in this country is pure and simple discrimination. Many Americans ignorant of the plight of these refugees believe they should not be in our country, and they are lazy, living on welfare. They also are often perceived as stupid because of their inability to speak English. Most Indochinese refugees in America have proven themselves to be fiercely independent, self-reliant, and hard-working individuals of normal intelligence. Negative stereotypes concerning Indochinese refugees stem from ignorance and xenophobia, conditions which may be remedied in part through education.

PERSONAL AND CAREER GUIDANCE COUNSELING NEEDS OF INDOCHINESE REFUGEES

Indochinese refugees in this country have experienced the horrors of war, near starvation, displacement, and untold other miseries. They, among other ethnic minorities, have special problems that schools and society need to recognize. First, sex roles are vastly different in America and Southeast Asia. This is a cause of family discord during adjustment to American life; Indochinese men are often disturbed that they are no longer the ultimate decision maker in the family. In the book, *From Vietnam* to America, Kelly (1977, p.119) reported that some Vietnamese men thought that "women in the United States have too much power." One counselor has noted that the greater the discrepancy between social standings in the old and new countries, the greater the stress for men. For many Indochinese men, the new culture is a great test of their resourcefulness, tolerance, and courage. Prestigious employment that took years to attain in their own country has vanished from their lives. Many refugee men weather the difficulties of supporting their families here in America by performing jobs for which they are vastly over-qualified.

Economic necessity often requires Indochinese women to work. In one family, after the wife began to work she became more outgoing and questioned her husband's household supremacy. Her husband resorted to sabotaging the family's second car to prevent his wife from working. The man was caught in a delicate dilemma. He must consider the economic necessity of having a two-income family simultaneously facing the possibility of losing rigid control over his wife. He is literally judged by his ethnic peers on his ability to exert control over his family, a large component of his "face" in the community. He must court voluntary agencies or sponsors by showing his cooperation while at the same time often resenting them for introducing "destructive" values in his family. Many men resolve this conflict by condemning the new culture, pointing especially to the high divorce rate. They then tighten the rein over their own family, justifying their increased control as merely trying to preserve the traditional values.

During the early adjustment period, Indochinese refugee children rapidly absorb their new culture through school, television, and American peers. The teenage sub-culture the children model challenges the dominance of Indochinese parents and contributes to stress within the family unit. Indochinese parents are especially distressed by their youngsters' rapid absorption of their new culture and their own inability to make meaningful and authoritative suggestions to guide them. A senior high school counselor of Indochinese adolescents spoke of a "power shift" within the family unit with the youngster gaining control due to a quicker command of the new language and culture. Parents have difficulty retaining control when they must interact with the world through the language skills of their children. The counselor suggested that such a situation be remedied by supplying the parents with skill and information to promote greater sharing of influence within the family unit.

Older generations, wanting to retain their familiar values, are especially frustrated by their children's adoption of new American values. Children with a quicker command of English and the culture begin to see the "imperfections" of their parents and elders and actively question their traditional supremacy in the family. The parents react by tightening the grips. For example, in many Vietnamese and Laotian families, an unspoken rule forbids English in the home. Parents struggling for day-to-day survival become more and more detached from the younger generations who desperately attempt to fit in with their American peers in fashion, behaviors, and values.

The result of this intergenerational cultural dilemma is an unspoken duality. Adolescents realize that in order to acculturate they must learn assertiveness and behaviors that are discouraged by their parents. They also know that they must learn and practice these values and behaviors outside of the family. Within their families, these adolescents go along with the status quo by not allowing their new values and behavior to show at home. Many successfully adjusted Indochinese families report a reconciliation over time between the two generations, with the younger generation retaining important aspects of their cultural heritage and the elders gradually accepting some aspects of the youths' assimilation into American society.

Another problem among Indochinese refugees is that of tremendous grief for families that were left behind. Many Indochinese feel guilt for "abandoning" family members and frustrations for not being able to help them. Refugees here in America often feel the need to help family members left behind by sending home money and gifts they can ill afford. One Vietnamese high school student recently dropped out of school because he felt he needed to work more to send money home to his family.

The double burden of supporting a family in America while sending money home causes extreme frustration for the refugee and a feeling of failure in comparison to those peers whose families are intact. This causes some refugees to feel bitter, withdrawn, and removed from their peers.

The intense feeling of guilt for abandoning family members often has profound deleterious effects on adjustment to American life. One Khmer girl became extremely withdrawn from her adjusting Indochinese peers. She refused to speak English while conversing with them and looked upon her slowly Americanizing friends with disgust. She reported that she felt her adjusting friends were betraying their heritages and had no right to enjoy themselves in this country while people such as her own family were suffering at home. For many of these refugees the intense sadness over their losses, compounded by feelings of guilt, leaves them embittered, unhappy, and less able to adapt to life in their new country.

Another case example is a Laotian family that arrived in the United States without their father. The eldest son, S., was an honor student in high school and excelled at a local community college. Financial support for the family was provided by a younger sister who worked to support S, his invalid mother, and younger sister. The stress and guilt S. felt finally became overwhelming and he dropped out of school. He now works at a toy factory to support the family. S. expressed bitterness and blamed himself for "failing" when he had less than three semesters left to complete his engineering degree.

Career Needs

Indochinese students are often at a distinct disadvantage because of the stereotypes held by school personnel. Counselors and teachers often assume these students will enjoy and excel in the physical sciences and mathematics. Because of their stereotypical perceptions, they often fail to expose these students to areas and career possibilities the Indochinese are reluctant to explore.

Indochinese students often try harder at math and physical sciences because these fields allow the student to operate at a high level with little command of the English language. Additionally, many Indochinese students believe to "follow the footsteps" of their elders, who often succeeded in math and physical science-related careers, is a necessity. Furthermore, Indochinese students were victims of unjust political and social systems during the war. Consequently, they are often cynical towards the social sciences and feel a certain degree of safety in the pure pursuit of scientific truth.

In assessing and assisting Indochinese students with their career needs, the single most important task is to encourage, guide, and teach Indochinese students how to become more assertive. Assertiveness is not encouraged or admired in the Asian and Indochinese cultures. While one may be successful in a technical career without having to assert oneself, the humanities require greater language fluency, confidence and, therefore, a greater degree of assertiveness. Assimilation, acculturation, and time remove some of the cultural barriers and give the student more confidence. Counseling and a concerted effort to expose Indochinese students to a wider variety of career choices may be needed to promote greater economic, political, and social influence among the Indochinese peoples.

COUNSELING SERVICES
FOR INDOCHINESE REFUGEES

Indochinese refugees in this country have a need for counseling services that are germane to the experiences they have suffered. Research has pointed to the fact that for a variety of reasons only a small percentage of Indochinese refugees use mental health services. Higgibotham (1980) suggested refugees do not have access to information about types of mental health services that are available or an understanding of the types of problems mental health services are meant to address. Cultural minorities in large part do not know mental health services exist nor are they referred to mental health facilities (Padilla, Ruiz, & Alvarez, 1975). In addition, Indochinese do not perceive mental health to be separate from physical health and therefore seek mental health assistance from medical practitioners.

One primary reason for non-utilization of mental health services is the notion in Indochinese culture that mental illness is a cause for ridicule for both the refugee and the family. The strong Asian concept of "face" within the ethnic community discourages many refugees from seeking help for their emotional problems. Additionally, talking to a stranger about private problems is not within the realm of experience of the refugee. Indeed, talking about feelings is simply not a Southeast Asian behavior. Tung (1985) related that although depression, regret, guilt, and shame weigh heavily on the Southeast Asian's mind and life, they are perceived as essentially private concerns.

Wong (1985, p. 348) found that "mental health services and support to Southeast Asian refugees have consisted of a hodgepodge of intervention attempts." The federal government funded projects in the early 1980s for mental health for Southeast Asian refugees, and in some areas of the country major projects such as the Bay Area Indochinese Mental Health Project trained mental health providers specifically to work with the special needs of Southeast Asian refugees.

Overall, however, only a paucity of trained professionals is available to help refugees with their unique problems. Robinson (1980) aptly stated that community mental health centers are inadequate in serving Indochinese refugees. Their staffs do not possess enough expertise in their particular concerns and culture and are not bilingual. Local voluntary agencies that provide translation services to refugees are generally overworked and understaffed and do not have the necessary time to translate for refugees' mental health problems. The voluntary agencies involved in refugee resettlement have precious little time to attend to finding housing, securing employment, obtaining clothing, arranging to medical appointments. The many related concerns of helping non-English speaking families begin life in a new country with no money and no resources push mental health services to the back burner.

Mutual Assistance Associations (MAAs) present in many Indochinese ethnic communities, are particularly helpful to the newly arriving refugee. These ethnic community groups help the refugee obtain necessary information concerning all aspects of life in America. Most importantly, the MAAs give a feeling of strength and support in absorbing the shock of being in a new country. Many leaders in these ethnic communities are the primary mental health providers for the refugee. Wong (1985) emphasized that these leaders are refugees themselves and are often dealing with concerns they themselves have recently experienced in the trauma of relocation and resettlement. These helpers are still struggling themselves and may have unresolved grief and conflict, an important fact to remember if, indeed, ethnic leaders are to be trained mental health providers.

For the resettled Southeast Asian refugee, appropriate and culture-sensitive counseling services are sadly lacking in America. Although some areas of the country have excellent programs and experts in refugee mental health, this is not true in the areas where the largest numbers of resettled Indochinese are located. Federal and state officials should be made aware of the needs of these newest members of our society.

THE HELPING PROFESSIONAL'S ROLE

The helping professional working with the Indochinese refugee must have an in-depth cultural sensitivity not only to characteristics of Southeast Asians, but also to the refugee status itself. Therapy will be irrelevant and possibly detrimental if these considerations are not taken into account.

Preferably, well-trained Indochinese mental health professionals and paraprofessionals should assist the refugee. However, as they are rarely available, American counselors assisting Indochinese refugees should be sensitive not only to the culture and to refugee status, but to many discrepancies between Eastern and Western thought. The cross-cultural counselor should be open and willing to look at emotional problems in a holistic fashion and possibly employ traditional Asian cultural means of helping the client. Often difficulties with Khmer refugees can best be dealt with through a Buddhist monk or through prescribed ritualistic actions. Duncan and Kang (1984) found simple Khmer ceremonies were helpful with unaccompanied refugee Khmer minors coming to this country; disturbing dreams and visits by hostile spirits were alleviated. Helman (1984) noted that in societies where ill health and other forms of misfortune were blamed on social causes (witchcraft, sorcery, or evil eye), or on supernatural causes (gods, spirits, or ancestral ghosts), sacred folk healers were particularly helpful. Westermeyer and Wintrob (1979) stated that mental disorder among Laotians was largely concerned with behavior viewed as desirable or undesirable in Laotian society. Williams and Westermeyer (1983) described an incident whereby a Southeast Asian refugee woman attempted suicide because her daughter had been disrespectful in allowing a Hmong boy to carry her books home from school.

The culturally-trained therapist working with Indochinese refugees should, if at all possible, try to use culturally relevant techniques and/or employ Buddhist monks, respected leaders in the ethnic community, elders, and those in the Indochinese community who may be able to ascertain if the presenting problem can be dealt with through traditional methods. If working with an ethnic healer or elder is impossible, the counselor working with the Indochinese refugee has many important considerations to bear in mind. Research indicates that therapeutic interventions with Indochinese refugees should focus on the present and the immediate future rather than on the past. Kinzie, Fredrickson, Ben, Fleck, and Karls (1984) found discussing past events with the refugee left them feeling worse, not better. Similarly, Boehnhein, Kinzie, Rath, and Fleck (1985) found among survivors of Cambodian concentration camps that detailed inquiry often intensified symptoms. They concluded that therapy should support avoidance of past events and encourage coping with current problems.

The Indochinese refugee is uncomfortable talking about feelings, particularly to a stranger. Our American concept of counseling and mental health is unheard of to the refugee. Aside from concentrating on the present, an important aspect, then, is for the counselor to be goal-directed and concrete in his or her counseling interventions. In addition, since problems or crises are often the result of inadequate knowledge of our culture, frequently all that is needed is to teach the refugee what is "proper" or "improper" behavior in our culture.

To summarize, in working with Indochinese refugee clients, the following suggestions are offered to American counselors:

1. Be thoroughly knowledgeable about the Indochinese refugee population. Know their culture, history, and current circumstances. This understanding will be your greatest asset as a counselor.

2. Concentrate on the present and future with the client. Avoid questions about their past.

3. Work toward a goal with the client. This fits into the Indochinese model of patient/counselor. Muecke (1983), Tung (1985), and Kinzie (1981) all pointed to the fact that use of medicine suggests to the Indochinese refugee patient something is being done. Similarly, working toward a goal gives the Indochinese client the feeling that the counselor is in control, as the client prefers.

4. Use ethnic leaders, monks, elders, or folk healers and employ traditional healing techniques with counseling interventions. Often a simple ritualistic ceremony may alleviate the suffering of visits from spirits and demons that are not within our own cultural realm of understanding.

5. Keep in mind that a problem or symptom may be the simple result of anxiety due to a misunderstanding or inadequate knowledge of the Indochinese refugee about our society/culture. Teach or model American behaviors to the refugee.

CONCLUDING REMARKS

Working as an American counselor with Indochinese refugees resettled in America is a challenging undertaking. Differences in culture, perspective, and the counseling process itself are all remarkable desperate. Although vast differences exist between cultures, the cross-cultural counselor is reminded of the words of Harry Stack Sullivan, "We are all more alike than different." Being sensitive to the Indochinese refugees' overwhelming concerns while at the same time acknowledging their incredible strength and endurance is one way the counselor can encourage and support the refugee. Above all, a sincere belief that the refugee can build a new and fulfilling life in this country is the key to a positive counseling encounter with the newest members of our society.

EXPERIENTIAL ACTIVITIES

Individual Activities

Imagine that you are a member of an ethnic group that has been involved in several wars with a neighboring ethnic group. These wars have spanned many centuries. Yet, in America, many people repeatedly refer to you as a member of the other culture. When you correct their error you hear the reply, "Oh, whatever ..., " which completely discounts every facet of your culture as being significantly different from that of your traditional enemy. Write a one or two paragraph reaction to the above incident.

Small Group Activity

Break into pairs. Write down three sentences that represent part of a typical conversation that might occur during the course of a day, such as explaining a pain to a health care professional, asking directions to a location when you do not know the address, or attempting to explain a problem to a landlord. After writing down your three sentences, go back and cross out three of every six words. Now, by reading your abbreviated sentence to the other person, attempt to be understood. Use hand signals, draw in the air, and exchange looks until you get your point across, then change roles and repeat with a different sentence.

Outside Class Activity

Go to an "oriental grocery store" (or to any grocery store catering to an ethnic group with which you have no familiarity) and without help, select the ingredients for a meal. Prepare the meal without using a cookbook (or use a cookbook in a language you do not understand). Go ahead...enjoy the meal.

REFERENCES

Boehnhein, J.D., Kinzie, S.D., Rath, B.E, & Fleck, J. (1985). One year follow-up study of post-traumatic stress disorder among survivors of Cambodian concentration camps. *American Journal of Psychiatry. 141*, 645-650.

Doerner, W. (1985, July 8). "To America with skills: A wave of arrivals from the Far East enriches the country's talent pool." *Time.* pp. 84-85.

Duncan J., & Kang, J. (1984). Use of traditional Cambodian culture as a mental health program to help children cope with separation and loss. Paper presented at the Unaccompanied Minors Conference, Washington, DC.

Helman, C. (1984). *Culture, health and illness.* Bristol: Wright Publishing.

Higgibotham, H.N. (1980). Culture and the role of client expectancy in psychotherapy in Hammet and Brislin (Eds.), *Research in Culture and Learning: Language and Conceptual Studies.* Honolulu: East-West Center.

Kelly, G. (1977). *From Vietnam to America: A chronicle of the Vietnamese immigration to the U.S. Boulder, CO:* Westview Press.

Kinzie, J.D. (1981). Evaluation and psychotherapy of Indochinese refugee patients. *American Journal of Psychotherapy. 35*, 251-261.

Kinzie, J.D., Fredrickson, R.H., Ben, R., Fleck, J., & Karls, W. (1984). Post-traumatic stress disorder among survivors of Cambodian concentration camps. *American Journal of Psychiatry. 141,* 645-650.

McLeod, B. (1986, July). The oriental express: Asian-American immigrants are seen as a "model" minority on a fast track to success. Their own view is less idyllic. *Psychology Today.* 48-52.

Muecke, M.A. (1983). Caring for Southeast Asian refugee patients in the U.S.A. *American Journal of Public Health. 73,* 431-438.

Padilla, A. M., Ruiz, R. A., & Alvarez, R. (1975). Community mental health services for the Spanish-speaking/surnamed population. *American Psychologist. 30,* 892-905.

Robinson, C. (1980). Special report: Physical and emotional health care needs of Indochinese refugees. Washington, DC: Indochina Resource Action Center.

Tung, T.M. (1985). Psychiatric care for Southeast Asians: How different is different. In T.C. Owan (Ed.), *Southeast Asian mental health: Treatment, prevention, services, training and research.* National Institute of Mental Health.

U.S. Immigration and Naturalization Service. (1990). Statistical Yearbook. Washington, D.C.

Westermeyer, J., & Wintrob, R. (1979). "Folk" explanations of mental illness in rural Laos. *American Journal of Psychiatry. 136,* 901-905.

Williams, C.L., & Westermeyer, J. (1983). Psychiatric problems among adolescent Southeast Asian refugees: A descriptive study. *The Journal of Nervous and Mental Disease. 171,* 79-84.

Wong, H.Z. (1985). Training for mental health service providers to Southeast Asian refugees: Models, strategies, and curricula. In T.C. Owan (Ed.), *Southeast Asian mental health: Treatment, prevention, services, training and research.* National Institute of Mental Health.

Chapter 13

CUBAN-AMERICANS

Gerardo M. Gonzalez, Ph.D.

Gerardo M. Gonzalez is Associate Dean of the College of Education, University of Florida. Formerly he was Professor and Chairman of Counselor Education at the university. He is also the founder and past-president of BACCHUS of the U.S., Inc., a national college and community organization for the prevention of alcohol abuse. From 1977 to 1986, he served as director of the Campus Alcohol and Drug Resource Center and Assistant Dean for Student Services at the same university.

An authority on alcohol and drug abuse prevention, Dr. Gonzalez frequently conducts formal presentations on such topics as "Models for Alcohol and Drug Abuse Prevention" and "Substance Abuse Education Programs." His work has been described in numerous scholarly publications including The Journal of Alcohol and Drug Education, The Journal of Student Personnel, and the International Journal of the Addictions.

Active in multicultural counseling and education issues, Dr. Gonzalez is a founding member of the Latino Interest Group of the Association for Multicultural Counseling and Development. He has addressed national and international groups and published scholarly works on the Cuban-American experience and Hispanic concerns.

Born on September 24, 1950, in Las Villas, Cuba, Dr. Gonzalez immigrated to the United States with his family in February, 1962, and was later naturalized as an American Citizen. A graduate of the University of Florida, Dr. Gonzalez received his B.A. degree in psychology in 1973 and his Ph.D. in Counselor Education from the same university in 1978.

AWARENESS INDEX

Directions: Mark your choice of the best response to the following items. Check your responses with the scoring guide provided following the 12 items.

1. The first major exodus of Cubans to the United States occurred during

   a. the Cuban wars of independence.
   b. World War II.
   c. the Castro revolution.

2. In comparison with other Hispanic populations, as well as with the total U.S. population, Cubans are

   a. the wealthiest group.
   b. the most chauvinistic group.
   c. the oldest group.
   d. the youngest group.

3. Cuban women in the United States exhibit a high rate of

   a. fertility.
   b. labor force participation.
   c. anemia.

4. The majority of Cubans who arrived in the United States after the Castro revolution were professionals, landowners, and businessmen in Cuba.

    a. True
    b. False

5. The characteristics of Cubans who arrived in the United States during the 1980 port of Mariel boatlift were significantly different from earlier arrivals.

    a. True
    b. False

6. The majority of Cubans who arrived in the United States after the Castro revolution

    a. plan to go back as soon as possible.
    b. left because of economic conditions on the island.
    c. would like to go back for a visit.
    d. plan to acquire U.S. Citizenship.

7. An experience common to all Cubans who immigrated to the United States is

    a. the process of acculturation.
    b. discrimination.
    c. having to learn English.

8. The acculturation gap hypothesis refers to

    a. the distance between Cuba and the U.S.

    b. the difference in perceptions between Cubans and Americans.

    c. the different rates at which older and younger immigrants adapt to a new culture.

9. Family disruption among Cuban-Americans is often the result of

    a. Cuban girls wanting to go out without a chaperon.

    b. differential rates of acculturation within the family.

    c. having to live in small houses.

    d. inability to speak English.

10. One of the major problems confronting Cuban immigrants arriving in the United States is

   a. lack of family to provide support.

   b. discrimination from the Anglo community.

   c. lack of knowledge of the English language.

   d. not having a social security number.

11. Older Cuban Americans often experience the results of a cultural tradition of

   a. respect within the family.

   b. self-diagnosis and self-prescription for various ailments.

   c. never accepting assistance from government agencies.

   d. never discussing their problems with others.

12. Cuban American women often perceive the American way of life as

   a. extremely stressful.

   b. too permissive.

   c. free from traditional roles.

   d. none of the above.

Scoring Guide for Awareness Index

1. a, 2. c, 3. b, 4. b, 5. b, 6. d, 7. a, 8. c, 9. b, 10. c, 11. b, 12. a

INTRODUCTION

Many people in the United States have a vaguely defined, often erroneous, stereotypic perception of the Cuban-American community. Cubans are a heterogeneous people. Because of its European, African, and Indian roots, traditional Cuban culture was described by Diaz (1981) as *ajiaco* (a typical stew of vegetables, roots, and meat). This stew has been further complicated by the pervasive influence of American institutions, language, and culture upon Cuban-American life. As Cubans here struggle to retain some of their mores, values, language, and traditions, Cuban culture in the United States displays elements of Cuban traditional culture that may be disappearing in Cuba itself.

In order to assist and work effectively with Cubans in the United States, this unique culture and its traditions must be understood. In this section a description of the population characteristics, the cultural adjustment problems of immigrants, and special acculturation experiences of Cuban families will be discussed. The hope is that a greater understanding of the need for culturally sensitive social and interpersonal interactions with this diverse, dynamic, and growing ethnic group will emerge among readers.

POPULATION CHARACTERISTICS

Cuban migrations to the United States predate this century. By the late 1800s about 100,000 Cubans were concentrated mainly in New York City, Tampa, Key West, and other Florida cities. Fleeing the Cuban wars of independence (1868 to 1895), this first massive wave of immigrants established the tobacco industry in South Florida and largely remained there to become the first large enclave of Cuban-Americans (Diaz, 1981). However, the majority of Cubans residing in the United States today arrived in six stages of migration between 1959 and 1980, following the Cuban revolution.

Between 1959 and 1980 some 600,000 Cubans immigrated to the United States (Perez, 1985). Another 160,000 arrived between 1981 and 1990 (U.S. Census Bureau, 1992). According to the 1990 Census of the Population, a total of 1,044,000 persons were identified as Cuban-Americans based on the respondents who indicated that they were of Cuban origin or descent. Most of the Cuban population is urbanite with heavy concentrations in the South and South Atlantic States, most particularly Florida. Florida alone is home to 674,000 Cuban-Americans.

In comparison to other Hispanic populations, as well as to the total U.S. population, Cubans are the oldest group. Middle-aged and elderly persons are over-represented in the Cuban population, a totally atypical characteristic for a population that is largely composed of immigrants. The high proportion of elderly persons has led to the relatively widespread existence among Cuban-Americans of the three-generation family (Perez, 1985).

Of the 335,000 Cuban-American families in the country, 255,000 are comprised of married couples with or without children. In comparison with other Hispanic groups and the total U.S. population the Cuban-American population has the highest proportion of children under 18 living with both parents, a low number of single female heads of household (65,000), and the lowest incidence of mother-child subfamilies (i.e., mother and child residing within the larger family)(U.S. Census Bureau, 1992). In addition, Cuban-Americans are the most affluent of all Hispanic groups with a median income of $31,439. Forty-six thousand families (178,000 persons) fall below the poverty line, less than 14%, while nearly 60% have incomes above $25,000 per annum.

CULTURAL ADJUSTMENT PROCESSES

The majority of Cubans in this country arrived in various stages of migration beginning in 1959 after the Castro revolution. Starting with the professionals, landowners, and businessmen of the early 1960s, successive waves of the migrant flow have brought to the U.S. a virtual cross-section of Cuban society (Bach, Bach, & Triplete, 1981-1982). The largest migration occurred from 1965 to 1973 when more than one-quarter million Cubans were airlifted into the United States. The airlift group was larger than the group of Cuban immigrants who came to the United States between 1959 and 1965 (Azicri, 1981-1982). The airlift brought about a change in the characteristics of the Cuban-American population. While approximately one-third of the early Cuban refugees were professionals and managers, the rate was reduced by one-half in the early '70s and has not shown significant changes during the past decade. However, the image of a Cuban exodus made up of professionals, businessmen, and middle-class families prevailed until 125,000 Cubans migrated to Key West from the port of Mariel near Havana in the summer of 1980. In May 1980 alone, more Cuban refugees arrived in the United States than in all of 1962, the previous record year for Cuban immigration.

If one characteristic distinguishes the Mariel "Freedom Flotilla" —the latest influx of Cuban immigrants—from all preceding waves, it is the frustrating ambivalence with which the new exiles were received in the United States. Part of this ambivalence may be attributed to the changed conditions in the United States which conflicted directly with the open admissions policy of historical precedent. Already besieged with high unemployment, inflation, and recession, many in the U.S. perceived this dramatic influx as yet another burden. This perception was not alleviated when the Cuban press claimed the island was ridding itself of "social undesirables." However, an examination of the first 62,000 Mariel arrivals processed in and released directly to the Miami community did not warrant the various pejorative labels "socially undesirable," "scum," and "deviant" used by the Cuban government to describe this group of immigrants. In fact, Bach et al. (1981-1982) reported a bias toward underestimating the proportion of family groups, women, and persons with relatives already in the United States who were resettled relatively quickly. Moreover, the Mariel entrants appeared to be no different than previous Cuban refugees, especially when compared to those who arrived during the airlift period of 1965 to 1973. This contention was supported by Fernandez (1981-1982) who demonstrated that the major differences were in race and age. A larger number of the Mariel entrants (approximately 14%) were mulattoes and Blacks and were approximately ten years younger than previous refugees.

Insight into the adjustment problems of these refugees was provided by Portes, Clark, and Lopez (1981-1982) who studied a sample of 514 adult Cubans who arrived in the United States from the port of Mariel in 1980 and were interviewed in late fall 1983 and spring 1984. A comparison was made between this group and an earlier cohort of Cuban refugees who were followed during the 1970s (Portes et al., 1981-1982). The overwhelming proportion of the 1980 arrivals gave political reasons, such as escape from communism and lack of personal freedom, as their main cause for departure. These reasons were almost identical to those found among Cuban refugees arriving in the 1970s.

As reported by Portes, Clark, and Manning (1985), the modal major problems confronted since arrival by 1980 male refugees were unemployment, the inability to speak English, and other economic difficulties among males and among females. In both cases, the distribution of reported difficulties was similar to that among Cuban refugees who arrived ten years earlier. In 1983 as in 1973, language and economic difficulties were by far the principal problem encountered. Interestingly, one-fifth to one-fourth of respondents indicated that they had faced no major obstacles upon arrival.

One major difference between the 1980 and 1973 arrivals was the extent of family networks and family support experienced. The 1980 entrants had an average of only three relatives awaiting them in the United States. This number was only one-third of the corresponding figure among 1973 refugees. Moreover, the proportion reporting substantial aid from relatives during the first month in the United States was more than 10 points lower among 1980 entrants than among 1973 refugees. Close to one-half of the 1980 sample depended primarily on public agencies and private charities for their main sources of help.

The final set of questions in the Portes et al. (1985) study dealt with perceptions and attitudes. The overwhelming majority of the respondents from both the 1980 and the 1973 samples reported satisfaction with life in the United States despite the serious difficulties faced. Approximately one-fourth of both samples indicated discrimination in economic opportunities in the United States, and about 40% believed that the American way of life weakened the family. Despite these critical perceptions, over 70% of both samples indicated that they planned to acquire U.S. citizenship, a finding fitting the reported high levels of satisfaction.

ACCULTURATION PROBLEMS

Acculturation refers to the problem of adjustment—the borrowing, acquiring, and adopting of cultural traits from a host society by people immigrating from another society. Clinical experience with the Cuban immigrant community in Dade County, Florida, indicates that the acculturation process often results in family disruption (Szapocznik, Ladner, & Scopetta, 1979). Moreover, since youngsters acculturate more rapidly than their parents, this process often exacerbates intergenerational differences. As an outgrowth of family conflict resulting from different rates of acculturation, Szapocznik et al. (1979) found an increased tendency for Cuban youngsters to participate in social support networks influential in the choice of antisocial activities such as drug abuse and other delinquent behavior. While new groups of first-generation Cuban immigrants have continued to arrive in the United States since 1959, youth born in the U.S. are being brought up in the midst of two different and often conflicting cultures. The result has been a youthful Cuban-American population afflicted with a host of problems related to the process of maturation and acculturation.

Cuban parents often hold idealized values of the Cuban culture which emphasize moral and social conservatism and strong religious beliefs. However, their children have generally developed a greater affinity for American values and are thus faced with the demands of parents and other relatives on the one hand, and the expectations of their peer group on the other. These two forces often represent conflicting values and behavioral expectations resulting in high levels of dysfunction including juvenile delinquency, drug use, and school dropout problems, among Cuban adolescents. A concerted effort must be made to understand the special cultural pressures that impact on the

Cuban adolescent and to develop culturally sensitive strategies specifically designed to prevent and treat these dysfunctions.

The Older Cuban-American population, like other older Americans, is concerned with the problem of failing health, but they also are experiencing the diminishing traditional importance of their position in the family. As younger Cubans become more acculturated and socially mobile, the traditional function of the extended family as a source of support and acceptance for older Cubans is eroding. In addition, the rapidly growing numbers of older Cubans in America and the diminishing numbers of younger family members who are available for their care present a serious challenge to community agencies charged with the responsibility for services to this population.

SPECIAL NEEDS AND APPROACHES

The modern Cuban-American community is a community in evolution. Throughout 30 years of successive migration waves into the United States, Cubans have become a pluralistic group. The continuing arrival of the Cuban immigrants has broadened the need for counseling, employment services, training, and education that are culturally sensitive to the needs of this population. The following sections present some of the special needs of Cuban-Americans in each of these areas and provide examples of approaches which have been found effective in dealing with some of these problems.

Counseling and Family Interventions

Understanding the concept of acculturation is crucial to counseling with Hispanics generally and Cuban-Americans specifically (Ponterotto, 1987; Szapocznik, Scopetta, Kurtines, & Arnalde, 1978). Differential levels of acculturation among migrant families as a group have led to more than the usual levels of intra-familial conflict and stress. In a study of acculturative differences in self and family role perception among Cuban-American college students, Kurtines and Miranda (1980) suggested that when counseling migrants, treatment type and modality should be adjusted to deal with disruptive acculturative differences when they occur within families. In such cases, family therapy provides a useful adjunct to individual therapy, and role-playing techniques serve as a tool for reducing intra-familial role conflict.

Perhaps the most extensive work with regard to the effects of acculturation on the Cuban family has been done by Szapocznik and his associates at the Spanish Family Guidance Center in Miami, Florida. Two innovative, culturally sensitive counseling approaches developed and tested there are Bicultural Effectiveness Training (BET) (Szapocznik, Santisteban, Kurtines, Perez-Vidal, & Hervis, 1986) and One-Person Family Therapy (Szapocznik, Kurtines, Foote, Perez-Vidal, & Hervis, 1983). BET is based on a model of adjustment which says that individuals living in bicultural contexts tend to become maladjusted when they remain or become monocultural. In this model, Cubans who fail to learn how to, or do not want to interact within the Anglo American context tend to under-acculturate and experience related adjustment problems. On the other hand, individuals who reject the skills necessary to interact within the Hispanic American context tend to over-acculturate and lack the flexibility necessary to cope with their entire cultural milieu.

The One-Person Family Treatment approach addresses the possibility of achieving the goals of family therapy (i.e., structural family change and symptom reduction) by working primarily with one person. This approach is based on the notion underlying family therapy which says that changing a part of the system almost inevitably brings about changes in the whole system. In a study of the relative effectiveness of Conjoint Family Therapy (CFT) versus One-Person Family Therapy (OPFT) for a Cuban-American population, Szapocznik et al. (1983) proposed a redefinition of family therapy as "a treatment modality in which the therapist's interventions target on changing family systems, regardless of who is present at a particular therapy session" (p. 890). The results of this comparative study showed that the OPFT treatment group attended significantly more sessions than the CFT group. Szapocznik et al. attributed this to the difficulty of retaining entire families in therapy. However, both modalities were effective in bringing about improvement in family functioning and symptom reduction in the individual participant (IP) at the time of termination. Follow-up analyses provided further evidence of the continued efficacy of both modalities on family functioning and slightly greater efficacy of the one-person modality in symptom reduction in the IP in several areas of functioning. The researchers concluded that OPFT would be preferred over CFT where there is particular difficulty in scheduling the whole family for therapy (as is often the case in working with Hispanic groups), when one family member requires a great deal of strengthening, or when family members are unwilling to participate in the therapy process. Their strongest suggestion, however, was to combine both modalities whenever possible.

One implication of these studies is that Structural Family Therapy can be effective with a Cuban population. Further, the researchers demonstrated that participation by the entire family is not always required for this form of therapy. This is an important finding because Hispanics generally, and Cuban-Americans in particular, tend to underutilize mental health services. To obtain full family participation is difficult even when some family members are willing to seek therapy. Moreover, since one of the outcomes of the acculturation gap within Cuban families is family stress and disruption, effective forms of family therapy can make an important contribution to the overall adjustment and assimilation of Cuban-Americans to the new culture.

Cubans are usually mobilized for treatment by the onset of a crisis and expect the therapist to provide immediate problem-oriented solutions to the crisis situation. In general, Cubans hold a present-time orientation and tend not to endorse humanistic values (Szapopznik, Scopetta, & Arnalde, 1978). Rather than being motivated to seek treatment by the search for personal and spiritual growth, they are more likely to be motivated to treatment by concrete and obtainable objectives. Because Structural Family Therapy focuses on behavioral treatment goals, this action-oriented approach is imminently suitable for the population.

Vocational Development and Interest Inventories

One of the most pressing problems that Cuban-Americans face in the United States is finding employment in areas where they have a particular skill or personal interest. The aspirations of newly arrived Cubans for new occupations in the United States were higher than past attainments in Cuba. However, these high aspirations compared quite negatively with subsequent attainments. Almost one-half of the sample studied by Portes and his colleagues (1981-1982) worked in the lower blue collar sector after several years in the United States. Little more than one-half the population employed in professional or managerial occupations in Cuba held similar positions in the U.S. Mean occupational prestige as measured by a socioeconomic index was 10 points below that at arrival, indicating significant downward mobility.

One of the major concerns for counselors who work with Cuban-American clients is the selection of appropriate interest inventories for measurement and assistance with career development goals. Very few studies have examined whether vocational development theories and interest inventories that have norms established primarily on White Anglo samples have relevance to Spanish-speaking individuals (Harrington & O'Shea, 1980). The Spanish translations of English tests are not always appropriate. Butcher and Garcia (1978) warned that even when adequate translation is achieved, the assumption can not be made that the same constructs are being measured in a different culture. Being cognizant of these problems, Harrington and O'Shea (1980) conducted a study designed to determine the construct validity of Holland's hexagonal model with Spanish-speaking subgroups and to establish the construct validity of the Spanish form of their own Career Decision Making (CDM) instrument.

The subjects for this study were 267 Spanish-speaking persons who resided in the United States and indicated their ethnic background as Mexican-American, Puerto Rican, Cuban, or South American. The intercorrelation matrix of the six CDM scales was compared with that of Holland's Vocational Preference Inventory. The results provided confirmation of the Holland hexagonal model in this diverse Spanish-speaking sample. According to the researchers, "This suggests that Spanish-speaking cultures have present work models whereby crafts, scientific, artistic, social, business enterprises, and business detail interest can develop" (Harrington & O'Shea, 1980, p.249). Study results also suggested that vocational interests of the Spanish-speaking can be validly measured through the Holland scales. Therefore, the CDM Spanish form provides counselors with a Holland-based tool to explore career choices with the Spanish-speaking client. Research is needed to see whether the CDM scales can be used to help Cuban immigrants explore various career choices and obtain proper training for their choice of work in the United States.

Bilingual Education and School Achievement

The majority of Cuban immigrants arriving in the United States indicate that the lack of knowledge of the English language is the principal problem confronting them (Portes, Clark, & Lopez, 1981-1982). English comprehension among Cuban exiles is surprisingly low even after several years of residence in the United States. Only 24% of Portes' sample were fluent in English, even when a liberal definition was adopted. This finding is not entirely surprising when one considers the existence of a large immigrant community where knowledge of the host country language is not imperative for economic survival. However, the lack of knowledge of the English language does present some rather serious problems for economic advancement and school achievement.

To what extent lack of knowledge of the English language is responsible for the excessive school dropout rates which prevail among Spanish-speaking students is impossible to say. Despite the Supreme Court 1974 decision (Lau v. Nichols) which indicated that without help, students who do not speak the school language are effectively foreclosed from any meaningful education, numbers of Hispanic students enrolled in bilingual education are still lacking.

Many different approaches to bilingual education have been developed, most of which can be divided into two broad categories: transitional and maintenance. Under the transitional approach the student's native language is used as a medium of instruction only until the student can function in an English language classroom. Students are expected to stay in these transitional programs for one to three years, until they can be "mainstreamed" into regular classrooms. Unfortunately, since the language most often spoken at home and outside the classroom is Spanish, many of these students never become sufficiently fluent in English to properly compete with their Anglo counterparts in the schools. The results are lower school achievement and increased dropout rates.

Greater sensitivity and special programs are needed to help Cuban-American students cope with the pressures of a home and peer environment that promotes adherence to the native culture and language, and a school environment that demands optimal performance in the English language. The same is true for workers out of school who wish to receive special training or instruction for career advancement. Both of these groups need special English instruction presented in a culturally sensitive way. To be most effective this instruction must be presented by appropriate role models who can clearly communicate an appreciation for the cultural pressures experienced by Cubans while at the same time making clear the practical benefits of fluency in the English language.

Life Enhancement Counseling
With Older Cuban-Americans

As noted earlier, Cubans in the United States are a population older than the mean. The need is growing for social services which are sensitive to two sets of characteristics unique to this population: (1) cultural background and (2) advanced age. The concept of matching services, particularly counseling modalities, to client characteristics has been well established in the mental health field. Recognition of the need for counseling approaches designed specifically for the elderly Cuban-American population led Szapocznik, Santisteban, Kurtines, Hervis, and Spencer (1982) to develop a life enhancement counseling model that makes therapeutic use of specific characteristics of elders, such as the tendency to reminisce, and employs an ecological approach to allow the therapist access to the elder's social environment. The overall goal of this form of therapy is to enhance the meaningfulness of life for elders. It conceptualizes many of the psychological difficulties and "disorders" of elders as potentially reversible rather than inevitable consequences of the aging process. The life enhancement counseling model was evaluated by Szapocznik, Santisteban, Hervis, and Spencer (1981) for its effect in the treatment of depression among Cuban-American elders and was found to be effective both when used alone or in combination with pharmacotherapy. However, clients who received both medication and life enhancement counseling tended to improve more than those who received either form of therapy alone.

Validation of the efficacy of life enhancement therapy as an effective treatment model has important implications for the treatment needs of this population. Cubans in general have a strong tradition of self-diagnosis and self-prescription. This tradition has been traced to the historical development of the pharmacist as a quasi-medical practitioner in Cuba (Page, 1982). What began as a one-stop form of caregiving by physicians who diagnosed, treated, and dispensed medicines in the same place, later gave rise to the expectation that pharmacists would do the same. In the Cuban-American community today the one-stop pharmacist-practitioner represents a convenient means for the self-diagnoser to obtain reassurance that the identified malady and chosen course of treatment are correct. Thus, the potential over-reliance on legal drugs, which are often obtained without a doctor's prescription, should be taken into account when counseling with older Cuban-Americans. Very early in the development of the counseling relationship the client should be encouraged to obtain a complete medical examination that includes an assessment of drugs being consumed. Based on the results of this examination, the counselor can then develop a treatment plan that may include physician supervised pharmacotherapy in conjunction with life enhancement therapy, or life enhancement therapy alone as an alternative to self medication.

Changing Roles of Cuban-American Women

The strong Cuban tradition of self-diagnosis and self prescription combines with the acculturation pressures of immigration to the United States has had an important effect on another major group of Cuban-Americans: women. The role of women in traditional pre-Castro Cuban society was that of housekeeper and mother (Boone, 1980). However, the need for economic survival upon arrival in the United States made it necessary for increasing numbers of Cuban women to join the labor force. Employment in the U.S. labor force, however, was tantamount to a loss of prestige because the role of nonworking housewife carried prestige in the upper social strata in Cuba (Gonzalez & Page, 1981). Furthermore, participation in the labor force often led to the double burden of employment and domestic responsibility for Cuban women. One outcome of this discrepancy between the traditional maternal role and the present day worker/housekeeper dual role has been a significant increase in stress related symptoms and prescription drug use.

In a sample of 100 Cuban women, Gonzalez and Page (1981) identified exile uncertainty and acculturation problems as the two most important sources of stress-related drug use among Cuban-American women in Miami. All of the respondents in this study agreed that Cuban women drastically increased their use of tranquilizers and sedatives after immigrating. Apparently the Cuban tradition of self-medication and the use of various herbs to calm the nerves in concert with psychoactive chemicals available from pharmacists, friends, and relatives in the Cuban-American community increased use of these substances. These authors offered the following before and after perspective on generalized acculturation stress from a 65 year-old woman:

> Before Castro, I had no reason to suffer from nerves, we lived a very tranquil life. We were a very united family, and we all got along together. All of the siblings, in-laws, everybody got along well. It was a normal life. I didn't need to eat my meals in a hurry to get to work on time. So, I suppose that if I had stayed in Cuba and if Fidel hadn't been in power I could have enjoyed a much calmer life. (Gonzales & Page, p. 49)

The increased stress and drug use related to the change in life-style among Cuban women in the United States is not limited to the older segment of the population. Page (1982) offered yet another example of the effects of acculturation stress in the following passage

Well, I will tell you, I never knew what a sedative [calmante] was [in Cuba]. ... The way things are here with the use of pills is terrible. Of course, the pharmacies [in Cuba] sold them, but then everybody had their pills at home, but you took them once in a great while, when your head hurt or your wisdom teeth ached. But I see so many young girls here taking Valium and sleeping pills and their nerves are shattered. But I don't remember seeing young girls taking such things in Cuba, and I left when I was 43 years old.... It's the environment, the standard of living we live in that bothers people here. (p.68)

Clearly, Cuban women perceive the American way of life as extremely stressful. In counseling Cuban women, the helper should express an understanding of and an appreciation for the anxiety of migration, acculturation, loss of country of origin, and the demands of changing sex roles. The primary avenue for engagement of the Cuban female client may well be through focusing on the difficulties they experience here and the differences from their life in Cuba. However, once the client has been engaged and a therapeutic relationship has been established, the treatment must be decidedly present-time oriented. As with other Cuban groups, Cuban women are likely to be mobilized into treatment by the onset of a crisis and expect the counselor to provide immediate problem-oriented solutions to the crisis situation. The culturally sensitive counselor is cognizant of how to use crises to promote growth and alter self-destructive life-styles. If the use of drugs has become the primary means of dealing with stress generally, most likely drugs will be seen as a means to deal with the present crisis. The counselor must be ready to take charge of the counselor-client relationship and suggest behaviors to restructure the interactions of the client with her environment. Many traditional Anglo-American counseling interventions are based on a model of a growth-oriented, self-actualizing individual who is ready to take control of his or her destiny. In contrast, the counselor must relate to the Cuban client hierarchically, recognizing that the counselor's role is perceived by the client as a position of authority (Szapocznik, Scopetta, & Arnalde, 1978). Alternative ways of coping must be suggested which are concrete and obtainable.

Whenever possible, Cuban women suffering from acculturation stress and related depression also should be involved in group counseling with peers. Cubans generally have high levels of need for social approval (Tholen, 1974). The warm, culturally familiar atmosphere of the group, with peers and possibly a counselor who speaks their language helps the Cuban client to feel accepted and less depressed. The group activities should focus on the here and now, and provide concrete advice in dealing with problems. When environmental pressures or tensions are the source of the Cuban client's dysfunction, as is often the case with Cuban women, the counseling interventions need to help the client develop the skills necessary to restructure the interactions of the client with her environment. Because of the Cuban client's tendency to perceive self as unable to control or modify environmental circumstances, reinforcement and feedback from group members can be an important source of support in learning these new skills.

SUMMARY AND CONCLUSIONS

Cubans in the United States are a diverse group. Most have arrived here in successive immigration waves following Castro's revolution and takeover of power in Cuba in 1959. While some of the initial waves of Cuban immigrants were over-represented by professionals and upper middle class persons, later arrivals closely paralleled the demographics found in the Cuban population at large. Counselors, teachers, and others who work with this population need to dispel the myth that Cubans are a privileged, affluent minority with no special needs. The fact is that Cuban-Americans experience many of the problems associated with immigration and social deprivation found among other Hispanic groups.

All Cubans in the United States have in common the experience of acculturation pressures as they try to adapt to a new way of life. Ever since Homer's description of the wanderings of Ulysses and his weeping and rolling on the floor at the thought of home, many writers and investigators have been aware of the relationship between the process of cultural adjustment among immigrant groups and the presence of acculturative stress (Santisteban, 1980). Cuban-American immigrants are no exception, particularly in regard to the impact on the family, to parental roles, and to family organization. Discrepancies in the rate of acculturation within families have been found to have strong causative effects on family dysfunctions.

In this chapter several examples of approaches developed to respond to the various needs of Cuban-Americans were discussed. These examples were selected because of their cultural sensitivity, creative approach, research basis, potential for being replicated, and implication for further development and study. They do not represent an exhaustive review of effective approaches. Many other educational, therapeutic, and community responses must be explored and developed in order to meet the needs of the growing Cuban-Americans population. However, the basic premise underlying any type of interventions that may be developed for Cuban-Americans is that those interventions must be sensitive to the particular needs, expectations, and values of this culture-rich, complex, and diverse population.

EXPERIENTIAL ACTIVITIES

Individual Activity

What stereotypes do people hold concerning the "new" Cuban immigrants versus the "old" Cuban immigrants? Think of ten things you've heard or seen in the media regarding the differences between Cubans who immigrated to the U.S. during or after the 1980 Mariel boatlift and those who came before. Then, check your list against available empirical evidence regarding these two groups. How might these perceptions influence American attitudes toward Cubans in the United States?

Group Activity

Divide participants into small groups of 5 or 6. Provide each group with a list of six to eight situations that a counselor or teacher might encounter when working with Cuban or Cuban-American clients. Each scenario should show how the counselor or teacher handled the situation. Ask each participant in the small group to individually rank order the counselor or teacher responses from most culturally appropriate to least appropriate way to deal with the situation. Then, have the small groups discuss the individual rankings and arrive at a group consensus. Each small group presents their consensus ranking to the other small groups and a general discussion on culturally appropriate behavior follows.

Outside Activity

Identify a Cuban immigrant who came to the United States prior to 1980 and a Cuban-American born in the United States of Cuban immigrant parents. Interview each one of these individuals and make a list of how their values are alike or different. Consider the sources of the value similarities and differences.

REFERENCES

Azicri, M. (1981-1982). The politics of exile: Trends and dynamics of political change among Cuban-Americans. *Cuban Studies, 11 & 12*, 56-70.

Bach, R.L., Bach, J.B., & Triplete, T. (1981-1982). Flotilla "entrants": Latest and most controversial. *Cuban Studies, 11 & 12*, 29-48.

Boone, M.S. (1980). The uses of traditional concepts in the development of new urban roles: Cuban women in the United States. In E. Bourguigan, *A world of women: Anthropological studies of women in the societies of the world* (235-269). New York: J.F. Bergin Publishers.

Butcher, J., & Garcia, R. (1978). Cross-national application of psychological tests. *Personnel and Guidance Journal, 56*, 472-475.

Diaz, G.M. (1981). The changing Cuban community. *In Hispanics and grantmakers: A special report of Foundation News* (pp. 18-23). Washington, DC: Council on Foundations.

Fernandez, G.A. (1981-1982). Comment—The flotilla entrants. Are they different? *Cuban Studies, 11&12,* 49-54.

Gonzalez, D.H., & Page, J.B. (1981). Cuban women, sex role conflict and the use of prescription drugs. *Journal of Psychoactive Drugs, 13,* 47-51.

Harrington, T.F., & O'Shea, A.J. (1980). Applicability of the Holland (1973) model of vocational development with Spanish-speaking clients. *Journal of Counseling Psychology, 27,* 246-251.

Kurtines, W.M., & Miranda, L (1980). Differences in self and family role perception among acculturating Cuban-American college students: Implications for the etiology of family disruption among migrant groups. *International Journal of Intercultural Relations, 4,* 167-184.

Page, J.B., (1982). A brief history of mind-altering drug use in prerevolutionary Cuba. *Cuban Studies, 12,* 55-71.

Perez, L., (1985). The Cuban population of the United States: The results of the 1980 U.S. Census of the Population. *Cuban Studies, 15,* 1-16.

Ponterotto, J.G., (1987). Counseling Mexican Americans: A multimodal approach. *Journal of Counseling and Development, 65,* 308-311.

Portes, A., Clark, J.M., & Lopez, M.M. (1981-1982). Six years later, the process of incorporation of Cuban exiles in the United States: 1973-1979. *Cuban Studies, 11 & 12,* 1-28.

Portes, A., Clark, J.M., & Manning, R.D. (1985). After Mariel: A survey of the resettlement experiences of 1980 Cuban refugees in Miami. *Cuban Studies, 15,* 37-58.

Santisteban, D. (1980). Acculturation/assimilation and psychological stress: A review of the literature. Unpublished manuscript. University of Miami, Spanish Family Guidance Center, Miami.

Szapocznik, J., Kurtines, W.M., Foote, F.H., Perez-Vidal, A., & Hervis, O. (1983). Conjoint versus one-person family therapy: Some evidence for the effectiveness of conducting family therapy through one person. *Journal of Consulting and Clinical Psychology, 51,* 889-899.

Szapocznik, J., Ladner, R.A., & Scopetta, M.A. (1979). Youth drug abuse and subjective distress in a hispanic population. In G.M. Beschner & A.S. Friedman (Eds.), *Youth drug abuse* (pp. 493-511). Lexington, MA: Heath.

Szapocznik, J., Santisteban, D., Hervis, O., & Spencer, F. (1981). Treatment of depression among Cuban-American elders: Some validation evidence for a life enhancement counseling approach. *Journal of Consulting and Clinical Psychology, 49,* 752-754.

Szapocznik, J., Santisteban, D., Kurtines, W.M., Hervis, O.E., & Spencer, F. (1982). Life enhancement counseling: A psychosocial model of services for Hispanic elders. In E. E. Jones & S.J. Korchin (Eds.), *Minority mental health* (296-330). New York: Holt, Rinehart & Winston.

Szapocznik, J., Santisteban, D., Kurtines, W.M., Perez-Vidal, A., & Hervis O. (1986). Bicultural effectiveness training: A treatment intervention for enhancing intercultural adjustment in Cuban families. *Hispanic Journal of Behavioral Sciences, 6,* 317-344.

Szapocznik, J., Scopetta, M.A., & Arnalde, M. (1978). Cuban value structure: Treatment implications. *Journal of Consulting and Clinical Psychology, 46,* 961-970.

Szapocznik, J., Scopetta, M.H., Kurtines, W.M., & Arnalde, M.A. (1978). Theory and measurement of acculturation. *Interamerican Journal of Psychology, 12,* 113-130.

Tholen, J.F. (1974). An interactive approach to the study of outcome in group counseling: Matching conceptual level with degree of structure. Unpublished master's thesis, University of Miami.

U.S. Census Bureau, Department of Commerce. (1992). *Statistical abstract of the United States.* Washington, D.C.: United States Government Printing Office.

Chapter 14

WOMEN ENTERING OR REENTERING THE WORK FORCE

Helen B. Wolfe, Ed.D.

Helen B. Wolfe is Coordinator of the Counselor Education program and Associate Professor of Education at Western Maryland College, Westminster, Maryland. She was formerly Dean of Graduate Affairs and Associate Dean of Academic Affairs. Prior to her present employment, Dr. Wolfe was Executive Director of the American Association of University Women. Her career has actively involved her in counseling, politics, research, evaluation, and teaching. She holds degrees from the State University of New York at Albany, Cornell University, and the State University College at Buffalo. Her involvement in counseling women stems from the mid-sixties when she began studying the work values of women.

Whether consciously or unconsciously, we have all absorbed an attitude toward the phenomenon of large numbers of women entering or reentering the labor market. This attitude has been shaped by our past experiences, by the feelings of others around us, by the mythology of a previous generation concerning women, and by any reading or serious reflection we may have done. The following awareness index has been designed to assist the reader in separating fact from fiction in the specific attitude which one brings to the consideration of the problems confronting these American women.

AWARENESS INDEX

Directions: Mark each answer true or false. Compare your answers with the scoring guide at the end of the awareness index.

T F 1. Employed women now receive equal protection under the law.

T F 2. The work force of the 90s reveals significant diversity in the jobs women hold.

T F 3. Women are overrepresented among the adult poor.

T F 4. While the gender gap between wages of men and women has narrowed in a number of fields, it is still significant in the professions.

T F 5. Employed women experience more mental health problems than other women.

T F 6. Real job growth for women in the 80s occurred in the lowest ranks of the service industries.

T F 7. The legislative climate of the 80s and early 90s has not been beneficial for women.

T F 8. A by-product of women's paid employment has been a blurring of the spousal roles within the family.

T F 9. Promising career choices for women in the year 2000 lie in small business management, health care, finance, and law.

T F 10. Models of career development emphasizing the life-span approach and the holistic view of individuals are the most appropriate for counseling women.

Scoring Guide for Awareness Index

1. F, 2. F, 3. T, 4. T, 5. F, 6. T, 7. T, 8. T, 9. T, 10. T

CASE EXAMPLES

Both

Beth is a young woman in her early thirties who is pursuing a career as a lawyer in a high-powered metropolitan law firm. Her equally ambitious husband is a lawyer with a competing firm in the same city. They postponed having children until they could be well launched in their professions, but as they viewed the biological clock, they determined not to be childless. Now after a three month maternity leave Beth must decide whether to remain home with her baby, to return to her seventy hour a week law practice, or to scale back her occupational goals. What is to be done with the baby? Grandparents are too actively engaged in their own careers to offer a solution. The cost of a live-in nanny would consume most of one of their salaries. Does our society want such a young woman to be able to have it all, to achieve professional and personal fulfillment? Or must she be compelled to choose between vocation and motherhood?

Sarah

Sarah is a young nurse who worked in hospitals before her marriage and for several years afterward. When the children came, however, she decided to stay home with them. With two young children still at home, her husband decided to fulfill his dream of opening a sporting goods store. Nursing lends itself better than most professions to an interrupted career pattern, and so Sarah returned to work in order to help cushion the financial downswing caused by her husband's self-employment. Since she works nights and weekends, one of them is always able to be home with the children.

Carole

Carole was a happily married full-time homemaker with four children. She enjoyed her role and viewed marriage as her economic bedrock. When she reached her early forties, her husband died unexpectedly. Economic necessity forced her to enter the work force. She cleaned houses, as this was her only marketable skill. Now she has been able to find a part-time job as a short order cook.

Joan

Joan has a job as a secretary which she took in order to supplement her husband's salary and provide the family with some luxuries. She enjoys getting out and meeting people now that her school age children require less of her time. However, her husband recently lost his job and now she is the sole supporter for the household. Her supplemental income has become their sole income. It is not sufficient.

Marjorie

Marjorie is a college professor with a son in elementary school. She and her husband shared child care responsibilities until their divorce. Now, however, Marjorie is on her own, and providing child care coverage is a major problem. She worries about the necessity of the "latch key" between the time her son gets home from school and the time she is able to leave work. Leaving town for a professional conference requires careful planning and also a bit of luck. The day she counts on being able to leave immediately after he boards the school bus, he may wake up with a fever and not go to school at all. She earns enough to afford baby sitting fees but not enough for a housekeeper.

THE FEMINIZATION OF THE WORK FORCE

This chapter focuses on the needs and issues of women who become part of the work force, either willingly or under some compulsion. Who are they? They are your daughters, wives, mothers, sisters, friends, nieces, cousins, and perhaps yourselves.

Sixty percent of all women are currently in the work force. Such numbers cannot be ignored. During the past 20 years they have increasingly attracted the attention of those who provide counseling services. Significant societal changes, beginning in the 1960s and including higher divorce rates, increased educational attainment of women, expanding opportunities in the labor market, rising expectations among women, economic imperatives, and changing views concerning working women have resulted in a labor force participation approaching that of men. At the beginning of this century the rule was women at home and the exception was outside employment. Now the exception is the full-time homemaker (Betz & Fitzgerald, 1987). Projections for the year 2005 estimate that women's share of the total work force will continue to increase and that men's therefore will decline (*Outlook 2005*, 1990/1991). This increased participation will come from new entrants, reentry women, and more women holding more than one job.

A new picture of women, men, children, and families has taken shape. Our society is characterized by smaller families, reconstituted families, dual career families, and women as heads of households (Hagen & Jenson, 1988). However, we should not overestimate the progress women have made or ignore the barriers they still face in the world of work. The gender gap in earnings; the clustering of women in low paying, low skill jobs; the underutilization of their abilities; and the higher unemployment rates for women are all on-going reminders that some of the progress is more cosmetic than real. The bottom line is that 60% of women are still seeking equality in the world of work.

CURRENT PROBLEMS

Societal Constraints

The drastic changes in society and the 30 year trend away from female domesticity have not yet produced an environment conducive to the paid employment of women. Such an environment would provide significant support for women in nontraditional roles: gender role expectations would show greater flexibility; sex role stereotyping in education would be eliminated; and societal structures would be in place to help women cope with work and family. We have instead a *null environment* where society takes a neutral posture toward the dilemmas women face in the workplace (Betz, 1989). Characteristic of this null environment is the seeming invisibility of problems. Women are neither encouraged nor discouraged in the labor force despite the fact that social conditions no longer allow the majority of women to remain at home.

Women also encounter the problem of inequitable compensation. Data for 1991 from the Bureau of Labor Statistics showed that women earn $.74 for every $1.00 men earn. Although the disparity has narrowed in recent years as a result of the rising educational levels of women, labor shortages in some areas, and the decline in men's earnings, the wage gap is still of interest to working women and economists. The discrepancy comes not from differences in the work tasks performed by men and women, but rather in the assessment of the worth of those tasks and the resulting wage structures. Some women's organizations have promoted comparable worth theory, which contends that if dissimilar jobs are similar in worth to the employer the wages paid should be relatively equal. The movement toward comparable worth may help reduce pay inequities associated with gender.

Bradley (1989) stated that the feminist movement has always drawn the bulk of its support from the middle class elite. "This has meant that women have done better in pushing their way into middle-class male occupations than in desegregating working-class jobs" (p.236). While these middle class women can now afford to hire help to handle the chores at home, this advantage has not been extended to working-class women. The latter are still clustered in the gender typed, low paying jobs and cannot afford paid assistance with their household tasks.

Since the majority of women workers are married, raising young children, working throughout their middle adult years, and working full time throughout the year, the issues of child bearing and child rearing are at the center of many of their difficulties. Because 90% of all American women will bear a child, child care concerns are inevitable. Social supports for preschool and after-school care exist, but their cost is prohibitive for many families. As women have observed this harsh reality, the rise in the number of employed women has been accompanied by a sharp decline in fertility rates. For many women, perhaps most, motherhood versus personal ambition represents the heart of the feminine dilemma.

Is it unfair for a woman to expect that her desire to be a full-time mother should be accommodated for an unspecified number of years?

Should another woman avoid motherhood entirely in order to secure the full chance that any man might have for economic autonomy and satisfying work?

Does a society that understands the need for successive generations have a moral obligation to ease the way for a woman intent on fulfilling both aspects of her dual purpose ambition? (Brownmiller, 1984, p. 231)

When a woman decides to combine motherhood with a career, her protection under the Federal Pregnancy Discrimination Amendment (1978) is limited. The law requires all employers who have disability plans to treat pregnancy as any other disability. However, not all private employers are required to provide disability coverage; therefore, many employed pregnant women are not covered.

Further constraints are related to the failure of academic disciplines to develop models of career development relevant for today's women. Poole and colleagues (Poole, Langan-Fox, Ciavanella, & Omodei, 1991) claim that career theory has focused on life-span development, self-concept, the matching of personality and work environments, social learning and decision making. These authors have contended that researchers have addressed neither additional constraining social and economic forces nor the multiple paths that women take in the world of work.

Workplace Constraints

Sexual harassment in the workplace is personally and professionally costly to women, whether or not they decide to report it. Some individuals quit; others avoid the harasser (to the detriment of their work); and still others find their productivity and satisfaction with work affected. Gutek (1985) noted that sexual harassment has been viewed in four ways: as a consequence of sexism in society; as reflecting unequal, exploitative power relationships at work; as a personal matter that occasionally gets out of hand; or as aberrant and nonprofessional behavior. Organizational policies prohibiting sexual harassment evolved in the early 80s as a response to Equal Employment Opportunity Commission guidelines. Research by Haavio-Mannila, Kauppinen-Toropainen, and Kandolin (1988) revealed that "Harassment was mainly dependent on an eroticized atmosphere in the workplace ....[that] becoming an object of sexual harassment was related to the sex structure of the workplace" (p. 135). Isolated and single women were objects of the most harassment. When Riger (1991) examined this issue, she noted that often the structure of the institution facilitated or supported sexual harassment. The college campus is an example of such a structure: the faculty is autonomous; authority is diffused; and women in positions of authority are scarce. So who is to monitor sexual harassment? Riger's conclusion was that the best way to eliminate sexual harassment is to create an organizational culture that sincerely promotes equal opportunities for women. The obverse, of course, is the imposition of sanctions for negative behavior.

The term "glass ceiling" was coined to describe the invisible barrier that women in mid-management positions encounter as they attempt to move to top management jobs. By a logical extension of meaning, the term connotes the underutilization of women's abilities by the work force in general. Women find themselves still trying to match management's model of *worker*. A model developed exclusively with males in mind, this worker model does not take into account the demands of child rearing or home management. Schwartz (1989) envisioned a two tier system for women which would identify *career primary* women and *career-and-family* women, a group subsequently dubbed by critics as "the mommy track." Schwartz advocated the accommodation of both groups through organization policies addressing the distinct needs of each group. Faludi (1991) reported that the furor with which this dual track system was greeted makes it unlikely to be a viable response to helping women find jobs commensurate with their training.

Moreover, the decision to have a child frequently jeopardizes a woman's employment status because she puts at risk her seniority and employee benefits. Guarantees are not present that she will be able to return to her same job after the birth. This is but another reminder that, in spite of the sentimentality surrounding Mother's Day, motherhood is accorded little status in the world of work. Noting the negative impact it has had upon others, many women have opted to delay motherhood until their careers have stabilized.

In the past decade, however, more organizations have adopted favorable policies on family leave. Swanson (1992) demonstrated that support from supervisors concerning family issues and child care (regardless of location) resulted in less on-the-job absenteeism because the work/family conflict was lower. Unfortunately, there are still relatively few modifications of rigid work schedules and little assistance with child care in most work settings. A bright spot on the horizon is the recent passage of the Family Leave Act of 1993 by the Clinton administration that requires up to 12 weeks leave upon delivery or adoption of a child for both mothers and fathers.

Finally, more women in management positions has resulted in more women working for women. O'Leary's (1988) examination of this phenomenon demonstrated that female subordinates evaluate women bosses differently than they do male bosses. There are many reasons for this, some of which are linked to the lack of power female bosses hold, the higher expectations female managers have for their subordinates, and the abandonment of "feminine characteristics" by the women bosses. Whatever the reason, there has been little change in women's preference for a male boss.

Personal Constraints

Personal constraints to full, happy, and profitable employment often begin early and are reinforced throughout life. These are the perceptions that women have related to their self-esteem, self-efficacy, and identity. For example, women tend to define themselves in relation to others (Gilligan, 1982; Forrest & Mikolaitis, 1986). Since women base many decisions on their relationships with people, when they prioritize work values they assign the highest rankings to social factors. This helps explain the dearth of women in mathematics and science, stereotypically male occupations, the stereotype being that of the male scientist working with things rather than with people (Lips, 1992). Doubts that women may have about themselves in these areas are remediable. Cantor and Bernay (1992) pointed out that a strong sense of self allows women to take risks and pursue nontraditional occupations. Single women and childless women have fewer personal constraints that interfere with their careers. However, married women with children and those who are heads of families articulate a variety of role conflicts that are in part societal and in part personal. For example, women find themselves with less transition time between work and home, less leisure time, and greater household responsibilities than do their spouses or partners (Sullivan, 1992). "Women's increasing participation in the work force is unreciprocated by men's involvement in the tasks of maintaining a home and family. Thus, women are still doing the majority of the housework and childcare" (Voydanoff, 1989, p.78).

HISTORY OF EMPLOYMENT LEGISLATION AND CAREER COUNSELING FOR WOMEN

Until recently unless a woman was enrolled in an educational institution that offered counseling and guidance services, she generally received no counseling from any source. Moreover, the availability of counseling services for working women tended to follow federal dollars. Money was allocated according to whether or not the country needed "Rosie the Riveter" during a war-time economy. Janeway (1974) pointed out that "one aspect of the war between the sexes not often noted is its manipulative use of women by the State and the Establishment. Wars put women into the labor market and recessions and depressions put them out of it" (p.79).

As a profession, counselors too often have allowed federal dollars to establish their priorities; thus they have followed more frequently than they have pioneered. After World War II a great effort was made to integrate veterans into a post-war society, but few were concerned about the working women who were pushed out at the same time. The launching of Sputnik in the late-fifties dictated that counselors master the techniques required to guide qualified persons into scientific and technological careers. In the early 1960s some legislative advances for women, such as the Equal Pay Act of 1963, were achieved, and a few governmental commissions were appointed to focus upon the changing roles of women. In 1965, I attended a conference sponsored by the Women's Bureau of the Labor Department to examine the counseling needs of women and girls. Female counselors and counselor educators met with the Women's Bureau, but the profession as a whole showed little interest.

The civil rights movement helped rekindle the women's movement, but funding primarily emerged for Blacks rather than for women. However, the specific drive for passage of the Equal Rights Amendment in the 70s generated enough energy to create crucial legislation for women in reproductive rights and employment. The Women's Educational Equity Act of 1974 allocated much needed funds for women's counseling. In 1975, Title IX of the Educational Amendments Act of 1972 was passed. With the intention of elimination, sexual discrimination in college admissions, financial aid, physical facilities curricula, sports, counseling, and employment in educational institutions receiving Federal funds, but lax enforcement and the narrowing of the scope of the legislation by subsequent court decisions resulted in minimal effects for women.

In the late 1970s and early 80s the Comprehensive Education Training Act (CETA) provided programs to retrain women who suddenly found themselves in the work force after many years as homemakers. The program was designed to address the particular educational and/or training women required in order to become economically self-sufficient. CETA programs were limited and tended to perpetuate occupational segregation for women, but ended entirely by the Reagan administration in the early 80s.

The general apathy toward the plight of women by the counseling profession caused feminists to take up the slack in providing counseling services in the 1960s and 70s. The advent of women's studies in higher education, elimination of gender stereotypes in standard elementary school textbooks, and the initiation of women into unions and professional societies increased the visibility of women and represented a greater commitment by major components of society to meeting their needs.

Women became important consumers for institutions of higher education concerned about declining enrollments from the traditional pool of high school graduates. Colleges and universities offered career/life planning services to recruit nontraditional students. Women embarking on a first career or a change of career comprised a large proportion of this population. Professional counselors in the 1980s then jumped on the bandwagon to provide a variety of services for women aimed at increasing their marketability as workers.

The failure of the effort to ratify the Equal Rights Amendment in the early 80s, however, accompanied by a 12 year vacuum in Federal leadership, resulted in the stagnation and erosion of women's rights. This theme is echoed in the examination of the backlash phenomenon that was the focus of a comprehensive study in the 1980s (Faludi, 1991). Faludi reminded us that the quest for gender equality was far from over. Hope lies, however, in the feminization of the counseling profession and in the demographics of the labor force, making it highly unlikely that the profession will return to the apathetic treatment given to women's career problems that characterized the prior generation of counselors.

THE HELPING PROFESSIONAL'S ROLE

In addition to counseling skills and techniques, counselors require a strong cognitive base that incorporates knowledge of the best careers for women in the future. Aburdene and Naisbitt (1992) identified the "hot" careers as owning one's own business, health care, finance, teaching (especially higher education), the food service industry, medicine, and law. A counselor's cognitive base also will include resources important to women as they integrate work and family, e.g., knowledge of child care and elder-care services. In addition, the counselor must be sensitive to the effect that the changes in women's roles bring to the lives of men. Faludi (1991) observed that employed women challenge men's masculinity, in part defined as being a good provider. Two groups of men seem most bitter about women in the work force, blue collar workers and younger baby boomers. In addition to an information base, the professional counselor engages in an on-going process of self-evaluation. Even the influx of women into the counseling profession does not preclude the need for all counselors to ensure that we do not constitute a barrier for women seeking to close the gap between their aspirations and the realities of life. Counselors must examine their own perceptions about women's development and their role in contemporary society. An important procedure is to help women to see real alternatives so that they can continue to move beyond traditional barriers in the workplace. Good, Gilbert, and Scher (1990) urge counselors to conceptualize problems within society's framework and to respect clients' freedom to choose roles that are most satisfying to them.

Although all women face similar economic and social conditions, it would be a mistake to assume that their responses are all alike. The personal and career needs of women are highly individual, and as a group they are no more homogeneous than men. Counselors should operate from the premise that women have many choices in creating their life patterns. Role models are diverse and numerous. Women can choose domesticity or nondomesticity with or without children. Their participation in the labor force may be full-time or part-time. Their work patterns may be stable or interrupted. Whatever the specific choice, what is predictable is the need for assistance in life planning, decision making, and goal setting.

Women perceive and construe social reality differently than do men (Gilligan, 1982). Gerson (1985) observed that "in order to justify their own embattled positions, domestic and nondomestic women denigrated each other's choices and the tradition of men's careers taking precedence over women. Many women may feel a trace of guilt when they go to work, and this guilt must be dealt with" (p. 171). Guilt is manifested in the tendency to compensate by becoming Superwoman, having the need to do it all—the job plus the myriad of other tasks that the wife and mother who is not employed performs. A few exceptional women are able to do these tasks without damage to themselves, but we should not assume they are the majority. Most women need to share tasks with their husbands and/or children. The employed mother also may seek to assuage guilt by over-indulging the children and should have an opportunity to examine this issue. Counselors can help women define their priorities and live comfortably with a series of compromises and fewer absolutes involving meal preparation, child care, housecleaning, and social life.

In working with women on career issues, group counseling is an effective technique for providing a feeling of mutuality. Women have been conditioned by society to minimize their own qualifications. In group they may be encouraged to discuss what they can do. Here they are taught that communication skills, including self-promotion, are part and parcel of labor force participation. Counselors and others can help women move toward greater self-awareness and refine their ability to project confidence.

In addition to the cohort support that single-sex group counseling can provide, family counseling takes on a greater role for counselors working with married women who are employed or seeking employment. We have now seen that the participation of both husband and wife in the labor force is the present norm in American society. Yet despite the challenges, options, and roles of the two-earner family with children, 74% of counselors exclusively use individual counseling. In one review of intervention modes used with women on career issues, family counseling was not even mentioned (Spokane & Hawks, 1990)! Both partners can benefit from exploring strategies that allow them to combine careers, marriage, and parenting more effectively. Spousal discussion of time management, role overload, childbearing plans, role conflict, identity issues, and career orientation can enhance the work/family connection.

Diversity in occupational choice also may be presented to women through career counseling. Almost one-half of all women work in jobs that are 80% female (Blankenship, 1991). Clearly, attaining diversity is important for women at large. For example, the job outlook in some traditionally female occupations is bleak. Increasing computerization, for example, forecasts elimination of secretarial positions. Using occupational card sorts instead of the traditional interest inventories and experiential activities such as shadowing workers, speakers, and internships promotes a wider variety of job choices and explores new career territory (Betz, 1989: Brooks & Haring-Hidore, 1988). The counselor must be careful, however, to adequately prepare women entering nontraditional fields for both the challenges and the obstacles they can encounter. Hammer-Higgins and Atwood (1989) have developed a simulation game to increase the client's awareness of potential problems and psychological pressures incumbent in these vocations.

Career planning is as important for women as it is for men. Because women tend to have a history of short-range planning, they may initially have difficulty with sequential, long-range planning. The counselor who understands this heritage that women bring to counseling, rather than erroneously assuming this is "just the way women are," teach the value of a long range view in career decision making. Careful discussion of life stages and selected readings also can promote the concept of long range planning.

The task of integrating career and family has been described earlier as one of the major constraints women face. McDaniels and Gysbers (1992) describe a variety of techniques counselors can use in exploring work/family issues. One of these is the *Life-role Analysis* which encourages the client to contrast where she was five years ago, where she is now, and where she expects to be five years hence. Another is the *Typical Day Assessment* based on Adler's work. In it the client details all events occurring in a typical day. This assessment is useful in helping women examine how they organize their lives. A third technique recommendation is the use of a *career genogram* which connects generations of family members by occupation. Its purpose is to enhance the client's understanding of work-family dynamics and implications for her career situation.

Interest, aptitude, and ability tests today have less relevance for mature women than mature men. Although test publishers have made significant revisions, the dependency upon the relevance of the male role model and the assumption of the female as deviant rather than different continue to be problems. The decision concerning test use, therefore, must be highly individual and done with an awareness of the appropriateness and validity of these measures.

The counselor, also, has a significant role in assisting women to make the transition from school to work. Since educational institutions have deliberately extended their outreach to women, the decision to seek further education appears to generate less stress in women today than a few years ago. Schools have discovered the importance of improving students' self-esteem. There are, however, some older women for whom interventions to strengthen one's self-esteem are crucial for their successful performance in the workplace. The marketplace imposes its own expectations, but women can address these by acquiring effective job-hunting skills and seeking assurance concerning self-efficacy.

SUMMARY

Counselors can be optimistic about the future of women in the labor market. Goldin (1990) cites the confluence of the percentages of males and females graduating from college, the similarities in the majors they select, and the percentages seeking postbaccalaureate education as signs of greater equity in the workplace. Today's young women have greater employment continuity, a sign of decreasing in the disparity between male and female earnings.

> If I have assigned a large role to the forces of economic development, it is because, in the long run at least, these factors are preeminent in explaining changes in labor force participation, earnings, and occupations. But I have also recognized that women can achieve real equality only when judged as individuals. Thus gender equality may be fostered by economic progress but must be assisted by legislation and social change. (Goldin, 1990, p. 217)

Counselors can play a significant role in this process as advocates and change agents.

James Michener (1972) wrote a book entitled *The Quality of Life*. In reflecting upon educational and occupational opportunities for minorities he made the telling point that our society cannot afford to cut anyone short of his or her full potential for we all have too much at stake. What great novel has not been written because we block the full potential of someone through destructive stereotypes? What cure for cancer might have been discovered by a woman? What improvements in the quality of life have we lost by this suicidal cutting off of the brain of a large part of our population? Because of their sensitivity to human personality, and their skill in surmounting problems, counselors as a group are in a position to be pioneers in the task of helping women achieve their full potential. Full integration in the workplace is a vital starting point.

EXPERIENTIAL ACTIVITIES

Individual Activity

Determine the work/family issues that you face in your own career by using either the Life-role Analysis, the Typical Day Assessment, or the career genogram. These are the interventions described by McDaniels and Gysbers (1992) earlier in this chapter.

Group Activity

Divide the class into groups of four. Imagine that it is the year 2005. Discuss what current issues mentioned in this chapter will still be unresolved. Create a profile of the woman worker of 2005 and share with the class.

Outside Class Activity

Interview a woman in a nontraditional occupation. Discuss the constraints she faces in her career. Identify those that are gender related and those that are uniquely individual. Share your findings with the class and contrast these findings with the research.

REFERENCES

Aburdene, P., & Naisbitt, J. (1992). *Megatrends for women.* New York: Villard Books.

Betz, N.E. (1989). Implications of the null environment hypothesis for women's career development and for counseling psychology. *The Counseling Psychologist, 17,* 136-144.

Betz, N.E., & Fitzgerald, L.F. (1987). *The career psychology of women.* Orlando: Academic Press.

Blankenship, K.M. (1991). Book Reviews. *Signs, 16,* 606-610.

Bradley, H. (1989). *Men's work, women's work.* Minneapolis: University of Minnesota Press.

Brooks, L. & Haring-Hidore, M. (Eds.) (1988). Career interventions with women. *Journal of Career Development, 14,* 221-293.

Brownmiller, S. (1984). *Feminity.* New York: Linden Press.

Cantor, D., & Bernay, T. (1992). *Women in power: The secrets of leadership.* Boston: Houghton Mifflin.

Faludi, S. (1991). *Backlash: The undeclared war against American women.* New York: Doubleday.

Forrest, L., & Mikolaitis, N. (1986). The relational component of identity: An expansion of career development theory. *Career Development Quarterly, 35,* 76-88.

Gerson, K. (1985). *Hard choices: How women decide about work, career, and motherhood.* Berkeley: University of California Press.

Gilligan, C. (1982). *In a different voice.* Cambridge: Harvard University Press.

Goldin, C. (1990). *Understanding the gender gap: An economic history of American women.* New York: Oxford University Press.

Good, G.E., Gilbert, L.A., & Scher, M. (1990). Gender aware therapy: A synthesis of feminist therapy and knowledge about gender. *Journal of Counseling and Development, 68,* 376-380.

Gutek, B.A. (1985). *Sex and the workplace: Impact of sexual behavior on women, men and organizations.* San Francisco: Jossey-Bass.

Haavio-Mannila, E., Kauppinen-Toropainen, K., & Kandolin, I.(1988) The effect of sex composition of the workplace on friendship, romance, and sex at work. In B.A. Gutek, A.H. Stromberg, & L. Larwood (Eds.), *Women and work: An annual review,* Vol. 3 (pp. 123-137). Newbury Park: Sage Publications.

Hagen, E., & Jenson, J.(1988) Paradoxes and promises: Work and politics in the postwar years. In J.Jenson, E. Hagen, & C. Reedy. (Eds.), *Feminization of the labor force: Paradoxes and promises* (pp. 276-287). New York: Oxford University Press.

Hammer-Higgins, P., & Atwood, V. A. (1989). The management game: An educational intervention for counseling women with nontraditional career goals. *The Career Development Quarterly, 38,* 6-13.

Janeway, E. (1974). *Between myth and morning: Women awakening.* New York: Morrow.

Lips, H.M. (1992). Gender and science-related attitudes as predictors of college students' academic choices. *Journal of Vocational Behavior, 40,* 62-81.

McDaniels, C., & Gysbers, N.C. (1992) *Counseling for career development: Theories, resources, and practice.* San Francisco: Jossey-Bass.

Michener, J. (1972). *The quality of life.* New York: Fawcett.

O'Leary, V.E. (1988). Women's relationships with women in the workplace. In B.A. Gutek, A.H. Stromberg, & L. Larwood (Eds.), *Women and work; An annual review,* Vol. 3 (pp. 189-213). Newbury Park: Sage.

Outlook 2005. *Occupational Outlook Quarterly.* (Winter/1990-91). Washington: United States Government Printing Office.

Poole, M.E., Langan-Fox, J., Ciavanella, M., & Omodei, M. (1991). A contextualist model of professional attainment: Results of a longitudinal study of career paths of men and women. *The Counseling Psychologist, 19,* 603-624.

Riger, S.(1991). Gender dilemmas in sexual harassment: Policies and procedures. *American Psychologist, 46,* 497- 504.

Schwartz, F. (1989). Management women and the new facts of life. *Harvard Business Review, 67*, 65-76.

Spokane, A.R., & Hawks, B.K. (1990). Annual review: Practice and research in career counseling and development, 1989. *The Career Development Quarterly, 39*, 98-122.

Sullivan, S.E. (1992). Is there a time for everything? Attitudes related to women's sequency of career and family. *The Career Development Quarterly, 40*, 234-243.

Swanson, J.L. (1992). Vocational behavior, 1989-1991: Life-span career development and reciprocal interaction of work and nonwork. *Journal of Vocational Behavior, 41*, 101-161.

Voydanoff, P. (1989). Work and family: A review and expanded conceptualization. In E.B.Goldsmith (Ed.), *Work and family: Theory, research, and applications* (pp. 1-22). Newbury Park: Sage.

Chapter 15

PREPARATION FOR HELPING PROFESSIONALS WORKING WITH DIVERSE POPULATIONS

Larry C. Loesch, Ph.D., N.C.C.

Larry C. Loesch is currently a Professor and Graduate Coordinator in the Department of Counselor Education at the University of Florida, Gainesville. He received his undergraduate and graduate degrees from Kent State University and has been at the University of Florida since completion of his doctoral program in June of 1973. Dr. Loesch has had over 70 articles published in professional journals, including more than a dozen specifically relating to the professional preparation of counselors. His recently co-authored book, Counseling: A Professional Orientation, was released in 1993 by Accelerated Development Publishers. From 1984 through 1986 Dr. Loesch served as a member of the Council for the Accreditation of Counseling and Related Educational Programs. He also is actively involved in several counseling and educational organizations and is the current Research and Evaluation Coordinator for the National Board for Certified Counselors, Inc. He and his wife, Barbara, have four daughters.

Diverse populations are by definition unique: they differ significantly in one or more regards from "typical" client groups. In order for helping activities to be effective with persons from diverse populations, those activities also must be unique. Therefore, to speak of the basic facets, or commonalities, in the professional preparation of persons intending to work with special groups is to raise an inherent contradiction. Fortunately this situation is not without resolution.

If a certain perspective is maintained, then commonalities can be discussed. This perspective holds that the implementation of a preparation method is unique with regard to diverse populations rather than to the method itself. Therefore, it is not unique training methods that are needed, but rather unique applications of existing training methods. Thus, many of the methods used to train counselors for work with typical populations can be effectively adapted for training helpers for diverse populations. Emphasis in training is thus shifted from a focus on the nature of the activity to a focus on the method of implementation. By the same token the preparation method selection process may be shifted from evaluation of the relative merits of various methods to evaluation of the ease with which any chosen method may be implemented with a given special population.

This discussion should not be construed to mean that innovative preparation methods are not needed or do not exist. On the contrary, innovative training methods are an excellent complement to established methods. When preparing to help any client group, a solid foundation must be built before the garnishments are added (Christensen, 1989; D'Andrea & Daniels, 1991; McRae & Johnson, 1991). Preparation methods offered in this chapter, however, fall in the proven or established category because space does not permit allusion to all possible methods. A helpful procedure in reading this chapter may be to keep a particular special population in mind in order to consider the question, "How do the points or suggestions made apply to this group?" This consideration will provide a more practical frame of reference for the reader.

POTENTIAL COUNSELING FUNCTIONS

The professional preparation of helping professionals who intend to counsel persons from diverse populations must necessarily take into account potential professional duties (Sue, 1991; Sue, Arrendondo, & McDavis, 1992). For what are these trainees being prepared?

For current purposes, a convenient categorization of functions is provided in the professional preparation standards used by the Council for the Accreditation of Counseling and Related Educational Programs (CACREP, 1988). These standards identify six major counselor functions: individual counseling, group counseling, vocational counseling, assessment, consultation, and research. In order to be as comprehensive as possible, two additional functions also will be considered: special types of counseling (e.g., marriage, family, life-style, leisure) and teaching.

1. Individual Counseling

The helping professional's functioning in individual counseling is typically dictated by a preferred orientation, degree of directiveness, or both. When counseling with persons from diverse groups, the question is not whether individual counseling is appropriate, but rather which approach is potentially the effective one. For example, the suggestion has been made that more structured individual counseling approaches are more effective with Asian Americans and African Americans. Selection of the "right" counseling approach is a tenuous proposition at best: little empirical data are available. Regardless of the approach taken, however, consideration of the client's cultural context is essential (Fukuyama, 1990; Ivey, 1987; Lee & Richardson, 1991; Locke, 1992; Vontress, 1988).

2. Group Counseling

Like individual counseling, group counseling has been viewed as a common helping function. It has the advantages of maximizing the helping professional's use of time and providing clients with simultaneous multiple interactions and perspectives. It has the disadvantages of reduced individual client-counselor interaction and confidentiality. Theoretically, any concern which might be covered in individual counseling also might be covered in a group counseling context.

The helping professional's functioning in the group context is dictated by preferences for various possible orientations, and thus preferences also are an issue here. In addition, the group context brings into consideration interactions among group members. Persons from some special populations are much more willing to interact in group counseling circumstances than are others. Accordingly, the social interaction characteristics of a group are an important issue in the group counseling process (Atkinson, Morten, & Sue, 1989; Ponterotto & Sabnani, 1989; Sodowsky & Plake, 1992).

3. Vocational Counseling

The key issues in vocational counseling with persons from diverse populations center on the unique characteristics of those persons (Campbell & Hadley, 1992; Cheatam, 1990). To what extent do these unique characteristics (values, history, education, family construct) affect the vocational development of these persons? How about their ability to capitalize on vocational opportunities? What can the counselor expect in regard to career maturity, previous career exploration, or employment discrimination with a special group? What part will counseling for self- esteem play with these individuals? Questions such as these will be faced by any helping professional working with persons from diverse populations.

4. Assessment

More than any other function, assessment has been, and remains, at the center of controversy within the helping professions (Lonner, 1985). Assessment procedures range from unobtrusive measures to performance or behavioral criteria. Yet, regardless of the procedures employed, some evaluation is made.

Bias is the term applied when the comparison process is deemed unfair. Typically, bias in assessments with persons from diverse populations centers on socio-linguistic differences, which in extreme cases may invalidate the assessments. This does not necessarily mean that assessments should not be made with such persons. Rather, it suggests that assessments (and subsequent evaluations) should be made carefully (Lonner & Ibrahim, 1989).

5. Consultation

The function of the helping professional as a consultant is an emerging one. Perhaps more than any other functional area, consultation activities allow helping professionals to influence very large numbers of persons (Conley & Conley, 1991). The major concerns associated with the consultation function are that the helping professional is one step removed from the people to be affected by the consultation and that the consultant may assume several roles. The consultant helps one or more persons help still other persons in the community. This distance between source and impact raises significant questions about which (consultation) tactics have the greatest potential for success. Should the consultant assume an educative, counseling, advice-giving, or source of information role for the consultee? The unique characteristics of the diverse population, as well as those of the intermediary, further compound the difficulty. For example, what is a perfectly logical, reasonable, and effective course of action for one group may have deleterious effects for another. An intervention may very well have social or political ramifications; therefore, careful examination of all facets of a consultation is essential.

6. Research

The research function in the helping professions is another which has been a source of controversy, although certainly not to the extent of assessment. The need for research in counseling is generally acknowledged and widely espoused (Ponterotto &

Casas, 1991). However, only a minute segment of helping professionals actually engage in research projects. Moreover, only a small portion of the research is specifically concerned with applications or implications for diverse populations.

A major issue in research concerning counseling diverse populations has been the lack of significant numbers of persons from which to derive data (Atkinson, 1985; Casas, 1985). Relatively large samples of subjects are difficult to obtain because large groups often are not available in readily accessible geographic areas. More recently, some special population groups have resisted participation in research endeavors because of concern about the validity of previous research done with or applied to them. These situations necessitate caution and sensitivity from helping professionals engaging in quantitative research activities as well as use of sensitive qualitative research methodologies (Casas, 1985; Ponterotto & Sabnani, 1989)

7. Special Types of Counseling

The rapid growth of the helping professions and the increasing recognition of their positive values in society have allowed for the development of many specialized areas of helping. The more recent innovations (at least in terms of relatively widespread practice) include marriage and/or family counseling, bereavement counseling, life-style counseling, leisure counseling, mid-life and pre-retirement counseling, assertiveness training, stress management, and health/wellness counseling. While services such as these have expanded greatly, their implementation with persons from diverse populations has lagged (D'Andrea & Daniels, 1991; Pedersen, 1987, 1991). This latency is probably in fact a positive phenomenon. Thorough understanding of the pertinent characteristics of a particular population (e.g., familial dynamics, typical leisure patterns and values, or religious tenets about grieving) and empirical support for the effectiveness of specific techniques with a particular group should be established before these special types of counseling are implemented. In view of the rapidly expanding knowledge base in the counseling professions, the implementation lag is probably a temporary phenomenon.

8. Teaching

The teaching function is not one normally associated with the counseling segment of the helping professions. Helpers, however, teach in a variety of ways: modeling, interpretation, demonstration, and bibliotherapy to name a few. In concert with the reasoning throughout this chapter, teaching methods used in counseling with persons from diverse populations must be uniquely adapted to them. Some of the more common teaching activities that can be readily adapted in this regard include use of literature (e.g., pamphlets, articles, or books), role-playing, visual media (e.g., videotapes or films), and experiential activities (e.g., field-trips or attendance at social functions). Similarly, assessing, gaining and evaluating cultural knowledge, investigating ethnic literature, and using specific behaviors to increase sensitivity to ethnic minorities also are applicable to direct service work with diverse cultural groups (Parker, 1987; Pedersen, 1988).

EVALUATING FUNCTIONS FOR USE

The eight functions described are all potentially useful for working with persons from diverse populations. The word *potential* must be emphasized because each of the functions will not necessarily be helpful for groups. Indeed, some of the preceding chapters have provided specific examples of functions that would have little or no utilitarian value for work with certain ethnic or minority groups. The appropriateness (and therefore potential for success) of any of these eight functions for a given population may be easily evaluated by considering three basic questions:

1. Is use of the function *feasible* with the person(s) in question? Is the function one that could be implemented? If not, the evaluation process obviously stops here. An affirmative response, however, raises another question.

2. Is the use of the function *necessary*? Feasibility in and of itself is insufficient justification for the application of an

intervention. A definable need must be established. Again, a negative response stops the evaluation process while an affirmative response raises another question.

3. Is the use of the function *cost effective?* A particular function may be feasible, desirable, and necessary, but its implementation costs may far exceed the potential benefits to be derived. To engage in a counseling function under such conditions is to be highly inefficient. A negative response to this question implies either termination of the evaluation or reevaluation of the second question; perhaps an alternative approach is more appropriate. Of course an affirmative response suggests that the function should begin.

Effective preparation programs will provide helping professionals with the skills and knowledge necessary to provide sound answers to these questions. This, then, is a good time to consider the components of an effective preparation program.

COMPONENTS OF A TRAINING PROGRAM

Preservice and inservice training programs for helping professionals intending to work with diverse populations must encompass a multitude of dimensions and experiences. In order to acknowledge the complex interrelations among these dimensions and experiences, a training program may be more appropriately described in terms of its major components: knowledge acquisition, attitude awareness, experiential interaction, and skill development. Obviously these components are related integrally in actual practice, but they are separated here for the purpose of clarity.

1. Knowledge Acquisition

A strong cognitive base is an acknowledged foundation for any aspect of the helping professions (Pedersen, 1990b). Indeed, for this particular type of preparation program, a significant portion of the trainees' time will be spent in attempting to answer the question. What makes a particular ethnic, racial, or minority group unique?

A helping professional must be grounded in the cultural and/or sociological characteristics of the diverse population (Hoare, 1991; Jackson & Sears, 1992; Pedersen, 1987; Thomason, 1991). What, if anything, is unique to the group in terms of appearance, dress, or self presentation? Where do they live? What are the identifying characteristics of their life-styles? Are common personality traits present? Do they have within group socioeconomic, political, or religious similarities? In general, the helping professional needs to learn how the diverse population is *both* similar to and different from other groups.

In like manner, a helping professional needs to be informed about the normative behaviors within diverse populations. What behaviors are idiosyncratic within a given population? Do they have unique speech patterns or specific vocabulary? Do they use common gestures, facial expressions, or body movements? In essence, the helping professional needs to know what is and is not acceptable behavior within the diverse population and how such behavior differs from that of other groups.

If effective interaction with persons from diverse populations is to be achieved by helping professionals, then they also must be familiar with the socio-political functioning within each population. Who are the leaders? Which persons earn the greatest respect? More importantly, why are these persons influential? With regard to direct contact helping functions (e.g., individual counseling), helping professionals must be knowledgeable of preferred modes of interaction (Draguns, 1989). What helping techniques have been proven to be effective? Which have been ineffective? Which have been as yet untried or evaluated?

Finally, the helping professional needs a thorough knowledge of professional ethics as well as the informal ethics within the diverse population. Would these sets of ethics ever come into conflict? In what ways are they similar? This type of knowledge will, to a great extent, enable helping professionals to avoid situations which are both personally and professionally compromising. In summary, a strong knowledge base may be described as a "necessary but not sufficient" condition for effective helping. Accordingly, this foundation must be complemented by the second major component in the preparation process.

2. Attitude Awareness

Attitude awareness has been deemed especially important for working with persons from diverse populations (Parker, 1987). This awareness includes personal attitude awareness as well as awareness of general attitudes of the population and its members. This emphasis is typically based on an assumption of attitudinal differences between helping professionals and clients in cross-cultural situations. If such differences exist, they may interfere with helping processes. Given the need for professional preparation in terms of attitude awareness, the question then becomes of which attitudes should the helping professional be aware? For our purposes, five types of attitudes will be considered.

a. The Professional's Attitude about Self. The first type of attitude of which the helping professional should be aware is attitude about self (Pedersen, 1987, 1988, 1991). Those helping professionals who are able to assess and evaluate accurately their own attitudes generally are more effective in helping others because they are aware how their attitudes affect their counseling activities (Sue, 1992).

b. The Professional's Attitudes about the Diverse Population. Helping professionals must be aware of their own biases, positive or negative, if they are to be able to work effectively with persons from diverse populations (Lee, 1991; Pedersen, 1990a). This type of attitude awareness enables the helping professional to be authentic, a characteristic generally understood to be necessary for competent helping. Further, it enables professionals to compare their attitudes about the diverse population with their attitudes about themselves. This comparison then provides a framework from which to approach their helping activities, or if the differences are too great, to move toward referral.

c. Diverse Population's Attitudes about Helping Professionals. Perceptions of the worth and value of the helping process (as typically conceived) vary greatly across populations. Some groups readily enter into the helping process while others do so only if forced. Development of awareness of such attitudes is essential for the counselor, particularly in the initial stages of the helping process.

d. Society's Attitude about the Diverse Population. A fourth type of attitude of which helping professionals should be aware is society's attitude about the diverse population. Particularly important in this regard are stereotypes (Pedersen, 1988). Which characteristics of the diverse population are typically stereotyped? What validity, if any, is present in the stereotypes? How do such stereotypes relate to, or affect, people's behaviors? Which of society's attitudes about the diverse population are evolving or changing? What characteristics of the diverse population seem to be the basis of stereotypes? Answers to questions such as these allow the helping professional to have a perspective on the society in which the special population exists. This perspective should, in turn, enable the helping professional to understand some of the realities of people within the group, thus facilitating the helping process.

e. Diverse Population Members' Attitudes about Themselves. The last type of attitude to be considered is the diverse population members' attitude about themselves. What do these individuals perceive as their positive and negative characteristics—their self-perceived strengths, weaknesses, assets, and liabilities? What is the nature of their collective self-concept? And perhaps most important, how do these attitudes interact with the other attitudes previously mentioned?

The establishment of a comprehensive cognitive base and the development of valid attitude awareness are absolutely essential for the effective preparation of helping professionals who intend to work with diverse populations. Moreover, their worth will be diminished if they are not grounded in reality for the trainee. Thus they serve as the basis for the third preparation component.

3. Experiential Activities

An effective preparation program will provide helping professionals with a broad set of experiences with diverse populations (D'Andrea & Daniels, 1991; McRae & Johnson, 1991; Nwachuku & Ivey, 1991). These experiences are important because they allow trainees to validate their own knowledge base and attitude awareness. They also aid in gaining appreciation for diverse life-styles and have the subtle benefit of allowing people from diverse populations to interact with potential helping professionals. Thus, experiential activities play a significant role in the preparation process by benefiting both trainees and persons from special populations.

The most obvious type of experiential activity to be incorporated into a training program is direct, supervised interaction with a particular population (Sue, 1991; Sue, Arrendondo, & McDavis, 1992). Beyond laboratory types of experience, helping professionals also should be provided with opportunities for less formal interactions, including visiting typical homes, social gathering places, or work locations. Trainees should note the environment, social and familial atmospheres, and behaviors present in order to solidify their impression of the life-styles of the population.

A related set of experiences allow helping professionals to interact formally and informally with persons from various groups (D'Andrea & Daniels, 1991). Formal activities might include participating in vocational activities or formal social meetings. Informal activities might include casual conversations, participation in leisure activities, or going to informal social events. The intention of these types of experiences is to allow the helping professional to become aware and practice ways of establishing rapport with persons from different cultural groups.

Another important set of experiences for helping professionals is for them to interact with other groups who have reason to interact with persons from the diverse population. These experiences should be similar to those described previously, particularly in the areas of formal and informal interactions. These types of experiences will provide helping professionals with two additional first hand perspectives.

Observations concerning how the diverse population is perceived and received by members of other groups enable trainees to gain appreciation and understanding of the life circumstances of the population.

While experiences such as these generally add significantly to the preparation of helping professionals, some caution should be exercised. In any preparation program only a relatively limited number of experiences with any given diverse population will be possible because of time and/or resource constraints. Accordingly, these experiences should be carefully selected and developed so that maximum benefit may be achieved (Sue, Arrendondo, & McDavis, 1992). At the same time, helping professionals should be cautioned against overgeneralizing from very small samples. That is, they must realize that such experiences may have only limited representative value across diverse populations. If helping professionals do not realistically evaluate the nature of their experiences, the experiences may do more harm than good.

Strong cognitive and experiential bases and attitude awareness do much to aid helping professionals in their professional interactions with persons from diverse populations. Yet knowledge, perspective, and social interaction skills are not enough. A professional must by definition have specific, identifiable skills. The development of these skills constitutes the fourth preparation component.

4. Skill Development

A major portion of the professional literature in the helping professions is devoted to the theoretical development, practical application, and subsequent evaluation of a variety of helping skills. These processes have led to the identification of a large number of such skills; however, they also have fostered considerable debate concerning what constitutes basic helping skills, particularly for use with persons from diverse populations (Ivey, 1987; Nwachuku & Ivey, 1991). At best, the resolution of these debates seems to be that the basic skills are what any particular author believes them to be. The ones presented here are no exception. It is important to remember, also, that the skills themselves are not unique. Rather, the ways they are used with particular individuals are unique. Accordingly, each of the following skills should be considered in regard to their potential for use with persons from various populations.

Active Listening. Active listening (facilitative responding) skills have been cited by numerous authors as being at the heart of helping. However, to assume that active listening, from within the context of a nondirective approach, will be effective with all persons would be incorrect (Holiman & Lauver, 1987). Indeed, some research shows that for persons from some populations a highly directive approach may be necessary. Consequently, helping professionals should receive training in directive helping approaches and approach discrimination so that they will be able to use an appropriate approach with a given individual.

Individual and Group Appraisal. Individual and group appraisal (i.e., measurement and evaluation) skills also are among the commonly cited basic helping skills. The considerable debate surrounding the validity of appraisals made on persons from diverse populations suggests that helping professionals should receive two related but distinct types of appraisal preparation. The first type is preparation for the more common methods of appraisal, i.e., standardized testing. This training is important because helping professionals will (1) sometimes use standardized testing procedures because such procedures will in fact be the most appropriate, and (2) need to know whether standardized testing procedures are the most appropriate or if some other procedure would be more appropriate. The second type of preparation is for the less common methods of appraisal: unobtrusive measures, behavioral observations, self reports, structured interviews, and the like. For many diverse populations this latter type of appraisal may be the best possibility. Failure to provide thorough training in both types would seriously limit trainees' eventual professional effectiveness.

Vocabulary Adjustment. A third basic skill in which helping professionals should be trained is vocabulary adjustment. Diverse populations, like any other societal group, have elements of speech interpretable only in the context of the group (Pedersen, 1987, 1988). Helping professionals must be aware of dialectical patterns and subtleties not for the purpose of learning a new language but as a means for gaining understanding and appreciation for differences in communication patterns. Likewise, nonverbal communication behaviors and their associated interpretations often differ dramatically across societal subgroups. Helping professionals must gain an understanding and appreciation of the differences in both verbal patterns and nonverbal behavior interpretations if they are to achieve acceptance and work effectively with persons from diverse cultural groups.

Confrontation. The last of the basic skills to be considered is confrontation. Use of confrontation within helping processes is indeed difficult for several reasons. First, it at least temporarily places the helper and the helpee in an adversarial position. Second, it often raises feelings of defensiveness and withdrawal in the helpee. Third, some helping professionals interpret confrontation as license to be aggressive and punitive. And fourth, for the previous reasons, confrontation is a common cause of premature termination of a helping relationship. Thus the use of confrontation is potentially dangerous in any helping relationship. This potential is increased with persons from special populations because of the greater possibility for communication misinterpretation. Nonetheless, confrontation also is an extremely powerful method of bringing about psychological movement within a helping relationship. Accordingly, helping professionals should have careful and thorough training in the use of confrontation.

Effective Preparation. Effective training in these basic skills should allow helping professionals to be at least minimally competent in their helping efforts with persons from special groups. One must remember, however, that these are only basic skills. Other skills, including those specific to particular diverse populations, also should be included in the preparation process. Space does not permit discussion of these other skills, save acknowledgment of their importance to thoroughly trained helping professionals. Suffice it to say that professional preparation is an extensive, lifelong process although it need not to be a difficult one if careful attention is given to planning and implementation.

EXPERIENTIAL ACTIVITIES

Activities for Cognitive Base Preparation

The first stage of the preparation process should provide a broad base of cognitive knowledge about diverse populations. Obviously a careful reading of this book is a first step toward establishing such a base. Following are some related activities which might be used to supplement this reading and lead toward the same goal.

1. Reread any two chapters of this book and develop a list of similarities and differences between the two populations described.

2. Select any chapter and create an *annotated* bibliography of at least seven current references appropriate for that chapter.

3. Select any particular point made by an author and write a paper, complete with references, arguing the opposite point of view. For example, you might argue that intelligence tests are not unfair to Mexican-American children because these children must exist and function within the majority society.

4. Select any chapter of interest and then create five multiple-choice, factual questions not covered in either the "Awareness Index" or questions in the "Experiential Activities."

5. Identify ten sources of information (e.g., books, journal articles, or other media) about a particular population which are not cited in this book.

6. Assume that you have the opportunity to interview some persons from a diverse population of interest to you. Develop a set of at least ten questions that will enable you to obtain factual information from the persons you will interview.

7. Assume that you have been asked to describe a given diverse population to a class of fifth graders. Prepare a ten minute presentation you could use to fulfill this request.

8. Select any chapter of this book and attempt to recreate the outline the author(s) used to write it. Then identify other pertinent topics which might have been included.

9. Identify a particular diverse population. Then write a paper, complete with references, defending the use of a particular helping orientation with persons from that group.

10. Examine the reference lists from any two chapters of this book. Then identify the references from one chapter which might apply (approximately equally) to the other chapter; repeat for the second chapter.

Activities for Attitude Awareness Preparation

1. Identify any particular diverse population and then create a list of at least ten stereotypes you think people hold about that group (exclude stereotypes presented in the pertinent chapter of this book).

2. Assume that you have the opportunity to interview some persons from a particular diverse population and that you would like to know what they are *really* like. Create a list of questions that you would ask each person.

3. Assume that you are an arbitrator between a group of persons from a diverse population and a group of persons from the White, middle-class majority. Compose a *treaty* to settle the differences between the two groups.

4. Assume you have the power to enact legislation that would benefit a particular diverse population. List and explain the laws you would enact.

5. Assign each person in a group to be representative of a different diverse population. Conduct a mock United Nations activity by having the representatives create a plan for the world wide enrichment of the human condition.

6. Select any particular diverse population and then ask children from different grade levels (e.g., third, seventh, and twelfth) to describe a person from that group. Compare and contrast the responses.

7. Select any two diverse populations and interview at least five persons from each group concerning their attitudes about the other population.

8. Select any diverse population and interview at least five persons from that diverse population about their attitudes regarding helping professions. Include a question concerning how they feel about being interviewed.

9. Create a *self-attitude awareness* activity which would be effective for use with a given population group.

Experiential Activities for Preparation

1. Visit, individually or with others, a restaurant catering primarily to persons from a particular diverse population.

2. Attend a religious ceremony intended primarily for members of a particular population.

3. Interview an identified political leader from a particular cultural group. Incorporate questions about current issues and problems as well as future political actions within the group.

4. Observe a group of children from a particular diverse population while at play. Note consistent behavior patterns and interaction styles.

5. Interview at least five persons from each of three different diverse populations concerning their favorite leisure activities. Compare and contrast their responses.

6. Interview a helping professional from a particular diverse population. Inquire about the professional problems and issues the professional most frequently encounters in helping activities.

Supervised Practice as Preparation

The final stage in the preparation process is supervised practice in helping relationships with persons from diverse populations. Note that these activities should be used only after participants have successfully completed the first three recommended stages.

1. Have one person role-play the part of a helping professional and another the part of a person from another population. Have a third person serve as an observer. Role-play a helping session for approximately five minutes. Then stop and critique the activity. Change roles in the triad and repeat two more times.

2. Have one person role-play the part of a helping professional and several other persons role-play the parts of people from a given population. Simulate a group helping session for approximately 20 minutes. Critique the simulation. Change roles (i.e., of the helping professional) and repeat as time allows.

3. Prepare a critique, individually or with others, of an audio or video tape of a session between a helping professional and a person from a particular diverse population.

4. Solicit volunteers from various diverse populations. Role-play the part of a helping professional working with them.

These culminating activities should allow helping professionals to put into practice all that they have learned from their previous learning experiences.

Continuous Preparation

Successful completion of each of these preparation stages should result in a helping professional with adequate competencies to undertake unsupervised professional interactions. For many professionals this preservice or inservice training terminates the preparation process. Truly competent professionals, however, continue the preparation process across their professional life spans through additional training.

This training should take the form of a continuation of all aspects of the preservice preparation program (D'Andrea & Daniels, 1991). Unfortunately, however, such training typically focuses only on the development of new skills at best and on relearning old skills at least. To expand continually a repertoire of skills is a noble effort, but to develop these skills on a foundation of knowledge that is continually becoming outdated is to diminish their potential utilitarian values. Thus, additional training should provide for extension and improvement in all the preparation areas: cognitive knowledge, attitude awareness, experiential interaction, and skill development. To do less is to foster imbalanced professional growth.

REFERENCES

Atkinson, D.R. (1985). A meta-review of research on cross-cultural counseling and psychotherapy. *Journal of Multicultural Counseling and Development, 13*, 138-153.

Atkinson, D.R., Morten, G., & Sue, D.W. (1989). *Counseling American minorities.* Dubuque, IA: William C. Brown.

Campbell, N.K., & Hadley, G.B. (1992). Creating options: A career development program for minorities. *Journal of Counseling and Development, 70*, 645-647.

Casas, J.M. (1985). A reflection on the status of racial/ethnic minority research. *Counseling Psychologist, 13*, 581-598.

Cheatam, H.E. (1990). Africentricity and career development among African-Americans. *Career Development Quarterly, 38*, 334-346.

Christensen, C.P. (1989). Cross-cultural awareness development: A conceptual model. *Counselor Education and Supervision, 28*, 270-289.

Conley, J.C., & Conley, C.W. (1991). *Consultation: A guide to practice* (2nd ed.). New York, NY: Pergamon.

Council for the Accreditation of Counseling and Related Educational Programs (CACREP). (1988). *Accreditation procedures manual and application for counseling and related educational programs.* Alexandria, VA: Author.

D'Andrea, M., & Daniels, J. (1991). Exploring different levels of multicultural counseling training in counselor education. *Journal of Counseling and Development, 70,* 78-85.

Draguns, J.G. (1989). Dilemmas and choices in cross-cultural counseling: The universal versus the culturally distinctive. In P. Pedersen, J.G. Draguns, W.J. Lonner, & J. Trimble (Eds.), *Counseling across cultures* (pp. 3-22). Honolulu, HI: University of Hawaii Press.

Fukuyama, M.K. (1990). Taking a universal approach to multicultural counseling. *Counselor Education and Supervision, 30,* 6-17.

Hoare, C. (1991). Psychosocial identity development and cultural others. *Journal of Counseling and Development, 70,* 45-53.

Holiman, M., & Lauver, P.J. (1987). The counselor culture and client-centered practice. *Counselor Education and Supervision, 26*(3), 184-191.

Ivey, A. (1987). Cultural intentionality: The core of effective helping. *Counselor Education and Supervision, 26*(3), 168-172.

Jackson, A.P., & Sears, S.J. (1992). Implications of an Africentric worldview in reducing stress for African-American women. *Journal of Counseling and Development, 71,* 184-190.

Lee, C.C. (1991). Empowerment in counseling: A multicultural perspective. *Journal of Counseling and Development, 69,* 229-230.

Lee, C.C., & Richardson, C. (Eds.). (1991). *Multicultural issues in counseling: New approaches to diversity.* Alexandria, VA: American Counseling Association.

Locke, D.C. (1992). *Counseling beyond U.S. borders. American Counselor, 1*(2), 13-17.

Lonner, W.J. (1985). Issues in testing and assessment in cross-cultural counseling. *Counseling Psychologist, 13*, 599-614.

Lonner, W.J., & Ibrahim, F.A. (1989). Assessment in cross-cultural counseling. In P. Pedersen, J.G. Draguns, W.J. Lonner, & J. Trimble (Eds.), *Counseling across cultures* (pp. 229-334). Honolulu, HI: University of Hawaii Press.

McRae, M.B., & Johnson, S., Jr. (1991). Toward training for competence in multicultural counselor education. *Journal of Counseling and Development, 70,* 131-135.

Nwachuku, U., & Ivey, A.E. (1991). Culture-specific counseling: An alternative training model. *Journal of Counseling and Development, 70,* 106-111.

Parker, W.M. (1987). Flexibility: A primer for multicultural counseling. *Counselor Education and Supervision, 26,* 176-180.

Pedersen, P. (1987). Ten frequent assumptions of cultural bias in counseling. *Journal of Multicultural Counseling and Development, 15,* 16-24.

Pedersen, P. (1988). *A handbook for developing multicultural awareness.* Alexandria, VA: American Counseling Association.

Pedersen, P. (1990a). The constructs of complexity and balance in multicultural counseling theory and practice. *Journal of Counseling and Development, 68,* 550-554.

Pedersen, P. (1990b). The multicultural perspective as a fourth force in counseling. *Journal of Mental Health Counseling, 12,* 93-95.

Pedersen, P. (1991). Multiculturalism as a generic approach to counseling. *Journal of Counseling and Development, 70,* 6-12.

Ponterotto, J.G., & Casas, M. (1991). *Handbook of racial/ethnic minority counseling research.* Springfield, IL: Charles C. Thomas.

Ponterotto, J.G., & Sabnani, H.B. (1989). "Classics" in multicultural counseling: A systematic five-year content analysis. *Journal of Multicultural Counseling and Development, 17,* 23-37.

Sodowsky, G.R., & Plake, B.S. (1992). A study of acculturation differences among international people and suggestions for sensistivity to within-group differences. *Journal of Counseling and Development, 71,* 53-59.

Sue, D.W. (1991). A model for cultural diversity training. *Journal of Counseling and Development, 70,* 99-105.

Sue, D.W. (1992). The challenge of multiculturalism: The road less traveled. *American Counselor, 1*(1), 6-14.

Sue, D.W., Arrendondo, P., & McDavis, R.J. (1992). Multicultural counseling competencies and standards: A call to the profession. *Journal of Counseling and Development, 70,* 477-486.

Thomason, T. (1991). Counseling Native Americans: An introduction for non-Native American counselors. *Journal of Counseling and Development, 69,* 321-327.

Vontress, C.E. (1988). An existential approach to cross-cultural counseling. *Journal of Multicultural Counseling and Development, 16,* 73-83.

INDEX

INDEX

special needs 302-11
treatment approaches 303-4
women, change 308-11
Culture
  encapsulation 12-3
  infusion 14-6
  learning 12-6
  learning model 13-4

D

D'Andrea, M. 340, 344, 350, 359
Daniels, J. 340, 344, 350, 359
Dank, B. 156, 173
DeCecco, J.P. 159, 173
DeVaney, S.B. 1, 199
Diaz, G.M. 296, 297, 314
Different by religion 29-60
Disability
  individuals with a physical
    251-71
Disengagement stereotype 99
Diverse populations
  definition 340
  preparation for helping 339-58
Dock, R. 275
Doerner, W. 278, 291
Douthis, J. 230, 249
Drag Queens 158
Draguns, J.G. 27, 347, 359, 360
Draguns, W.J. 359
Drew, C.J. 262, 271
Duberman, M. 154, 174
Duignan-Cabrera, A. 164, 174
Duncan, J. 288, 291
Dworkin, S.H. 170, 174

E

Economic Opportunity Act 5
Education for All Handicapped
  Children Act 261
Educational Amendments Act of
  1972
Egan, M.W. 262, 271
Elementary and Secondary
  Education Act of 1965 5
Ellis, L. 158, 174
Ellis, R. 179-80
Encapsulation, cultural 12-3

Engel, J.W. 157, 174
Equal Pay Act of 1963 327
Equal Rights Amendment in the
  70's 327
Exclusion Act of 1882 68
Experiential activities
  See specific diverse population
  in training program 350-1

F

Faludi, S. 325, 328, 329, 335
Family, Amish 39-40
Family Leave Act of 1993 325
Federal Pregnancy Discrimination
  Amendment 1978 323
Feelings 64-6
Fernandez, G.A. 299, 314
Ficke, S.C. 107, 115
Fitzgerald, L.F. 321, 334
Fleck, J. 288, 291, 292
Fogel, B.S. 115
Follow-up 241
Fong, S.L.M. 73, 85
Foote, F.H. 303, 315
Forrest, L. 326, 335
Frank, A.C. 77, 88
Fredrickson, R.H. 288, 292
Freiedman, A.S. 315
Fricke, A. 160, 161, 174
Fry, P.S. 99,. 115
Fukuyama, M.K. 341, 359
Fuller, J O. 9
Furino, A. 115

G

Gaia's Guide 162, 174
Gaines-Carter, P. 232, 249
Ganikos, M. 103, 105, 116
Garcia, R. 305, 313
Garfinkle, E.M. 154, 175
Gay population 147-72
  career needs 167-8   Title IX 327
  counseling needs 165-7
  current problem 159-65
  experiential activities 171-2
Gay women
  definition 152
Gay Yellow Pages 162, 174

legal changes 261-4
mobility 267
negatively stereotyped 256
normalization 258-61
personal and social disposition
267
personality 256-7
physical or body requirements
267
reflections 253-4
stigma 254-5
time 267
Individuals with disabilities
Education Act (IDEA) of 1990 262
Indochinese refugee
See Southeast Asian refugee
Inflexibility
stereotype 100
Influences
historical 4-6
Infusion 14-6
Ino, S. 73, 77, 87
Intelligence
measurement of minorities
129-30
Isaacson, L.E. 212, 215
Ivey, A. 341, 351, 359
Ivey, A.E. 350, 351, 360

J

Ja, D. 79, 88
Jackson, A.P. 347, 359
Janeway, E. 327, 336
Jenson, J. 321, 336
Johnson, S. 340, 350, 360
Johnson, V. 157, 175
Jones, E.E. 86, 315
Jourard, S. 237, 249

K

Kaahumanu, L. 151, 174
Kandolin, I. 324, 335
Kaneshige, E. 77, 86
Kang, J. 288, 291
Karls, W. 288, 292
Kauppinen-Toropainen,K. 324, 335
Kelly, G. 282, 291
Kennedy, E. 152, 174

Kinsey, A. 154, 175
Kinzie, J.D. 288, 289, 291, 292
Kinzie, S.D. 288, 291
Kitson, G.C. 204, 215
Kleinman, A. 88
Knowledge acquisition 346-8
Korchin, S.J. 89, 315
Kramer, B. 85
Kuo, W. 78, 86
Kurtines, W.M. 302, 303, 307, 314,
315

L

Ladner, R.A. 301, 315
Lanbda Update 151, 175
Langan-Fox, J. 323, 336
Larwood, L. 335, 336
Lasakow, P. 237, 249
Lauritson, J. 169, 175
Lauver, P.J. 352, 359
Learn
culture 12-6
culture model 13-4
Lee, C.C. 341, 348, 359
Lee, F. 78, 86
Lesbian population
career needs 167-8
counseling needs 165-7
current problems 159-65
experiential populations 171-2
population 147-72
Lesbians
definition 152
Leung, P. 69, 86
Levine, G.N. 73, 86
Lew, C. 79, 88
Lewis, M.I. 101, 110
Leyden, P. 164, 174
Life-role analysis 332
Lin, T.Y. 88
Lips, H.M. 326, 336
Listening
Locke, D.C. 51, 60, 242, 249, 341,
360
Loesch, L.C. 8, 339-40
Long, S.M. 144, 146
Longstreet, S. 122, 146
Lonner, W.J. 27, 343, 359, 360
Lonner, W.M. 360